SPANISH PHONOLOGY

# SPANISH PHONOLOGY

JAMES W. HARRIS

Research Monograph No. 54
THE M.I.T. PRESS
Cambridge, Massachusetts, and London, England

*To Lucy, Corinne, Bessie, and Florence*

# Foreword

This is the fifty-fourth volume in the M.I.T. Research Monograph Series published by The M.I.T. Press. The objective of this series is to contribute to the professional literature a number of significant pieces of research, larger in scope than journal articles but normally less ambitious than finished books. We believe that such studies deserve a wider circulation than can be accomplished by informal channels, and we hope that this form of publication will make them readily accessible to research organizations, libraries, and independent workers.

HOWARD W. JOHNSON

# Acknowledgments

Of the many people to whom I owe a debt of gratitude for direct and indirect contributions to this book, I shall single out only three: Noam Chomsky, Morris Halle, and my wife, Florence. Chomsky's contribution is indirect but enormous. In the course of engaging in particular linguistic discussions and advancing particular linguistic arguments, it is easy to lose sight of the fact that Chomsky has almost singlehandedly enriched the content and raised the general level of these very discussions and modes of argumentation to an extent that is well nigh incalculable. Halle's contribution is both indirect and direct. He is surely the most perceptive and provocative phonological theorist of the generation and has brought about a general revolution in phonological theory. More directly, he is my phonological mentor and has given generously of his valuable time to discuss the problems with which this book is concerned. My wife's contribution is direct. She has attended to the technicalities of editing and seeing a difficult manuscript into print and has forced me to rewrite many stretches of impenetrably bad expository prose.

The research reported in this document was made possible in part by support extended the Massachusetts Institute of Technology, Research Laboratory of Electronics, by the National Institute of Mental Health (Grant 1 PO1 MH13390–02).

# Contents

# SPANISH PHONOLOGY

# 1. Introduction

Of the major world languages, Spanish is perhaps the least well studied in the context of recent linguistic theory. With regard to Spanish phonology in particular, few studies relevant to current theoretical issues have found their way into print. The present work strives to remedy this lack by examining the phonological component of a transformational generative grammar of a major Spanish dialect. The purpose here is twofold. First, there is an attempt to gain deeper insight into the widely studied facts of Spanish pronunciation by presenting a theory of these facts in the form of a generative grammar. Such precise and explicit formulation can lead to the discovery of serious deficiencies in our understanding of the data and may have the heuristic value of suggesting a principled way to remedy such defects. Second, a large and detailed body of data is made available in a form appropriate for testing certain parts of the universal phonological theory whose most recent and comprehensive statement is found in Chomsky and Halle (1968), *The Sound Pattern of English*.[1] At present

---

[1] The development of this theory can be traced, in part, in such works as the following: Chomsky, Halle, and Lukoff (1956), "On Accent and Juncture in English"; Jakobson and Halle (1956), *Fundamentals of Language*; Chomsky (1957), *Syntactic Structures*; Halle (1959), *The Sound Pattern of Russian*; Halle (1962), "Phonology in a Generative Grammar"; Jakobson, Fant, and Halle (1963), *Preliminaries to Speech Analysis*; Chomsky (1964), *Current Issues in Linguistic Theory*; Katz and Postal (1964), *An Integrated Theory of Linguistic Descriptions*; Chomsky (1965), *Aspects of the Theory of Syntax*; Chomsky and Halle (1965), "Some Controversial Questions in Phonological Theory"; Chomsky (1967), "Some General Properties of Phonological Rules"; Postal (1968), *Aspects of Phonological Theory*. It is assumed in the present study that the reader is familiar with such works.

this theory can best be tested, sharpened, and enriched by being examined in the light of phonological studies of the widest possible range of languages. Such studies, however, must approach if not exceed in both scope and depth Chomsky and Halle's study of English. Otherwise it is not likely that they will provide the kinds of evidence that bear on the correctness of the abstract phonological principles proposed by Chomsky and Halle. At various points in the following exposition, observations are made regarding the empirical adequacy of the phonological theory in question. Difficulties are pointed out, but detailed proposals for their solution would, in most cases, be premature. The intention here, then, is to make a contribution to the large body of reasonably clear empirical data that must underlie future theoretical revisions.

The discussion includes what I believe to be a fairly comprehensive account of the rules for perhaps most of the central and crucial phonological processes of Spanish. In addition, there is a more detailed examination of certain areas in which it is plausible to assume that all the relevant data have been considered and which, furthermore, promise to contribute to our understanding of the sound structure of Spanish and to phonological theory in general. It is only in the light of some knowledge of the total grammar that intensive exploration of particular areas can be carried out with a reasonable assurance of relevance. It seems to me that lack of such assurance greatly reduces the interest of some recent work in Spanish phonology, such as that done by Foley (1965), Sableski (1965), and Saporta (1965).[2]

Examples of areas to which considerable attention is given in this study are the formulation of rules that express generalizations concerning the assimilation of nasals to following obstruents, the phonological and phonetic representation of glides, and the characterization in terms of distinctive features of the various flapped and trilled r-type phones of Spanish. On the other hand, no rules are proposed to account for the distribution in phonetic representations of tenser and laxer vowel allophones, since it seems unlikely that study of this topic would lead to any results of general interest. Nor is there any attempt

---

[2] Saporta (1965) himself acknowledges this weakness: "The rules for Spanish are largely illustrative. In the absence of much of the relevant material, it is not clear what modifications might be required, for example, in the underlying representations. These changes would not alter the main line of the argument" (p. 220). The present work, taken as a whole, does provide much though not all of the relevant material and, if even approximately correct, raises serious questions about the validity of the basis for much of Saporta's discussion. More specific remarks will appear at appropriate points in the exposition.

to give a full account of many morphophonemic phenomena that traditionally have been considered irregular or exceptional, such as irregular preterit and present tense forms of verbs. While apparently irregular and exceptional forms may be of value in dealing with questions whose solutions are underdetermined by the data provided by clearly regular forms, it seems misguided to attach much weight to irregularities until at least the outlines of a theory of regular cases are clear.

I should like to point out once again that this study purports to be neither definitive nor exhaustive. Rather, it must be considered to provide a basis for the formulation of significant questions, a foundation, heretofore seriously inadequate or altogether lacking, upon which serious work on Spanish may begin to be more fruitful than it has been in the past.

The dialect of Spanish described is that of a few Mexican friends whose speech I believe to be typical of educated speakers from Mexico City. This dialect was chosen out of necessity. There does not exist for Spanish anything equivalent to, for example, Kenyon and Knott (1953), *A Pronouncing Dictionary of American English*, and the state of the study of Spanish dialectology is deplorable by the standards of such work in other major languages. Therefore the only body of data accessible to me in sufficient breadth and detail is that with which I am familiar from firsthand experience. Information about other dialects plays almost no role in this study. The extent to which the results of this investigation may carry over to other dialects is, of course, an empirical question and must be left to future research.

The concentration here on one narrowly delimited dialect calls for a few further comments. It has been suggested by Halle (1962) that dialectology may profitably be pursued by focusing on "the grammars of the dialects, i.e., on the ordered set of statements that describe the data, rather than on the data directly" (p. 342). Further, "since grammars consist of ordered sets of statements, differences among grammars are due to one or both of the following: (a) different grammars may contain different rules; (b) different grammars may have differently ordered rules" (p. 343). Following the lead of Halle and of Keyser (1963), Saporta (1965) has stated that "the grammatical description of a given dialect may be *converted into* [italics mine] an adequate description of a related dialect by the addition, deletion, or reordering of a relatively small number of rules" (p. 219), and "it should be made explicit that the choice of underlying forms and rules is motivated by the desire to account for the greatest number of facts in a manner as straightforward as possible" (p. 220). If I understand

Saporta, he is saying that dialectology will be best served if, in postulating a phonological description of a particular dialect, consideration is given to related dialects, that is, underlying forms and rules should be chosen such that the greatest number of facts *in all dialects* is accounted for by the simplest set of rules *for all dialects together*. It is not clear to me precisely how the notion of converting one dialect into another in the first quotation relates to that of overall simplicity implied in the second, but presumably it is a desideratum that the conversion be effected by the smallest possible number of rule additions, deletions, and reorderings. The remainder of Saporta's discussion adds no substantial clarification, but related work by Sableski (1965), cited with approval by Saporta, contains a number of statements that support my interpretation of Saporta's position. Sableski asks: "Which real or hypothetical dialect of Spanish will serve as the most efficient base from which to derive other dialects?" (p. 12). "In determining the underlying representation [N.B., singular] from which to derive the dialects [N.B., plural] of a language, it is necessary to select the *one* [italics mine] which will permit the simplest possible phonological rules [for the set of all dialects together?]" (p. 13). Sableski concludes that "Castilian Spanish is chosen as the underlying dialect . . . entirely on the grounds of simplicity and generality [of the rules needed to derive a dialect of rural Panamanian Spanish from Castilian]" (pp. 14–15).[3]

Both Saporta and Sableski clearly consider their work to support and provide further exemplification of Halle's views. However, if my interpretation of their position is correct, their proposals go far beyond anything Halle has ever suggested and, unfortunately, in a direction that renders Halle's actual suggestions immune to empirical test and reduces his approach to dialectology to near vacuity. If a grammar is taken to be an explicit theory of a speaker's internalized linguistic competence, then anything that is irrelevant to the latter is also irrelevant to the former. Presumably, a speaker's linguistic competence arises, in a way that we have little understanding of at present, from the interaction of (a) whatever innate equipment the speaker brings to the task of language learning, (b) the linguistic data to which the speaker has access, and (c) perhaps other factors we know little about. Surely

---

[3] Incidentally, Sableski's description of Castilian does not always agree with that of Navarro Tomás (1965), the best-known and most careful treatment of Castilian in existence. Compare, for example, Sableski's statement of the distribution of tense and lax allophones of /e/ (pp. 25–26) with that of Navarro (pp. 52–53). It is worth noting that the discrepancies are in the direction of making Sableski's rules simpler rather than more complex.

particular facts about a dialect the speaker has never heard can in no way figure in any of (a), (b), or (c). Just as surely, particular facts of one dialect have no bearing on the justification of a grammar of another dialect. This is not to say, of course, that a linguist seeking to formulate a grammar for a particular dialect may not get bright ideas from other dialects, from known historical rules, from dreams, or from any source whatever. The point is rather that the motivation and justification of a grammar of a particular dialect must be based on data from that dialect and no other if the grammar is to have any intelligible relation to the linguistic competence of speakers of the dialect of which the grammar is a theory. In short, grammars of the type apparently proposed by Saporta and actually written by Sableski are unable to make truth claims about human linguistic competence. Furthermore, since all conclusions that might have come out as empirical results of a comparison of independently motivated and justified grammars are built in from the start, such an approach in effect guarantees that nothing can be learned about how dialects are related as systems of rules. In particular, all questions are begged concerning the relation to Castilian Spanish of the Panamanian dialect studied by Sableski since it was assumed a priori that the two dialects are related in a certain way, namely, that the grammar of the Panamanian dialect *is derived from* a putative grammar that gives the phonetic output of Castilian (which the Panamanian speakers have never heard) by certain adjustments on the rules. It is of course logically possible that the grammar of the Panamanian dialect is correct (that is, that it could be justified by evidence internal to the dialect) and hence that its relation to a grammar of Castilian is exactly the one claimed. But this has been assumed, not demonstrated. Neither general phonological theory nor dialectology has much chance of being advanced by such apriorism.

# 2. Some Consonantal Phenomena

## 2.1 Styles of pronunciation: Largo, Andante, Allegretto, Presto

In this chapter we shall be concerned with certain well-known facts that are presented, in varying degrees of detail and explicitness, in almost every treatment of Spanish pronunciation. Common knowledge of these facts, however, has not generally been accompanied by a real understanding of them, and careful studies, several of which will be cited later, have generally ended up in puzzlement and irreconcilable disagreement.

Consider, for example, familiar instances of variant pronunciations such as the following: *es viudo*, "he's a widower," may be heard as [esbyuðo], [ezbyuðo], or [ezβyuðo]; both *hay una*, "there is one," and *ayuna*, "(he) is fasting," may be heard as [aẙuna] or [ayuna] ([ẙ] has fricative noise, [y] does not); *bien, gracias*, "fine, thanks," may be heard as [byengrasyas] or [byeŋgrasyas].

Stockwell, Bowen, and Silva-Fuenzalida (1956), whose examples and transcriptions I have deliberately borrowed, argue that one might ascribe such cases to:

> free variation at this [phonemic] level, presumably controlled by stylistic choice . . . [This] solution is easily eliminated because it is equivalent to saying that the variation cannot be described systematically even when it can be . . . we would not object to

6

recognizing free variation in an instance of this sort, where there is fair assurance that the variation will actually be statable on a stylistic level. . . . It is, of course, recognized that no one has, to our knowledge, actually described the conditioning on this higher level (pp. 408–409).

Evidence will be adduced here that suggests that the alternations illustrated, and others as well, not only *can* but *must* be described in terms of stylistic levels. Native speakers agree that [esbyuðo] and [ezβyuðo], for example, are not free variants in any intuitive, non-technical sense; rather, [esbyuðo] represents a "more careful" and [ezβyuðo] a "less careful" pronunciation. (The non-Spanish-speaking reader may perhaps be helped to appreciate the Spanish speaker's feeling by comparing *Betty* pronounced with a medial aspirated [tʰ] and pronounced with a medial voiced alveolar flap in American English.) Certainly a reasonably complete phonological description must take such facts into account. Furthermore, and more pertinent to our purpose here, it will be shown that careful examination of the kinds of alternations under discussion leads to some interesting questions about the form and organization of phonological rules.

To establish a framework for discussion, I give in (1) an impressionistic description of a hierarchy of "styles" of pronunciation in Spanish:

(1)

*Largo:* very slow, deliberate, overprecise; typical of, for example, trying to communicate with a foreigner who has little competence in the language or correcting a misunderstanding over a bad telephone connection.

*Andante:* moderately slow, careful, but natural; typical of, for example, delivering a lecture or teaching a class in a large hall without electronic amplification.

*Allegretto:* moderately fast, casual, colloquial. In many situations one might easily alternate between Andante and Allegretto in mid-discourse or even in mid-sentence.

*Presto:* very fast, completely unguarded.

We will be concerned primarily with Andante and Allegretto but will mention Largo and Presto at various appropriate points.

The dialect under consideration—educated Mexico City speech— is generally thought of among Latin Americans as being not only prestigious but also hypercareful and even slightly affected in pronunciation. Consider the examples given in (2):

| (2) | MEXICO CITY | HAVANA |
|-----|-------------|--------|
| Largo | [mismo] | [mismo] |
| Andante | [mis$^z$mo] | [mis$^z$mo] |
| Allegretto | [mis$^z$mo] | [mifimo] ([ɦ] = voiced [h]) |
| Presto | [mizmo] | [mĩ:mo] |

The difference in span of divergence from Largo to Presto in the two dialects in (2) provides an interpretation of the Havana speaker's impression that unguarded Mexico City pronunciation is somewhat artificial.

With this background, we will now proceed to investigate in some detail alternations of the type illustrated in the opening paragraphs of this chapter. As the exposition develops, the informal characterizations of stylistic levels given in (1) will be replaced by sets of rules that explicitly describe each style, and a few tentative observations will be made concerning the notions "style" and "stylistic level" as these are reflected in the formal differences among the sets of rules.

## 2.2 Nasal assimilation

In treatments of Spanish pronunciation one frequently finds statements to the effect that nasal consonants assimilate to the point of articulation of a following consonant. In this section we shall examine in some detail the distribution of nasals in preconsonantal position. We shall see that a close study of this well-known phenomenon leads to several interesting theoretical questions, such as the appropriateness of a new set of distinctive features proposed by Chomsky and Halle (1968).

In all styles of speech, *m*, *n*, and (palatal) *ñ* occur distinctively before vowels: *cama*, "bed"; *cana*, "gray hair"; *caña*, "cane." Unassimilated *n*—that is, before a vowel and before pause—is alveolar [n], not dental [ṇ]. Labiodental [ṃ], dental [ṇ], and velar [ŋ] occur only as the result of assimilation. For further details, each "style," as characterized in the preceding section, must be considered separately.

### 2.2.1 *Largo*

In Largo, word-final *n* does not assimilate to the initial consonant of the following word: *un beso* [unbeso], *un cacto* [unkakto]. Thus we

*(margin handwritten note: 3 unassimilated nasals: m, n, ñ / the rest are results of assimilation)*

may restrict our attention to forms such as those in (3), in which there is assimilation within a word before obstruents but not before nasals, liquids, or glides:[1]

(3)

| NASAL BEFORE: | BILABIAL | LABIO-DENTAL | DENTAL | ALVEOLAR | PALATAL | VELAR |
|---|---|---|---|---|---|---|
| Obstruent | *campo* | *triũfo* | *cuãto* | *canso* | *rãcho* | *aŋca* |
| | *cambio* | | *cuãdo* | | | *gaŋga* |
| | | | | | | *ajeŋjo* |
| Nasal | *inmenso* | | | *innato* | | |
| | | | | *columna* | | |
| Liquid | | | | *honra* | | |
| | | | | *enlace* | | |
| Glide | *nuevo* | | | | *nieto* | |

In the sense that [p,b,f,t,d,s,č,k,g,x] are the only obstruents that occur after nasals, (3) is exhaustive. It is immediately obvious that there is complete neutralization of nasals before obstruents: that is, only homorganic clusters of nasal plus obstruent occur, with the apparent exception of the cluster *nch*. It is striking that the nasal that occurs before palatal [č] is not palatal [ñ], although the phonetic inventory of the dialect does include [ñ], as previously noted. The nasal that occurs before [č], for which I have chosen the noncommittal symbol [ṅ], is auditorily indistinguishable from alveolar [n], but quite different from [ñ]. Articulatorily, the tongue tip makes contact with the alveolae for [ṅ] just as for alveolar [n], but not for palatal [ñ]. The area of lingual contact extends slightly farther back for [ṅ] than for [n], though not so far back as the dorsopalatal contact of [ñ]. Informants uniformly assert that the nasal before [č] is *n* and, furthermore, that the cluster [ñč] is impossible. In short, it seems quite out of the question to identify the nasal that occurs before [č] as palatal

[1] Throughout the book it is assumed that the reader is familiar with standard Spanish orthography. For the sake of readability, the transcription of examples will depart from standard orthography only to the extent required for clarity in a particular discussion. Mixed representations will occur frequently: for example, orthographic *habrá* might be written *haβrá* rather than [aβrá], since in the latter representation the word may not be as easily recognized as in the former. Where confusion might result from not knowing whether a character is a letter or a phonetic symbol, one or more phonetic symbols will be enclosed in brackets within a sequence of letters: for example, orthographic *proteger* might be written *prote*[x]*er*.

*diffuse = front = SPE anterior*
*grave = peripheral = SPE [−coronal]*

[ñ] since it is closer to alveolar [n] auditorily and articulatorily, as well as intuitively for native speakers.[2]

Let us now attempt to formulate rules that capture the facts of nasal assimilation shown in the examples in (3). In the familiar theory of distinctive features in which the traditional four primary points of articulation for consonants are characterized by the two features [diffuse] and [grave], four nasals may be distinguished, as in (4):

(4)

| | LABIAL | DENTAL | PALATAL | VELAR |
|---|---|---|---|---|
| | m | n | ñ | ŋ |
| diffuse | + | + | − | − |
| grave | + | − | − | + |

The auditory and articulatory facts that were given previously indicate that the nasal that occurs before [č] must be characterized as [+diffuse, −grave] in terms of (4). Thus, ignoring the bilabial-labiodental and dental-alveolar distinctions, which cannot be stated in the theory that includes (4), we may formulate rule (5) to express the generalizations illustrated in (3):[3]

(5)

$$[+\text{nasal}] \rightarrow \begin{bmatrix} +\text{grave} \\ \alpha\text{diffuse} \end{bmatrix} \Big/ \underline{\hspace{2em}} \begin{bmatrix} +\text{obstruent} \\ +\text{grave} \\ \alpha\text{diffuse} \end{bmatrix}$$

We must specify [+grave] rather than [βgrave] in (5) in order to exclude assimilation before palatal [č].

Now consider sets of words such as in (6):

(6)
| | | |
|---|---|---|
| consu[m]ir | consu[ns]ión | consu[n̆t]o |
| to consume | consumption | consumed |
| presu[m]ir | presu[ns]ión | presu[n̆t]ivo |
| to presume | presumption | presumptive |
| redi[m]ir | rede[ns]ión | rede[n̆t]or |
| to redeem | redemption | redeemer |

---

[2] The literature abounds in statements to the effect that [ñ] does in fact occur before [č]. See, for example, Campbell (undated, pp. 27 ff.), Saporta and Contreras (1962, pp. 30 ff.), Alarcos Llorach (1961, pp. 175 f.), Foley (1965, p. 27), Navarro Tomás (1965, p. 133), Sableski (1965, p. 32), Stockwell and Bowen (1965, p. 83). These references, however, describe some dialect other than that of Mexico City, although some give descriptions that presumably apply across dialects. On the other hand, King (1952, p. 55) states explicitly that the same nasal allophone occurs before [č] as before [s]. We return briefly to the question of other dialects in note 6.

[3] The notational conventions used throughout this work are those of Chomsky and Halle (1968), with which the reader is presumed to be familiar. Therefore, no explanation will be given here.

Evidently the words in (6) have the stems *consum-*, *presum-*, and *redem-*, with the final *m* appearing as alveolar [n] or dental [ň] before an affix beginning with an alveolar or dental obstruent.[4] (The vowel alternations can be handled by a very general rule which will be given in Chapter 4.) Thus rule (5) must somehow be adjusted to include the effect of (7):

(7)
$$m \rightarrow n \ / \ \underline{\quad} \begin{bmatrix} +\text{obstruent} \\ -\text{grave} \\ +\text{diffuse} \end{bmatrix}$$

A rule with the effect of both (5) and (7) might be formulated as in (8), among other conceivable alternatives:

(8)
$$[+\text{nasal}] \rightarrow \begin{cases} [-\text{next rule}] \ / \ \underline{\quad} \begin{bmatrix} -\text{diffuse} \\ -\text{grave} \end{bmatrix} & a \\[2em] \begin{bmatrix} \alpha\text{diffuse} \\ \beta\text{grave} \end{bmatrix} \ / \ \underline{\quad} \begin{bmatrix} +\text{obstruent} \\ \alpha\text{diffuse} \\ \beta\text{grave} \end{bmatrix} & b \end{cases}$$

There are, however, at least two difficulties with rule (8). First, use of the device [ − next rule] is rather suspect on theoretical grounds.[5] Second, and perhaps more important, (8) does not rule out [mč], [ňč], and [ŋč], which not only do not occur but are in fact impermissible sequences rather than fortuitous gaps. Thus an *ad hoc* statement to this effect would have to be added to a grammar containing (8). These difficulties can be avoided in a formulation like (9):

(9)
$$[+\text{nasal}] \rightarrow \begin{bmatrix} \alpha\text{diffuse} \\ \beta\text{grave} \end{bmatrix} \ / \ \underline{\quad} \begin{bmatrix} +\text{obstruent} \\ \gamma\text{diffuse} \\ \beta\text{grave} \end{bmatrix}$$

CONDITIONS: if $\gamma = \beta$, then $\alpha = +$
if $\gamma \neq \beta$, then $\alpha = \gamma$

However, the set of conditions on (9) is extremely complex for an otherwise very simple rule.

Let us turn now to consider how the data presented so far relate to the revision of distinctive feature theory proposed by Chomsky and Halle (1968, Chapter Seven). In this modified framework, those

[4] Fuller discussion of such forms is presented in Section 5.2.3.2.

[5] See Chomsky and Halle (1968, Chapter Four, Section 2.2, and Chapter Eight, Section 7).

obstruents [p,b,f,t,d,s,č,k,g,x] which occur after nasals, as illustrated in (3), are characterized in part as in (10):

(10)

|  | p,b | f | t,d | s | č | k,g,x |
|---|---|---|---|---|---|---|
| coronal | − | − | + | + | + | − |
| anterior | + | + | + | + | − | − |
| back | − | − | − | − | − | + |
| distributed | + | − | − | + | + | + |

The seven nasals that have been distinguished phonetically are characterized as in (11):

(11)

|  | m | m̆ | n̆ | n | ṅ | ñ | ŋ |
|---|---|---|---|---|---|---|---|
| coronal | − | − | + | + | + | − | − |
| anterior | + | + | + | + | − | − | − |
| back | − | − | − | − | − | − | + |
| distributed | + | − | − | + | + | + | + |

In this framework not only are we able to distinguish bilabial [m] from labiodental [m̆] and dental [n̆] from alveolar [n], but we may also distinguish an alveolopalatal [ṅ] from both alveolar [n] and palatal [ñ]. Moreover, [ṅ] has the same point-of-articulation features as [č]. The acoustico-articulatory description of the nasal before [č] given previously leaves no room for doubt that this nasal should be assigned the features listed for [ṅ] in (11).[6]

Rules (8) and (9) may now be replaced by (12), which states simply that only homorganic clusters of nasal plus obstruent occur:

(12)

$$[+\text{nasal}] \rightarrow \begin{bmatrix} \alpha\text{cor} \\ \beta\text{ant} \\ \gamma\text{back} \\ \delta\text{distr} \end{bmatrix} \Big/ \underline{\qquad} \begin{bmatrix} +\text{obstr} \\ \alpha\text{cor} \\ \beta\text{ant} \\ \gamma\text{back} \\ \delta\text{distr} \end{bmatrix}$$

A comparison of rules (8) and (9) with rule (12) shows that the relatively small and straightforward set of data presented so far provides

[6] Trager (1939) observed that "/n/ is . . . alveolopalatal ([ṅ], different from [ñ]) before /č/ . . . /ñ/ is prepalatal with no apicalization" (p. 219). With the possible exception of a much less explicit statement by Silva-Fuenzalida (1952, p. 160), Trager's observation is, to my knowledge, unique in the literature. In view of (10), (11), and (12), it would seem entirely appropriate to assume that all dialects of Spanish have [ṅ] before [č]. If this is correct, then all the references of note 2 except King either have not observed very carefully or have swept phonetic detail under the rug for the sake of an elegant description. (The former but not the latter accusation may be leveled against King.)

rather strong support for Chomsky and Halle's revision of distinctive
feature theory. To begin with, the features of (4) afford no way of
distinguishing between bilabial [m] and labiodental [m̆] or between
dental [n̆] and alveolar [n], although the data demand that these
distinctions be made if even a moderate degree of phonetic accuracy
is to be achieved. But this is a relatively minor problem that one might
dispose of by relegating it to the limbo of phonetic detail rules in which
the coefficients of features are integers rather than plus or minus.[7] Note
that in the theory that includes (11), the increase in the number of
phonetic distinctions available is simply a consequence of the increase
in the number of parameters in the system—exactly what one would
expect. This gain is offset by a serious loss, namely, that of the strength
of the claims made about language: the extremely restrictive, and
hence interesting, claim that all languages operate with only four
significant points of articulation for consonants has been abandoned.

The real gain in the theoretical revision under discussion is not that
certain phonetic distinctions can be made without the use of integral
feature coefficients, but rather that the straightforward process of
nasal assimilation can be described in one simple rule that requires
neither devices like [−next rule] nor complex "if-then" conditions,
both of which are extremely powerful and must be severely con-
strained. Furthermore, the nonoccurrence of [mč], [ñč], and [ŋč] is
not only accounted for by rule (12), but it is in fact explained. Even if
there were no [č] in the language, rule (12) would still have to be stated
exactly as it is, feature by feature. Thus the rule automatically predicts
the quality of the nasal that does in fact occur before [č]. This situation
stands in sharp contrast to that of rules (8) and (9), where the difficulties are caused solely by the existence of [č].

Finally, it is important to bear in mind that Spanish was not included
in the very wide range of languages on the basis of which Chomsky
and Halle's theoretical changes were proposed. Linguistic theory is
obviously not advanced greatly by making *ad hoc* adjustments every
time some recalcitrant fact turns up in a language not previously
investigated. Any theoretical innovation constitutes a prediction that
data not yet considered will contain generalizations that would be lost
in the former framework but can be captured in the revised theory.
Only when such predictions are borne out can we feel that progress
has been made. We have seen that some of the predictions of the
theoretical changes proposed by Chomsky and Halle have been fulfilled

[7] Some discussion of integral feature values may be found in Chomsky and Halle
(1968, p. 65, p. 383) and Postal (1968, pp. 65 ff.)

in a particularly clear way by the facts presented in this section. (In Section 2.4.5.3 we shall come across further support for these revisions.)

At this point we shall abandon the use of the feature framework that includes [diffuse] and [grave] in favor of the new set of features proposed by Chomsky and Halle.

Incidentally, the facts presented here concerning the distribution of [m,m̃,n̆,n,ñ,ŋ] before obstruents provide evidence against a "taxonomic phonemic" level of representation which is slightly more complicated but entirely analogous to Halle's (1959) much quoted argument based on the distribution of [t,d,č,ǰ] in Russian. Note that *m* and *n* (and *ñ*) contrast "phonemically" in at least one environment, namely, before vowels (*cama*, "bed," versus *cana*, "gray hair"), while [m̃], [ŋ], etc., never contrast. Thus, one committed to "taxonomic phonemics" would insist that the general rule (12) be replaced by two less general rules, the first relating "morphophonemic" to "phonemic" representation, and the second relating "phonemic" to phonetic representation: for example, morphophonemic *redemtor*, phonemic *redentor*, phonetic *redentor*. Just as in Halle's example, this loss of generality is a consequence solely of the linguistically unmotivated requirement that a grammar provide a "taxonomic phonemic" level of representation.

## 2.2.2 *Andante*

In Andante the distribution of nasals within a word is exactly as in Largo, as illustrated in (3) and (6). Unlike Largo, however, Andante has partial assimilation across word boundaries, a phenomenon that merits careful examination.

The following passage from Navarro Tomás (1965) is a description of Castilian Spanish, but in every detail relevant to nasals it carries over to the Mexican dialect under consideration. It will be quoted in full because of its unique lucidity and attention to phonetic detail.

*Nasal ante labial.* —En contacto con las consonantes *p, b,* la *n* final de una palabra anterior se pronuncia corrientemente *m*, sin que en este sentido pueda advertirse diferencia alguna entre expresiones como, por ejemplo, *con padre* y *compadre*, pronunciadas ambas [kompáðre], o entre *con placer* y *complacer*, pronunciadas [komplaθér]. La *n* final mantiene, sin embargo, su propia articulación, . . . cuando por lentitud o vacilación en el lenguaje aparece desligada de la consonante siguiente. Suelen darse asimismo, según la rapidez con que se hable, *formas intermedias de asimilación en que la* n, *sin perder enteramente su articulación alveolar, resulta en parte cubierta por la oclusión de los labios* [italics mine]. En la conversación ordinaria, la transformación de la *n* en *m* ante las oclusivas bilabiales *p*, *b*, se produce de una manera regular y constante.

[Footnote:] Los gramáticos han discutido extensamente sobre si la *n* ante *p*, *b*, se pronuncia *n* o *m*. La realidad da apoyo, como se ve, para varias opiniones. Todo depende de la forma de pronunciación que se tome por base . . . (p. 89).

Let us make the following obvious associations with the "formas de pronunciación," or styles, which Navarro mentions: his "lentitud o vacilación" corresponds to Largo, where there is no assimilation across word boundaries; his "conversación ordinaria" corresponds to Allegretto, where, letting the exposition get ahead of itself, the same distribution of nasals is found over word boundaries as within words. We are left with Navarro's "formas intermedias de asimilación," which we assign to Andante. Navarro's descriptions of the assimilation of nasals to other than bilabial obstruents are not as detailed as the one quoted, but, in general, they support the stylistic assignments made here.

Now let us consider how the nasal assimilation rule (12) presented for Largo applies in the case of Andante. By a general convention on the application of phonological rules, the presence of a word boundary in a string blocks the application of a rule that would otherwise apply unless the boundary is explicitly mentioned in the rule.[8] Thus, in Largo, rule (12) is correctly blocked from applying to representations such as *con padre* and *con placer*, although it does apply to *con+padre* and *con+placer*, for example, since the boundary + does not block application of a rule. The same is true in Andante: rule (12) will apply correctly to forms such as *con+padre* and *con+placer*, giving *com+padre* and *com+placer*. To account for the additional partial assimilations that occur in Andante, then, there evidently must be another, presumably later, rule that applies across word boundaries to assign appropriate feature values to nasals followed by obstruents in the next word. At this stage of our knowledge, little more can be said about what these "appropriate feature values" are. They might be integers, for example. Yet it seems that Navarro's careful description points to a type of coarticulation that has not yet been studied in the framework of distinctive features, in particular, a nasal in which bilabial closure is superimposed on alveolar closure. Other dialects provide even more striking cases. For example, many Cubans pronounce *enfermo* as [e$\tilde{\eta}$fermo], where the first nasal, presumably systematic phonemic *n*, is realized with no alveolar contact at all, but rather

[8] See Chomsky and Halle (1968, Chapter Three, Section 1.3.1).

with a labiodental articulation superimposed on a dorsovelar articulation. Current phonological theory includes no device for assigning a feature specification that would reflect the auditory and articulatory properties of the segment represented as [m̆ŋ] and capture in some way the phonological processes involved, namely, the [ŋ] component as a prejunctural phenomenon and the [m] component as an assimilation to the following [f]. It must be left to future research to explore the significance of such data.

### 2.2.3 *Allegretto*

In Allegretto the distribution of nasals within a word is again just as in (3) and (6). To this, however, we must add the data of (13), which illustrate that in Allegretto the distribution of nasals over word boundaries is precisely the same as that within words, with certain apparent exceptions which will be discussed shortly. (*Un* is the masculine singular form of the indefinite article; before vowels it occurs as [un], as in *un oso* [unoso], "a bear.")

(13)

| BILABIAL | LABIO-DENTAL | DENTAL | ALVEOLAR | ALVEOLO-PALATAL | VELAR |
|---|---|---|---|---|---|
| um *peso* | um̆ *foco* | un̆ *tío* | un *saco* | un̆ *charco* | uŋ *cacto* |
| um *beso* | | un̆ *día* | | | uŋ *gato* |
| | | | | | uŋ *juego* |

Thus we may propose that while Largo and Andante have rule (12), Allegretto has rule (14). This rule is identical to rule (12) except for the presence of (#) in the environment, allowing it to apply across word boundaries as well as within words.

(14)

$$[+\text{nasal}] \rightarrow \begin{bmatrix} \alpha\text{cor} \\ \beta\text{ant} \\ \gamma\text{back} \\ \delta\text{distr} \end{bmatrix} / \underline{\quad\quad} (\#) \begin{bmatrix} +\text{obstr} \\ \alpha\text{cor} \\ \beta\text{ant} \\ \gamma\text{back} \\ \delta\text{distr} \end{bmatrix}$$

Actually, a fair amount of complexity has been glossed over in (14) with the use of the symbol (#). Even if it is correct in the case of the examples in (13) that before any phonological rules have applied "word boundary" is represented by the symbol #, which is itself an abbreviation for a bundle of features,[9] this is certainly not correct in

---

[9] For discussion of the feature composition of boundaries see Chomsky and Halle (1968, Chapter Three, Section 1.3.1).

other cases to which rule (14) must apply. Consider the examples in (15):

(15)

| | |
|---|---|
| *canta*m̆ *bien* | (they) sing well |
| *crece*m̆ *flores* | flowers grow |
| *tiene*ñ *dientes* | (they) have teeth |
| *ven zopilotes* | (they) see buzzards |
| *so*ǹ *chinos* | (they) are Chinese |
| *Jua*ŋ *canta* | John sings |

The variety of structures illustrated in (15) all have more complex representations than the single symbol # in the positions indicated by orthographic word divisions. These representations are provided by universal conventions.[10] However, we will maintain for the moment the simplifying fiction that all orthographic word divisions are correctly represented as #.

We turn now to apparent exceptions to the fact that in Allegretto the distribution of nasals is the same across word boundaries as within words. Consider the examples in (16), in which nasals occur before glides:

(16)

| BEFORE [y] | BEFORE [w] |
|---|---|
| *miel* [myel] | *muevo* [mweβo] |
| honey | I move |
| *nieto* [nyeto] | *nuevo* [nweβo] |
| grandson | new |
| *un hielo* [uñyelo] | *un huevo* [uŋweβo] |
| an ice (cube) | an egg |

It would seem from the data in (16) that we must add to rule (14) a case with the effect of (17), which assimilates nasals to a following glide across a word boundary but not within a word:

(17)

$$[+\text{nasal}] \rightarrow \begin{bmatrix} -\text{cor} \\ -\text{ant} \\ +\text{distr} \\ \alpha\text{back} \end{bmatrix} \Big/ \underline{\qquad} \# \begin{bmatrix} G \\ \alpha\text{back} \end{bmatrix}$$

However, it is not at all a straightforward matter to collapse (17) with (14). Note, first of all, that the # in (14) is optional, while the same boundary in (17) is obligatory. Furthermore, (17) alone or combined in some way with (14) provides no insight into these apparently quite odd assimilations, since it has no more independent motivation and is not simpler than (18), for example:

[10] For discussion see Chomsky and Halle (1968, Chapter One, Section 5.3).

(18)

$$[+\text{nasal}] \rightarrow \begin{bmatrix} +\text{cor} \\ +\text{ant} \\ -\text{distr} \\ \alpha\text{back} \end{bmatrix} / \underline{\quad} \# \begin{bmatrix} G \\ \alpha\text{back} \end{bmatrix}$$

In other words, the only advantage of (17) over (18) is that (17) apparently expresses the facts correctly while (18) does not: (17) contributes nothing toward an explanation of the facts. We leave the matter in this unsatisfactory state until Section 2.4, which contains a fuller discussion of glides.

There is one further problem concerning nasals in Allegretto, which must be left unresolved. In all styles the cluster *mn* is phonetically [mn]: *columna, himno, omni-, alumno, calumnia, solemne, circumnavegar*, etc. On the other hand, the cluster *nm* is phonetically [nm] only in Largo and Andante. For the situation in Allegretto, I again cite Navarro Tomás (1965), whose description of Castilian once more carries over to the dialect under study:

> En el grupo *nm* la articulación de la primera consonante, en la conversación ordinaria [i.e., Allegretto], va generalmente cubierta por la de la *m*: la lengua realiza, de manera más o menos completa, el contacto alveolar de la *n*; pero al mismo tiempo la *m* forma su oclusión bilabial, siendo en realidad el sonido de esta última el único que acústicamente resulta perceptible: *inmóvil* [i$_n^m$móβil], *conmigo* [ko$_n^m$míɣo] (p. 113).

Thus we have another example of the type of coarticulation mentioned in Section 2.2.2 with regard to nasal assimilation across word boundaries in Andante. This time the situation is asymmetrical: *m* is unaffected before *n*, but *n* assimilates partially to a following *m*.


## 2.3 Lateral assimilation

In the dialect under study there is presumably only one systematic phonemic lateral, *l*. Initially, intervocalically, finally, and before labial, labiodental, alveolar, and velar obstruents, *l* is alveolar. Within a word in Largo and Andante, and across word boundaries as well as within a word in Allegretto, *l* assimilates to the point of articulation of a following dental ([t,d]) or alveolopalatal ([č]) obstruent. Thus we might propose, as first approximations, rule (19) for Largo and Andante and rule (20) for Allegretto:

(19)
$$1 \; \rightarrow \; \begin{bmatrix} \alpha\text{ant} \\ \beta\text{distr} \end{bmatrix} \; / \; \underline{\hspace{1cm}} \; \begin{bmatrix} +\text{obstr} \\ +\text{cor} \\ \alpha\text{ant} \\ \beta\text{distr} \end{bmatrix}$$

(20)
$$1 \; \rightarrow \; \begin{bmatrix} \alpha\text{ant} \\ \beta\text{distr} \end{bmatrix} \; / \; \underline{\hspace{1cm}} \; (\#) \begin{bmatrix} +\text{obstr} \\ +\text{cor} \\ \alpha\text{ant} \\ \beta\text{distr} \end{bmatrix}$$

Furthermore, in Allegretto *l* is realized as palatal [λ] before *y* across a word boundary, but as alveolar [l] before *y* within a word: *al hielo* [aλyelo], *aliento* [alyento]. Thus, apparently, in Allegretto (20) must be supplemented by (21):

(21)
$$1 \; \rightarrow \; \begin{bmatrix} -\text{cor} \\ -\text{ant} \\ +\text{distr} \end{bmatrix} \; / \; \underline{\hspace{1cm}}\#y$$

The similarity between (19), (20), (21) and (12), (14), (17), respectively, is striking. In fact, the *l*-assimilation data are just a subset of the nasal assimilation data. Rather clearly there is a significant linguistic generalization here: noncontinuant sonorants become homorganic with a following obstruent, within the limits set by certain constraints (there are labial, labiodental, and velar nasals, but no labial, labiodental, or velar *l*'s). This generalization is obviously not captured by the pairs of rules (12) and (19), (14) and (20), and (17) and (21), which treat the nasal and lateral assimilations as unrelated phenomena.

Ignoring for the moment the question of assimilation before glides, one might propose the following solution to the problem just posed. Consider a grammar that includes the nasal assimilation rule (22), which assimilates nasals to the major point of articulation of a following obstruent:

(22)
$$[+\text{nasal}] \; \rightarrow \; \begin{bmatrix} \alpha\text{ant} \\ \beta\text{cor} \end{bmatrix} \; / \; \underline{\hspace{1cm}} \begin{bmatrix} +\text{obstr} \\ \alpha\text{ant} \\ \beta\text{cor} \end{bmatrix}$$

In Allegretto the environment of (22) would of course be: $\underline{\hspace{1cm}}$ (#) ... Then a separate sonorant assimilation rule (23) assimilates nasals and *l* in features of phonetic detail with a following obstruent with which they already agree in major point of articulation. (In (23) the abbreviation [cont] stands for the feature "continuant.")

(23)

$$\begin{bmatrix} -\text{obstr} \\ -\text{cont} \end{bmatrix} \rightarrow \begin{bmatrix} \alpha\text{ant} \\ \beta\text{back} \\ \gamma\text{distr} \end{bmatrix} \Big/ \begin{bmatrix} \underline{\phantom{xx}} \\ \delta\text{cor} \end{bmatrix} \begin{bmatrix} +\text{obstr} \\ \alpha\text{ant} \\ \beta\text{back} \\ \gamma\text{distr} \\ \delta\text{cor} \end{bmatrix}$$

It is clear, however, that (22) and (23) fail to accomplish what they were invented to accomplish. *Ceteris paribus*, a grammar containing (22) and (23), or the obvious Allegretto analogues, will not be more highly valued than a grammar containing (12) and (19), or their Allegretto variants. *why not?*

These facts may well point to a defect in current phonological theory. It would seem reasonable to argue that it should be possible to state a phonological rule as something like (24):

*cant one state a rule thusly?*

(24)      ASSIMILATE: $\begin{bmatrix} \underline{\phantom{xx}} \\ \text{l,n} \end{bmatrix}$ [+obstr]

Such a rule would be interpreted to mean that *l* and *n* take the values of the features of any following obstruent, within the limits set by universal constraints. Thus (24) would yield, for example, labial and velar nasals, but not labial and velar *l*'s, before labial and velar obstruents. More generally, it seems that phonological theory should be revised to allow rules that mention processes such as "assimilation," "palatalization," "strengthening," "lenition," "vocalization," and "consonantalization" and to include an evaluation measure such that rules of this type are in general less "costly" than other types of rules. The issues involved are complex, and we cannot go into them further here. However, the literature abounds in suggestive facts,[11] and it seems to me that the Spanish data just presented provide prima-facie empirical evidence that some revision of phonological theory along the lines vaguely suggested is warranted.

For the present, we will retain the rules of nasal assimilation and lateral assimilation as in (12), (14), (19), and (20).

*what exactly is Harris' criticism here.*

## 2.4 Glide-consonant alternations

In the preceding discussion of assimilation, we noted certain difficulties regarding glides, particularly with respect to rules (17) and (21). These observations provide a minimal introduction to some of the problems in this area that have caused considerable confusion and controversy in such careful works as Bowen and Stockwell (1955),

---

[11] See, for example, Fudge (1967).

Bowen and Stockwell (1956), Saporta (1956a), and Stockwell, Bowen, and Silva-Fuenzalida (1956).

We will begin our examination of glides here by stating the relevant phonetic facts as they are given in a number of modern descriptions. Original notations will be retained in all quotations.

### 2.4.1 *Representative descriptions*

2.4.1.1. King (1952) includes the following statements about phonemes with glide allophones.

The phoneme /i/ has, in addition to the syllabic allophone [i], the nonsyllabic allophone

> [i̯], occurring between vowel and consonant or between consonant and vowel: /siénsia/, /lasiudád/, /áidós/, /óiga/, /áire/ (p. 52).

The phoneme /u/ has, in addition to syllabic [u], the nonsyllabic allophone

> [u̯], occurring between vowel and consonant or between consonant and vowel: /lasuérte/, /antíguo/, /kuidádo/, /oyuélo/, /déudas/, /automóbil/ (p. 52).

The phoneme /w/, the class of labial semivowels, has the single allophone

> [w], *with varying amounts of voiced velar friction* [italics mine], occurring initially and medially before vowels: /áwa/, /manáwa/, /čiwáwa/, /suwánte/, /suswískis/, /laswértas/. In certain styles of speech [gu̯] and [w] are in contrast: /sónguántes/, /sónwápos/ (p. 53).[12]

The phoneme /y/, the class of palatal semivowels, has the two allophones

> [i̯], *with varying amounts of voiced palatal friction* [italics mine], occurring initially and medially before vowels: /áya/, /yéga/, /subyúga/, /losyéba/ (p. 53).

and

> [i̯ˣ], *with varying amounts of voiceless palatal friction* [italics mine], occurring before pause: /mebóy#/, /áy#/, /múy#/ (p. 53).

---

[12] It is not clear what King means here. In fact, [gu̯] and [w] are "in contrast" only because of King's decision to phonemicize them a certain way. The last two examples also occur as /sónwántes/, /sónguápos/, which, by King's own analysis, shows exactly the opposite of what he seems to be saying. That is, they show that [gu̯] and [w] contrast only stylistically, not phonemically. We return to this directly.

*yes, because they seem to be in free variation*

2.4.1.2. Bowen and Stockwell's (1960) pedagogical statement:

Spanish /y/ at the beginning of a word is often considerably more tense than English /y/, but not started as a stop consonant, rather like the /d/ sound, as the English /ĵ/ is. The reason it is sometimes heard as English /y/, sometimes as English /ĵ/ is precisely because it is partially similar to both, but not identical with either; it is, so to speak, between them ... (p. 81). Spanish /w/ is similar to Spanish /y/ in the relative tenseness of its pronunciation when it is the first sound in a word. Where initial /y/ suggests /dy/ or /ĵ/, initial /w/ is often heard as /gw/, and a few words are actually listed in the dictionaries with two variant forms, for example, *huaca* and *guaca* (p. 82).

2.4.1.3. Bowen and Stockwell (1955):

[y] before a vowel is an on-glide from high-front tongue position; [y̌] is the same combined with *palatal friction* [italics mine]; [w] before a vowel is an on-glide from high-back tongue position with lips rounded; [w̌] is the same with *velar friction* [italics mine]. The same symbols after a vowel denote off-glides toward high-front or high-back position (p. 400, note 2).

### 2.4.2 *Interpretation of the data*

It is not known, of course, how the segments just described as having voiced and voiceless palatal and velar friction, or as being "between" English /y/ and English /ĵ/, would have been characterized if the writers cited had been working within a phonological theory that countenanced distinctive features. The descriptions given, however, explicitly term these phones "semivowels" or "glides" with some sort of peculiar phonetic admixture of fricative noise. A radically different claim will be made here: in phonetic representations the segments produced with friction are obstruents, not glides. The remainder of this section will be devoted to clarifying this claim and to presenting evidence that supports it.

Since constrictions radical enough to produce friction noise are involved, the specification of these segments as obstruents is clearly necessary on phonetic grounds in any phonological theory in which the relationship between phonetic transcription and articulatory and acoustical data is taken seriously. Moreover, it will be seen that the decision to treat these segments as obstruents is further motivated in terms of the set of phonological rules of the language. It will also be shown that these rules are in part independently justified, that is, they would be necessary even if the segments under discussion did not exist in Spanish.

Before proceeding further, let us establish the uniform transcription shown in (25):

(25)

| KING | BOWEN AND STOCKWELL | HENCEFORTH |
|---|---|---|
| i̭ | y | y |
| ṷ | w | w |
| j̱ | y̌ | $\gamma_1$ |
| w | w̌ | $\gamma^w$ |
| j̱ˣ | | $x_1$ |

The intended interpretation of the symbols in (25) with respect to the relevant features is given in (26):

*[handwritten: aya    ay    lasuerte    awa    siensia]*

(26)

|  | y | $\gamma_1$ | $x_1$ | w | $\gamma^w$ |
|---|---|---|---|---|---|
| vocalic | − | − | − | − | − |
| consonantal | − | + | + | − | + |
| anterior | − | − | − | − | − |
| coronal | − | − | − | − | − |
| high | + | + | + | + | + |
| back | − | − | − | + | + |
| round | − | − | − | + | + |
| continuant | + | + | + | + | + |
| voice | + | + | − | + | + |

Let us now re-examine King's examples (Section 2.4.1.1) in the light of (26), beginning with the [−back] phones. (King's original transcription is changed to that of (25), and boundaries are indicated. The boundary = occurs between prefix and stem, # indicates word divisions, and the *ad hoc* symbol ‖ stands for pause, total cessation of phonation.)

(a) Examples with [y]: *syénsya, la#syudád, áy#dós, óyga, áyre*

(b) Examples with [$\gamma_1$]: *á$\gamma_1$a, $\gamma_1$éga, sub=$\gamma_1$úga, los#$\gamma_1$éba*

(c) Examples with [$x_1$]: *me#box$_1$‖, áx$_1$‖, mux$_1$‖*

Clearly, [y], [$\gamma_1$], and [$x_1$] are in complementary distribution as shown in (27):

(27)     *a.* [$x_1$] occurs in the environment ——‖

         *b.* [$\gamma_1$] occurs in the environment $\left\{ \begin{matrix} V \\ = \\ \# \end{matrix} \right\}$ ——V

         *c.* [y] occurs elsewhere

Implicit in King's data is the fact that neither [y] nor unstressed [i] occurs between vowels: [á$\gamma_1$a], but not *[áya] or trisyllabic *[áia]. Not revealed by the data is the existence of alternations between the unstressed simple vowel [e] and the diphthong [yé]: $p$[e]$nsamiento$, "thought (noun)," $p$[e]$nsamos$, "we think," $p$[yé]$nso$, "I think." Furthermore, there are alternations between unstressed [e] and [$\gamma_1$é]: [e]$ló$, "it froze," [$\gamma_1$é]$la$, "it is freezing"; [e]$rrar$, "to err," [$\gamma_1$é]$rra$, "(he) errs."

We now turn to King's examples of [+back] phones.

(a) Examples with [w]:  $la\#swérte, antígwo, kwidádo, o\gamma_1wélo,$
$déwdas, awtomóbil$

(b) Examples with [$\gamma^w$]:  $á\gamma^wa, maná\gamma^wa, či\gamma^wá\gamma^wa, su\#\gamma^wánte,$
$sus\#\gamma^wískis, las\#\gamma^wértas$

As far as these examples show, [w] and [$\gamma^w$] have exactly the same distribution as [y] and [$\gamma_1$], respectively (see (27)). (The absence of a [+back] analogue of [$x_1$] need not concern us now.) Also, like [y] and unstressed [i], [w] and unstressed [u] do not occur between vowels: [á$\gamma^w$a], but not *[áwa] or trisyllabic *[áua]. There are, furthermore, alternations between unstressed [o] and the diphthong [wé]: $s$[o]$ltamos$, "we release," $s$[wé]$lto$, "I release"; and between unstressed [o] and [$\gamma^w$é]: [o]$lor$, "odor," [o]$lemos$, "we smell," [$\gamma^w$é]$le$, "(it) smells."

As a summary of the data presented so far and as a basis for further discussion, let us tentatively propose the ordered set of informal rules shown in (28):

(28)

$a.$ $\left\{\begin{matrix}\text{É} \\ \text{Ó}\end{matrix}\right\}_1$ $\rightarrow$ $\left\{\begin{matrix}\text{yé} \\ \text{wé}\end{matrix}\right\}_1$ $(under\ certain\ conditions)$[13]

$b.$ $\left\{\begin{matrix}\text{y} \\ \text{w}\end{matrix}\right\}_1$ $\rightarrow$ $\left\{\begin{matrix}\gamma_1 \\ \gamma^w\end{matrix}\right\}_1$ $/$ $\left\{\begin{matrix}\text{V} \\ \left\{\begin{matrix}= \\ \#\end{matrix}\right\}\end{matrix}\right\}$——$\left\{\begin{matrix}\text{V} \\ \|\end{matrix}\right\}$  — how is this to be expanded?

$c.$ $\begin{bmatrix}\text{V} \\ +\text{high} \\ -\text{stress}\end{bmatrix}$ $\rightarrow$ G $/$ $\left\{\begin{matrix}——\text{V} \\ \text{V}——\end{matrix}\right\}$

$d.$ $\gamma_1$ $\rightarrow$ $x_1$ $/$ ——$\|$

For the moment (28) is simply another way of organizing the data; as the exposition continues and more data are accumulated, these rules will be modified considerably.

[13] Diphthongization will be treated more carefully in Section 6.2.1. For expository purposes, we will henceforth represent as upper case $E$ and $O$ those $e$'s and $o$'s that diphthongize when stressed.

/antiguo/ → [ɛu] →[ʷ]

Thus pure glides y + w are
derived from /underlying/ same
/i/ + /u/, respectively

d. modifies one out Out of b.)
'is derived' in final position is of

p.25 - 11B: Harris wants a single
lexical item to have the
same underlying form in all
styles of the dialect

...ment able w/ the rule, no numbers, w can take top row
combined w. bottom (top row
or vice versa $\left(\{=\} - V\right)$; or

top w. top $(V \_ V)$ or bottom w.
bottom $\left(\{\#\} - ||\right)$

The fact that certain of these don't
occur doesn't matter —

Thus, possible arguments w:
$y \rightarrow \delta'$ / V $\_$ V
/V $\_$ ||     (by d., this later
$\rightarrow$ x,)

p.24 - comment on the eigenvalues +
results of Rule (28) a - α -

a. = eigentheorems — to be discussed later

b. - $\begin{Bmatrix} y \\ w \end{Bmatrix} \rightarrow \begin{Bmatrix} \delta' \\ \gamma w \end{Bmatrix}$ . . . . . .

numbered parentheses mean; if take
y, must → γw δ' ; if take w,
must → γw δ' ;

$/ = — \lor$

$/ = — \,||$ (never occurs)
$/ \neq — \,||$ ( " )
$/ \neq — \lor$

Same for $w \rightarrow$

NB: this means tht $y + w$ are underlying, + that $f$, + $f^w$ can be produced by P-rules

c. takes care of situations like

### 2.4.3 *Andante*

Rules (28*a–d*) are a first approximation to a set of rules for careful speech only, that is, for the style of pronunciation we have been calling Andante. We turn to Allegretto in Section 2.4.4 after completing the discussion of Andante.

2.4.3.1. Let us now elaborate on King's (1952) statement that "in certain styles of speech [gu] and [w] are in contrast" (see note 12). In some dialects there is a contrast between the initial sound of words such as *guante, guapo* and the initial sound of words such as *huele, huevo*, at least in careful speech. In the dialect under study, on the other hand, no such contrast exists in Andante. The examples given are pronounced [γʷ]*ánte*, [γʷ]*ápo*, [γʷ]*éle*, and [γʷ]*évo*. In hypercareful speech, however—that is, in Largo—words written with initial *gu*V are pronounced with an initial stop.

Forms such as *olór*, "odor," and *olémos*, "we smell," show that the underlying phonological representation of the initial segment of *huéle*, "(it) smells," is *O*. Similarly, the underlying initial segment of *huévo*, "egg," is also *O*, as is shown by related forms such as *ovidúcto, ovifórme, ovíparo, ovulación*, and *ovário*.

The underlying phonological representation of the initial segments of words such as *guante* and *guapo* is not so clear. One might propose the following. In Largo, the underlying representations in question are /gwante/ and /gwapo/, essentially identical to the phonetic representations. In Andante, on the other hand, the underlying representations are /wante/ and /wapo/, with initial /w/ then being turned into [γʷ] by rule (28*b*). Such a proposal seems to me to be quite unattractive, however, since it makes the odd claim that a lexical item has different lexical representations in different styles of the same dialect. This claim might be made a little more acceptable by arguing that the Largo pronunciation with an initial stop is an artificial "spelling pronunciation" that is correctly accounted for by a phonological representation distinct from the normal one. It would seem much more natural, however, to assume that words such as *guante* and *guapo* have initial /gw/ in all styles.[14] Initial [γʷ] in Andante can then be accounted for with the help of rule (29):

$$(29) \qquad\qquad g \;\rightarrow\; \phi \;/\; \text{———w}$$

With rule (29) ordered before rule (28*b*), the derivation of *guapo* and *huevo*, for example, would include the steps shown in (30):

---

[14] See also Chapter 5, note 10.

(30)                          gwápo      Óvo
                                          wé       (28a)
                             φ                     (29)
                             $\gamma^w$   $\gamma^w$   (28b)
                             $\gamma^w$ápo  $\gamma^w$évo

*good!*

Presumably, rule (29) is missing in dialects that contrast the initial
sounds of *guapo* and *huevo* and in Largo in the dialect under study.
With this proposal, then, which I will accept until counterevidence is
found, the difference between styles is not due to differences in underlying phonological representations, but rather to differences in the set
of rules for each style.

2.4.3.2. The controversy in the well-known series of articles Bowen
and Stockwell (1955), Bowen and Stockwell (1956), Saporta (1956a),
and Stockwell, Bowen, and Silva-Fuenzalida (1956) centered around
the problem of the phonemicization of [i,y,$\gamma_1$,u,w,$\gamma^w$]. As has been
seen in the preceding sections, and as the authors mentioned would
no doubt now agree, the difficulties simply disappear when certain
linguistically unmotivated methodological restrictions of structuralist
phonemic theory are abandoned. It is interesting to note at this point
that although the work of King (1952) is cited in the series of articles
referred to, certain of his data did not figure in the later discussion,
and these facts might have altered the course of the controversy had
they been considered. I shall present these data now, both for their
own interest and for the role they will play in the sections to come.

King notes that there are contrasts among phonetic sequences
involving glides which are not accommodated by his phonemicization
of consonants, vowels, glides, and stresses. Expanding somewhat on the
list of examples King gives, we observe that *hiena*, "hyena," *hiato*,
"hiatus," and a few other words form nearly minimal contrasts with
words like *yema*, "yolk," and *yate*, "yacht." Words like *hiena* and *hiato*
are pronounced with initial glides—[yéna], [yáto]—or with shortened
vowels—[ĭéna], [ĭáto]—while words like *yema* and *yate* are pronounced
with initial [$\gamma_1$]—[$\gamma_1$éma], [$\gamma_1$áte]. Analogous examples may be found
in which there is a contrast between [w] or shortened [ŭ] and
[$\gamma^w$]: *huida* [wíða] or [ŭíða], "flight," versus *güira* [$\gamma^w$íra], "gourd."

*this is only for Andante*

Such contrasts pose no problem for the proposals being developed
here. For words like *hiena* and *hiato*, the systematic phonemic representations /iena/ and /iato/ may be assumed. Rule (28c) will then apply
to initial /i/, giving [yena] and [yato], respectively. For words like
*yema* and *yate*, the systematic phonemic representations /yema/, /yate/,
plus application of rule (28b) to the initial /y/, give [$\gamma_1$ema] and [$\gamma_1$ate],

*excellent!*

respectively. The examples with [w] and [$\gamma^w$] are accounted for analo-gously.[15] We will not consider the pronunciations with the shortened vowels [ĭ] and [ŭ] at this point: they are discussed at the end of Section 2.4.5.1.

The reason for the introduction of these examples here will become apparent in the next section.

### 2.4.4 *Allegretto*

The differences between Andante and Allegretto with respect to the segments that have traditionally been called "glides" are essentially the following:

(a)  In words like *hiena, hiato, huida,* which may have initial [ĭ], [ŭ] or initial [y], [w] in Andante, only [y] and [w] occur in Allegretto: [y]*ena*, [y]*ato*, [w]*ida*.

(b)  Where Andante has [$\gamma_1$] and [$\gamma^w$], Allegretto has [y] and [w], respectively. Thus, corresponding to Andante *ha*[$\gamma_1$]*a*, [$\gamma_1$]*ega*, *sub*[$\gamma_1$]*uga*, etc., we find Allegretto *ha*[y]*a*, [y]*ega*, *sub*[y]*uga*; corresponding to Andante *a*[$\gamma^w$]*a*, *Chi*[$\gamma^w$]*a*[$\gamma^w$]*a*, *las* [$\gamma^w$]*ertas*, etc., we find Allegretto *a*[w]*a*, *Chi*[w]*a*[w]*a*, *las* [w]*ertas*.

It would seem at first glance that the relevant difference between the sets of rules for Andante and Allegretto is simply that Allegretto lacks rule (28*b*), which turns *y* and *w* into obstruents. We shall see in the following sections, however, that this cannot be the case. We shall find evidence that the grammar of Allegretto must contain rules with the effect of (28*b*) and then later rules with the effect of (31):

$$(31) \qquad \begin{Bmatrix} \gamma_1 \\ \gamma^w \end{Bmatrix}_1 \rightarrow \begin{Bmatrix} y \\ w \end{Bmatrix}_1$$

It is somewhat inelegant that the grammar of Allegretto must have rules that turn glides into true consonants, (28*b*), and then other rules that turn the latter back to glides, (31), but this is demanded by the data that will now be presented.

2.4.4.1. In Section 2.2.3 it was pointed out that the distribution of nasals before glides was apparently quite odd and seemed to require a complicated formulation of the otherwise straightforward rule of nasal assimilation (14). We may add to the examples given in (16) the contrasts shown in (32):

---

[15] There are also instances of VV versus GV contrasts. For example, the contrast between trisyllabic *dueto* [dueto], "duet," and dissyllabic *duelo* [dwelo], "mourning," can presumably be accounted for by the underlying representations /du = eto/ and /dOlo/, respectively. For other kinds of examples, see Section 4.3.4.

(32)                     NASAL BEFORE [y]

    [ny]*eto*        versus      *u*[ñy]*elo*

    grandson                     an ice (cube)

    *so*[ny]*enas*     versus      *so*[ñy]*emas*

    (they) are                 (they) are

    hyenas                      yolks

*[handwritten: but I thought they assimilated across #!]*

                    NASAL BEFORE [w]

    [nw]*evo*       versus      *u*[ŋw]*evo*

    new                      an egg

    *si*[nw]*ida*      versus      *si*[ŋw]*ira*

    without                  without (a)

    flight                    gourd

Now, given the existence of rule (28*b*) and the addition of rule (31) to the grammar of Allegretto, the contrasts illustrated in (32) are accounted for without the questionable rule (17) or any other complication of the nasal assimilation machinery. Contrasts like those between [ny]*eto* and *u*[ñy]*elo* and between [nw]*evo* and *u*[ŋw]*evo* are handled as shown in the partial derivations in (33):

*[handwritten: nieto   un hielo   nuevo   un huevo]*

(33)    nÉto     un#Élo     nÓvo     un#Óvo

        yé         yé        wé        wé      (28*a*)

                 γ1                    γ$^w$      (28*b*)

                 ñ                   ŋ       (14)

                 y                   w       (31)

    *nyéto*    *uñyélo*    *nwévo*    *uŋwévo*

Contrasts like those between *so*[ny]*enas* and *so*[ñy]*emas* and between *si*[nw]*ida* and *si*[ŋw]*ira* are handled as shown in the partial derivations in (34):

*[handwritten: son hienas   son yemas   sin huida   sin wira]*

(34)   són#iénas   són#yémas   sin#uída   sin#wíra

                    γ1                    γ$^w$      (28*b*)

                  ñ                   ŋ       (14)

      y                    w               (28*c*)

                  y                   w       (31)

    *sónyénas*   *sóñyémas*   *sinwída*   *siŋwíra*

Rules (28*b*) and (28*c*) will be discussed further and formulated more carefully in Sections 2.4.5.1 and 2.4.5.2. First we turn to additional evidence in support of the present proposals for Allegretto.

2.4.4.2. In Section 2.3 it was pointed out that the distribution of laterals before glides corresponds in part to that of nasals before glides.

Thus we have in Allegretto *aliento* [alyento] but *al hielo* [aλyelo], and so on. It is obvious that the derivation of such forms is entirely analogous to those in (33) and that such a rule as (21) is unnecessary in a grammar that contains rules with the effect of (28*b*).

2.4.4.3. There is another set of data relevant at this point which will be sketched briefly now and then examined in detail in Section 2.5.2. In both Andante and Allegretto, *s* becomes partially voiced before certain voiced segments:

(a)  before obstruents—*dezde, loz dientes* (versus *hasta, los tientes*)
(b)  before liquids—*izla, loz lagos, Izrael, loz ricos*
(c)  before nasals—*mizmo, loz monos, azno, loz nuevos*

Additionally, *s* voices in Allegretto before glides across a word boundary but not within a word: *loz yates* versus *desyerto*; *loz wevos* versus *swevos*. Voicing of *s* never occurs before vowels, either across a word boundary or within a word: *los osos*.

If we omit glides from consideration, we may give (35) as a first approximation to the rule of *s*-voicing:

(35)
$$s \rightarrow z \ / \ \text{---}(\#)\begin{bmatrix}+\text{cons} \\ +\text{voice}\end{bmatrix}$$

In a grammar that does not have rules with the effect of (28*b*), rule (35) will apparently have to be supplemented by a rule with the effect of (36) in order to account for assimilation before glides:

(36)
$$s \rightarrow z \ / \ \text{---}\#\begin{bmatrix}-\text{cons} \\ -\text{voc}\end{bmatrix}$$

With rules (35) and (36), we are again faced with the now familiar difficulties of collapsing two rules, one of which has an optional # before certain segments other than glides and the other of which has an obligatory # before glides. On the other hand, a grammar that contains rules (28*b*) and (31) presents no such difficulty since rule (36) becomes unnecessary. The contrasting examples given earlier are then derived, in part, as illustrated in (37):

(37)

| los#yates | desyerto | los#wevos | swevos | |
|-----------|----------|-----------|--------|---|
| $\gamma_1$ | | $\gamma^w$ | | (28*b*) |
| z | | z | | (35) |
| y | | w | | (31) |
| *loz yates* | *desyerto* | *lozwevos* | *swevos* | |

Further contrasts involving *s*-voicing, analogous to those illustrated in (34) involving nasal assimilation, are exemplified by *las hienas* [lasyenas] versus *las yemas* [lazyemas] and *las huidas* [laswiðas] versus *las güiras* [lazwiras].

2.4.4.4. In each of the three cases just discussed, formal difficulties arise from the apparent necessity of adding to the rules in question a case in which the environment includes ——# $\begin{bmatrix} -\text{cons} \\ -\text{voc} \end{bmatrix}$, where # is not optional. However, such additions are otiose duplications of part of the work of (28*b*), which changes glides into obstruents in the environment #——. Thus, extremely strong support is provided for the inclusion of rules with the effect of (28*b*) in a grammar of Allegretto, even though this entails the seeming inelegance of rule (31), that is, a rule that reverses the effect of (28*b*). Add to this evidence the fact that certain "glides" are actually realized phonetically as obstruents in Andante and the case becomes even stronger. Furthermore, it will be argued in Section 2.6.2.4 that rules with the effect of (28*b*) are motivated quite independently of the data presented in the preceding sections.

### 2.4.5 *Further details*

2.4.5.1. A number of questions remain concerning rule (28*c*). First, consider the nearly minimal pair *c*[wi]*dádo–c*[yu]*dád*. Let us assume that prior to the application of (28*c*) the representations in question are *cuidado* and *ciudad*. In neither of the sequences of high vowels *ui* and *iu* is either vowel stressed. Hence, if the two cases of (28*c*) were unordered, the rule could apply to either vowel. The fact that (28*c*) must apply to the first vowel in each sequence seems to establish the order of the cases as they have been given.

But we have gone too quickly: we have not actually shown that (28*c*) is in fact a rule of Spanish. What has been noted is that, with a few marginal exceptions, Spanish does not have in phonetic representations sequences of the form $V_1V_2$ or $V_2V_1$ within a word where $V_1 = [+\text{high}, -\text{stress}]$. It is gratuitous to assume, however, that the only explanation for the absence of such sequences is that they are all converted into GV and VG, respectively, by rule (28*c*). There exists, in fact, evidence that this assumption may be false. We now turn to this evidence.

Foley (1965) proposed that stress in Spanish can be entirely accounted for (aside from marginal exceptions, of course) by the familiar Latin stress rule. There are difficulties associated with this proposal, a few of which will be discussed in Section 4.3. Nevertheless, for the sake of argument, let us assume that the Latin stress rule is one of the rules that play a role in assigning stress in Spanish and, in particular, that stress is assigned to nouns and adjectives by this rule. Now consider nouns and adjectives such as those in (38):[16]

(38)  a.  *láudano, náufrago, áulico, áureo, cáustico, hidráulico, cláusula, farmacéutico, Seléucidas, terapéutico, enfitéutico*
      b.  *alícuota, ventrílocuo, cónyuge, cuadríyugo, pléyade*

If all the segments in (38) that are spelled as vowels (and the *y* of the last three examples) were represented as vowels at the time the stress rule applied, then stress could not be assigned correctly: in every case stress would have to be assigned to the fourth vowel from the end of the word, but the Latin stress rule can assign stress no further to the left than the third vowel from the end of a word. Thus, either (a) the segments written *i, u, y* that are contiguous to a vowel are not vowels in the systematic phonemic representation of these words, or (b) there must be a rule with the effect of (39) that is ordered before stress assignment:

(39)
$$
\begin{bmatrix} V \\ +\text{high} \end{bmatrix} \rightarrow G \ / \ \left\{ \begin{matrix} \underline{\quad} V \\ V \underline{\quad} \end{matrix} \right\}
$$

*order :*
*1. (39)*
*2. stress assignment*
*3. (28c)*

Observe now that (28c) mentions [−stress] and therefore must be ordered after stress assignment. Thus, if alternative (b) is correct and both (39) and (28c) are in the grammar, we are left with two nearly identical rules that cannot be collapsed. When faced with such a situation, one might seriously question the existence of (28c). What we must now do, then, is examine other data that may shed light on the status of these two rules in the grammar.    *28c ≠ 39*

Examples such as those in (40) are common in Allegretto:

(40)          a.  *amplío, amplyámos, amplyár*
                  *vacío, vacyámos, vacyár*
                  *insinúo, insinwámos, insinwár*
                  *individúo, individwámos, individwár*

              b.  *país, paysáno*
                  *baúl, bawléro*

All the examples of (40a) are verb forms. *Amplío* is first person singular present indicative, *amplyámos* is first person plural present

---

[16] It is actually rather difficult to find relevant examples. The reader will note that the examples in (38a) contain only *aw* and *ew*. Aside from a handful of exceptions, some unique, there are no instances in the language of *ey, ow, iw, uw, iy, uy* within a word. Rules will be given in Chapter 3 that account for the absence of these sequences.

indicative, *amplyár* is the infinitive, "to enlarge." The other examples in (40*a*) are arranged in the same manner. The examples in (40*b*) show stress shifts accompanying the common suffixes -*ano* and -*ero*. Clearly the vowel-glide alternations in all these forms are determined by the position of stress; hence there must be a rule like (28*c*) which applies *after* stress is assigned.

In short, if alternative (b) is correct—that is, if rule (39) is in the grammar—then (39) must apply before stress is assigned and (28*c*) must apply after stress is assigned. Yet, as already mentioned, these two rules are apparently identical except that (28*c*) applies only to segments that are [−stress]. Furthermore, the question now arises as to why application of (39) does not remove all the cases to which (28*c*) might apply. For example, how do *país* and *baúl* escape (39)? (There is no reason that I know of to postulate phonemic representations like *paCis*, *baCul*, where some intervening consonant would block (39).) One particularly simple answer would be that (39) is not a rule of Spanish.

If rule (39) does not exist and if stress is assigned at least to nouns and adjectives by the Latin stress rule, then we seem to be left with alternative (a): the orthographic *i*'s and *u*'s contiguous to other vowels (and *y* in *cónyuge*, etc.) in (38) are not represented phonologically as vowels. Since these segments occur phonetically as glides, we must assume that they are represented phonologically as glides unless there is reason to do otherwise.[17] Thus we will have, for example, the underlying representations /lawdano/, /kawstiko/, /terapewtiko/, /konyuge/.

There is of course no a priori objection to the appearance of glides in underlying representations. In fact, Chomsky and Halle (1968, Chapter 9) consider VG and GV sequences to be less "marked" than VV sequences. I belabor the point simply because the argument presented here is, to my knowledge, entirely novel in the considerable literature concerned with glides in Spanish. If this argument is correct, it provides motivation for including glides in the inventory of systematic phonemes of Spanish in addition to that suggested in connection with contrasts of the type illustrated by *hiato* versus *yate*, namely, the positing of underlying /iato/ versus /yate/.[18]

As a final remark about rule (28*c*), it may be observed that the need for such a rule seems to be clearly established, in particular by the examples of (40), at least for Allegretto. However, the exact status of

---

[17] In *alícuota* and *ventrílocuo*, for example, the phonetic [w] represented by orthographic *u* may come from an underlying rounded velar: /alik$^w$ota/, /ventrilok$^w$o/. Rounded velars will be discussed in Section 5.2.5.3.

[18] Further motivation for underlying glides will be given in Section 4.3.2.

(28*c*) in Andante is problematic, as is the relation of (28*c*) in Allegretto to the phenomena to be mentioned briefly now. Several observers— for example, Stockwell, Bowen, and Silva-Fuenzalida (1956)—have noted the occurrence of extra short vowels (indicated here with the diacritic [˘]) immediately before another vowel: lĕón, pŏeta, lă odia. These shortened vowels give rise to a number of questions. For example, what is the difference, if any, between [ĭ] and [y] or between [ŭ] and [w]? Should [ĕ] and [ŏ] be characterized formally as nonsyllabic vowels, that is, should they be assigned the features of nonhigh glides? If so, should this treatment be extended to [ă]? Empirically justified answers to these questions and others are lacking at present. The available facts suggest that the distribution of extra short vowels is dependent on the assignment of stresses other than primary both within words and to longer stretches  However, the study of stress assignment of this type, and consequently the distribution of shortened vowels, has not progressed sufficiently to warrant further discussion at this time.[19] I shall therefore leave (28*c*) in the grammars of both Andante and Allegretto as a first approximation to the correct rules.

2.4.5.2. We will now examine rule (28*b*) in slightly more detail. Consider King's example *hoyuelo* (Section 2.4.1.1, second paragraph), a diminutive of *hoyo*, "hole," "hollow," which is pronounced [oywélo] in Allegretto and [oɣɪwélo] in Andante. *Hoyuelo* is presumably represented as *oy+Ólo* before, and as *oy+wélo* after, the application of rule (28*a*). The problem at hand is to refine rule (28*b*) so that it will apply to a representation like *oy+wélo* (as stated it will not) and yield the correct form [oɣɪwelo] and not *[oyɣʷelo] or *[oɣɪɣʷelo]. More generally, we must determine whether (28*b*) should apply only to the first of a sequence of two glides or only to the *y* in either of the sequences *yw* or *wy*. Unfortunately, no clear example of *wy* at this stage of derivation comes to mind. I will therefore assume, tentatively and somewhat arbitrarily, that the first alternative is correct, that is, that

---

[19] Some readers may be surprised at the blitheness with which one talks about contrasts among representations of the form VV, V̆V, GV, and possibly also VV̆, VG. The rhythm of Spanish utterances is of the type that has been called "syllable-timed," as opposed to "stress-timed" rhythm found, for example, in English. This means that in Spanish all syllables tend to be of the same length, regardless of position of stress, relative tenseness or laxness of vowels (there are no reduced vowels in Spanish), and so on. Thus any deviation from the typical machine gun flow of evenly spaced syllables can be perceived fairly readily. The only instance in which there is ever any question as to how many syllables there are in an utterance is the case of V̆V or VV̆, which seems intuitively to be intermediate between VV (obviously two syllables) and GV or VG (obviously one syllable).

(28*b*) should apply to the first glide in both of the sequences *yw* and *wy*. More explicitly, (28*b*) applies in the (unordered) set of environments of (41):[20]

(41)    *a.*    V——[−cons]    (*oyo, oywelo*)

   *b.*    V——‖    (*voy*)

   *c.*    $\left\{\begin{matrix} \# \\ = \end{matrix}\right\}$——[−cons]    (*sub* = *yuga, yweve*)

   *d.*    $\left\{\begin{matrix} \# \\ = \end{matrix}\right\}$——‖

Let us first assume that (28*b*) is a cyclical rule. Then, given the representations in (42), where only minimal assumptions are made about surface syntactic structure, (28*b*) would apply as shown:

(42)

| | | | |
|---|---|---|---|
| | | | 1ST |
| [#oywelo#] | [# [#ay#] [#wevos#] #] | [# [#ay#] [#una#] #] | CYCLE |
| $\gamma_1$ | —        $\gamma^w$ | — | (28*b*) |
| | | | 2ND |
| [#o$\gamma_1$welo#] | [##ay##$\gamma^w$evos##] | [##ay##una##] | CYCLE |
| — | — | — | (28*b*) |
| *o$\gamma_1$welo* | *ay$\gamma^w$evos* | *\*ayuna* | |

The rule thus yields an incorrect result for *hay una*, which should be [a$\gamma_1$una] rather than *[ayuna].

Let us now assume that (28*b*) is a rule of word-level phonology, that is, a rule that applies only once in a given derivation, when the level of the "phonological word" is reached.[21] It is easily seen from examination of (42) that *hay una* will again come out as *[ayuna] rather than as [a$\gamma_1$una].

Finally, let us assume that (28*b*) is somehow allowed to apply once, "across the board," ignoring sequences of any number of occurrences of #. We will then have the results shown in (43):

(43)        oywelo        ay wevos        ay una
        *o$\gamma_1$welo*        *\*a$\gamma_1$wevos*        *a$\gamma_1$una*

We have simply moved from one incorrect result to another. One plausible way out of these difficulties would be to split (28*b*) into the two (ordered) rules (44*a*) and (44*b*):

---

[20] The fact that there are no examples of (41*d*) suggests that something is wrong with the formulation of (28*b*), but we will ignore this for the moment.

[21] For fuller discussion see Chomsky and Halle (1968, Chapter Eight, Section 6.2).

(44)  a. $\begin{bmatrix} -\text{voc} \\ -\text{cons} \end{bmatrix} \rightarrow [+\text{cons}] \ / \ \begin{Bmatrix} \# \\ = \end{Bmatrix}$ ———

b. $\begin{bmatrix} -\text{voc} \\ -\text{cons} \end{bmatrix} \rightarrow [+\text{cons}] \ / \ \text{V}$ ——— $\begin{Bmatrix} (\#) \ [-\text{cons}] \\ \| \end{Bmatrix}$

However, review of the data for Allegretto, particularly Section 2.4.4, indicates that the first case of (44*b*) is unnecessary for this style and the second case is apparently optional. We therefore refine (44*b*) as (45):

(45)

$\begin{bmatrix} -\text{voc} \\ -\text{cons} \end{bmatrix} \rightarrow [+\text{cons}] \ / \ \text{V}$ ——— $\begin{Bmatrix} (\#) \ [-\text{cons}] \\ \| \end{Bmatrix}$   *a.* ANDANTE
   *b.* ANDANTE:
        *obligatory*
     ALLEGRETTO:
        *optional*

*[handwritten annotation: ie, top line applies only s. Andante, bottom line is oblig. f. andante + opt. f. allegretto]*

Somewhat surprising evidence in support of this solution will be given in Section 2.6.2.4. (In Section 2.8.2 the theoretical status of the *ad hoc* notation ‖ will be discussed.)

Recall, incidentally, that (44*a*) must precede rules (12) and (14), that is, the rules of nasal assimilation, as well as rule (35), *s*-voicing. (See the derivations (34) and (37).)

2.4.5.3. Let us compare the feature specifications of the segments $[\text{i,y,}\gamma_1\text{,u,w,}\gamma^w]$ in terms of the familiar distinctive feature framework containing the features [diffuse] and [grave] on the one hand, and in terms of the newer framework that includes the features [anterior], [coronal], [high], and [back] on the other.

| (46) | | i | y | $\gamma_1$ | u | w | $\gamma^w$ |
|---|---|---|---|---|---|---|---|
| | vocalic | + | − | − | + | − | − |
| | consonantal | − | − | + | − | − | + |
| *a.* | diffuse | + | + | − | + | + | − |
| | grave | − | − | − | + | + | + |
| *b.* | anterior | − | − | − | − | − | − |
| | coronal | − | − | − | − | − | − |
| | high | + | + | + | + | + | + |
| | back | − | − | − | + | + | + |

The data that have led to the postulation of rules (28*c*), (44*a*), (45), (29), and (31) point to a close relationship among the members of the set $[\text{i,y,}\gamma_1]$ and among the members of the set $[\text{u,w,}\gamma^w]$. It is immediately obvious that these relationships are formally expressed

*excellent!*

more adequately in (46*b*) than in (46*a*): (46*b*) reflects precisely the fact that the alternations $i \sim y \sim y_1$, $u \sim w \sim y^w$ are essentially alternations of major class features ([vocalic] and [consonantal]) and not of cavity (point-of-articulation) features. Thus further support is supplied for Chomsky and Halle's recent revision of distinctive feature theory discussed in Section 2.2.

### 2.4.6 *Summary of rules*

For convenience of reference, the rules proposed so far are collected here as the ordered list (47). (Summaries of rules will be provided at intervals throughout the exposition. A cumulative list of rules appears in Section 6.5.) To the right of each rule are the example numbers used for its major appearances in the preceding discussion.

Inasmuch as $\#$ is being used as a cover symbol for more complex representations, no distinction will be made between $\#$ and $=$. (The role of boundary symbols in the phonological rules of Spanish is discussed more fully in Section 2.8.1.) The reader is reminded that several of the rules will undergo considerable revision.

(47)

*a.* $\left\{ \begin{matrix} \text{É} \\ {}_1\text{Ó} \end{matrix} \right\}_1 \rightarrow \left\{ \begin{matrix} \text{yé} \\ {}_1\text{wé} \end{matrix} \right\}_1$　(*under certain conditions*) 　　　　　(28*a*)

*b.* $\text{g} \rightarrow \phi \ / \ \text{——w}$ 　　　　　(29)

*c.* $\begin{bmatrix} -\text{voc} \\ -\text{cons} \end{bmatrix} \rightarrow [+\text{cons}] \ / \ \#\text{——}$ 　　　　　(28*b*), (44*a*)

*d.* $\begin{cases} [+\text{nasal}] \rightarrow \begin{bmatrix} \alpha\text{cor} \\ \beta\text{ant} \\ \gamma\text{back} \\ \delta\text{distr} \end{bmatrix} \ / \ \text{——} \begin{bmatrix} +\text{obstr} \\ \alpha\text{cor} \\ \beta\text{ant} \\ \gamma\text{back} \\ \delta\text{distr} \end{bmatrix} \quad \text{ANDANTE} \qquad (12) \\[3em] [+\text{nasal}] \rightarrow \begin{bmatrix} \alpha\text{cor} \\ \beta\text{ant} \\ \gamma\text{back} \\ \delta\text{distr} \end{bmatrix} \ / \ \text{——} (\#) \begin{bmatrix} +\text{obstr} \\ \alpha\text{cor} \\ \beta\text{ant} \\ \gamma\text{back} \\ \delta\text{distr} \end{bmatrix} \quad \text{ALLEGRETTO} \qquad (14) \end{cases}$

(*continued*)

*(47 continued)*

$$e. \begin{cases} 1 \rightarrow \begin{bmatrix} \alpha\text{ant} \\ \beta\text{distr} \end{bmatrix} \Big/ \underline{\phantom{xx}} \begin{bmatrix} +\text{obstr} \\ +\text{cor} \\ \alpha\text{ant} \\ \beta\text{distr} \end{bmatrix} \quad \text{ANDANTE} \qquad (19) \\[4em] 1 \rightarrow \begin{bmatrix} \alpha\text{ant} \\ \beta\text{distr} \end{bmatrix} \Big/ \underline{\phantom{xx}} (\#) \begin{bmatrix} +\text{obstr} \\ +\text{cor} \\ \alpha\text{ant} \\ \beta\text{distr} \end{bmatrix} \quad \text{ALLEGRETTO} \qquad (20) \end{cases}$$

$$f. \begin{bmatrix} -\text{cons} \\ +\text{high} \\ -\text{stress} \end{bmatrix} \rightarrow [-\text{voc}] \Big/ \begin{Bmatrix} \underline{\phantom{xx}}V \\ V\underline{\phantom{xx}} \end{Bmatrix} \qquad (28c)$$

$$g. \begin{bmatrix} -\text{voc} \\ -\text{cons} \end{bmatrix} \rightarrow [+\text{cons}] \Big/ V\underline{\phantom{xx}} \begin{Bmatrix} (\#)[-\text{cons}] \\ \| \end{Bmatrix} \quad \begin{matrix} \text{ANDANTE} \\ \text{ANDANTE:} \\ \textit{obligatory} \\ \text{ALLEGRETTO:} \\ \textit{optional} \end{matrix} \qquad \begin{matrix} (28b), \\ (44b), \\ (45) \end{matrix}$$

$$h. \text{ s} \rightarrow \text{ z} \Big/ \underline{\phantom{xx}} (\#) \begin{bmatrix} +\text{cons} \\ +\text{voice} \end{bmatrix} \qquad (35)$$

$$i. \gamma_1 \rightarrow [-\text{voice}] \Big/ \underline{\phantom{xx}}\| \qquad (28d)$$

$$j. \begin{Bmatrix} \gamma_1 \\ {}_1\gamma^w {}_1 \end{Bmatrix} \rightarrow \begin{Bmatrix} \text{y} \\ {}_1\text{w} {}_1 \end{Bmatrix} \quad \text{ALLEGRETTO} \qquad (31)$$

## 2.5 Obstruents: further remarks

### 2.5.1 *Distribution of* [b,d,g,β,δ,γ]

The statement is frequently found in school grammars that *b*, *d*, *g* "normally" occur as [b,d,g] initially, after nasals, and after *l*, but as the nonstrident continuants [β,δ,γ] elsewhere.[22] Before clarifying what

[22] *B* versus *v* is an orthographic, not a phonetic, distinction. For example, *hierba*, "herb," "grass," and *hierva*, "boil (present subjunctive)," are homophones, as are *cabo–cavo* and other similar pairs. Although there is no [v] in Spanish, the *f* of *Afganistán, afgano* is voiced before the following voiced consonant. Similarly, in *un chef bueno*, "a good chef," the *f* of *chef* may be voiced. The voicing of *f* is of no great importance per se, but it will fall out automatically from an independently motivated extension of the *s*-voicing rule (47h) to be given in Section 2.5.2.

might be meant by "normally," let us demonstrate that the "elsewhere" part of the statement is true.

The pronunciations indicated in (48) are to be taken as illustrative of Allegretto:

(48)

|  | β | δ | γ |
|---|---|---|---|
| V— | haβa | haδa | haγa |
| l— | calβo | [d] | alγo |
| —l | haβla | aδláteres | aγlomerar |
| r— | árβol | arδe | arγamasa |
| —r | haβrá | paδre | aγrio |
| y— | jayβo | nayδen²³ | cayγa |
| —y | aβyerto | aδyestrar | siγyendo |
| w— | ewβolia | dewδa | zewγma |
| —w | aβwelo | aδwana | aγwero |
| $\begin{bmatrix} C \\ +\text{voice} \end{bmatrix}$— | aδβerso | aββomen | suββylotal |
| —[+nasal] | suβmarino | aδmiración | diaγnóstico |

*Handwritten margin notes:*
*seems contrary to p. 37, where b, d, g are [b,d,g]   /l—*
*[b,d,g]*
*Andante = word init al [b,d,g]*
*Allegretto = utt.*
*[b,d,g]*

In word-initial position *b*, *d*, *g* occur both as [b,d,g] and as [β,δ,γ]; for example, *Beatriz babea*, "Beatriz slobbers," may be pronounced [b]*eatriz* [b]*a*[β]*ea* or [b]*eatriz* [β]*a*[β]*ea*. The former is the more careful pronunciation, while the latter is more casual. Let us say that the former is Andante and the latter is Allegretto. Thus, for Andante, "initially" must be taken to mean both utterance-initially (||——) and word-initially (#——). In Allegretto, on the other hand, "initially" means only utterance-initially, since [β,δ,γ] occur in word-initial position internal to an utterance, unless, of course, preceded by a nasal or *l* in the previous word. Note, furthermore, that the bracketing of the example just given is [s [NP [N*Beatriz*]N ]NP [VP [V*babea*]V ]VP ]s. The break between *Beatriz* and *babea* is at precisely the point at which the greatest number of # boundaries might occur; still the initial *b* of *babea* is [β] in Allegretto.

2.5.1.1. Let us assume, perhaps incorrectly, that the directionality of the alternations *b–β*, *d–δ*, *g–γ* is from stop to continuant. Concentrating on Andante for the moment, we will make a first approximation to a rule—"Spirantization"—to account for these alternations. Since anything in the environment ||—— is also in the environment #——, we may propose the following as a first step (where [strid] abbreviates

²³ This form is substandard but not rare. No standard example could be found.

the feature "strident"):[24]

$$\begin{bmatrix} +\text{obstr} \\ -\text{tense} \end{bmatrix} \rightarrow \begin{bmatrix} +\text{cont} \\ -\text{strid} \end{bmatrix} \quad \text{EXCEPT} \ / \ \#\text{———}$$

As mentioned, spirantization does not occur after nasals: *bom*[b]*a*, *don*[d]*e*, *gan*[g]*a*. Our next step, then, is to extend the environment of spirantization as follows:

$$\text{EXCEPT} \ / \ \begin{Bmatrix} \# \\ [+\text{nasal}] \end{Bmatrix} \text{———}$$

After *l*, *d* occurs as a stop but *b* and *g* occur as continuants: *cal*[d]*o* but *cal*[β]*o*, *gal*[γ]*o*. Thus we further extend the environment of the rule:[25]

$$\text{EXCEPT} \ / \ \begin{Bmatrix} \# \\ [+\text{nasal}] \\ \langle l \rangle \end{Bmatrix} \begin{bmatrix} \text{———} \\ \langle +\text{cor} \rangle \end{bmatrix}$$

This formulation states the facts correctly but fails to reveal any significant generalization about the environments in which Spirantization occurs. In particular, it fails to explain why after *l* only *d* appears as a stop but *b* and *g* appear as continuants. Note first that the nasals and *l* comprise just the set of noncontinuant sonorants in the dialect of Spanish under study. Thus the environment of Spirantization can refer simply to [−obstruent, −continuant] segments, rather than having to specify [+nasal] plus all the features of *l*. Now recall that nasal-obstruent clusters are always homorganic and note that *d*, like *l*, is [+coronal] while *b* and *g* are [−coronal]. The complete generalization is now evident: *b*, *d*, *g* appear as continuants except initially and after homorganic noncontinuant sonorants. Therefore, by ordering Spirantization after the rule of nasal assimilation, the environment can be reformulated as:

$$\text{EXCEPT} \ / \ \begin{Bmatrix} \# \\ \left\langle \begin{bmatrix} -\text{obstr} \\ -\text{cont} \\ \alpha\text{cor} \end{bmatrix} \right\rangle \end{Bmatrix} \begin{bmatrix} \text{———} \\ \langle \alpha\text{cor} \rangle \end{bmatrix}$$

[24] Justification of [+ obstruent, − tense] in this rule rather than [+ obstruent, + voice] will be given in Section 2.5.2. The specification of [−strident] in the output is necessary in order to block the application of marking conventions that would otherwise yield strident *v* and *z*. See Chomsky and Halle (1968, Chapter Nine).

[25] The angled bracket notation made use of here is that of Chomsky and Halle (1968, pp. 76–77): either (a) both members or (b) neither member of the pair in angled brackets must be present, and the ordering of (a) and (b) is disjunctive.

Stating the environment affirmatively, the Spirantization rule for Andante can be given as (49):

*(handwritten: aft. an obstruent, aft a cont-inuant, etc.)*

*(handwritten: b, d, g → β, δ, γ /)*

*(handwritten left margin: (within words))*

(49) $$\begin{bmatrix} +\text{obstr} \\ -\text{tense} \end{bmatrix} \rightarrow \begin{bmatrix} +\text{cont} \\ -\text{strid} \end{bmatrix} \bigg/ \left\{ \begin{matrix} [+\text{obstr}] \\ [+\text{cont}] \\ \langle[-\alpha\text{cor}]\rangle \end{matrix} \right\} \begin{bmatrix} \underline{\quad} \\ \langle\alpha\text{cor}\rangle \end{bmatrix}$$

2.5.1.2. Turning now to Allegretto, we recall that spirantization does not take place utterance-initially but does take place word-initially, except, of course, after a nasal or *l* in the preceding word. We may therefore state the rule for Allegretto as in (50):

*(handwritten left margin: (across word boundaries))*

(50) $$\begin{bmatrix} +\text{obstr} \\ -\text{tense} \end{bmatrix} \rightarrow \begin{bmatrix} +\text{cont} \\ -\text{strid} \end{bmatrix} \bigg/ \left\{ \begin{matrix} [+\text{obstr}] \\ [+\text{cont}] \\ \langle[-\alpha\text{cor}]\rangle \end{matrix} \right\} (\#) \begin{bmatrix} \underline{\quad} \\ \langle\alpha\text{cor}\rangle \end{bmatrix}$$

### 2.5.2 *Voiced tense and voiceless lax obstruents*

The voiced obstruents *b, d, g* are sometimes realized as the voiceless nonstrident continuants which will be transcribed [$\beta^\phi$, $\delta^\theta$, $\gamma^x$]: *a*[$\beta^\phi$]*surdo, clu*[$\beta^\phi$], *a*[$\delta^\theta$]*quirir, se*[$\delta^\theta$], *A*[$\gamma^x$]*fa*, and *zigza*[$\gamma^x$].[26] It is immediately apparent that the voiced continuants [$\beta,\delta,\gamma$] become voiceless before voiceless obstruents and in final position (more precisely, in the environment ——‖). Further data, however, indicate that closer scrutiny is warranted. We will limit our observations to careful speech (Andante) since in more rapid speech (a) additional assimilations occur that complicate the picture, and (b) the fine distinctions discussed here, if they exist at all, are extremely difficult to perceive.[27]

*(handwritten left margin: ? )*

Consider the contrasts illustrated in the following examples (which, for simplicity, show dentals only, although similar contrasts exist among labials and velars):

(a)  voiceless [t]: *cuanto, etcetera, atleta, atroz*
(b)  voiced [t$^d$]: *atmósfera, étnico, fútbol*
(c)  voiced [d]: *cuando, donde*
(d)  voiced [δ]: *admiro, padre, adláteres, amígdalas*
(e)  voiceless [δ$^\theta$]: *adquirir, adscribir, adjunto* (*j* = [x]), *sed, ataúd*

---

[26] Although *club, Agfa*, and *zigzag* are not of native origin, they are in common use. I have cited them in order to illustrate assimilations of *b* and *g* not otherwise found because of limitations on the distribution of *b* and *g* in native words. Incidentally, in the dialect under study the plural of *club* is *clubs* [klu$\beta^\phi$s], not the expected *\*clubes*.

[27] The reader is also advised that not all dialects share every detail of the data presented here.

These could be marked as in (51):

| (51) | t | $t^d$ | d | $\delta$ | $\delta^\theta$ |
|---|---|---|---|---|---|
| continuant | − | − | − | + | + |
| tense | + | + | − | − | − |
| voice | − | + | + | + | − |

While the specifications indicated in (51) are sufficient to mark all the contrasts and are quite plausible, recent instrumental investigations suggest that (51) might well be refined in the direction of greater acoustico-articulatory accuracy.

Lisker and Abramson (1964) have measured the onset time of vocal cord vibrations in the vowels following the release of stop consonants in a number of languages, including Spanish. From their measurements it may be concluded that the onset times of vocal vibrations fall into four distinct categories:[28]

(a) onset of voicing precedes stop release
(b) onset of voicing substantially coincides with stop release
(c) onset of voicing lags moderately after stop release
(d) onset of voicing lags considerably after stop release

Lisker and Abramson have shown that in initial position Spanish [t] falls into category (b) and Spanish [d] falls into category (a). The span of prevoicing of Spanish [d] is on the order of 100 milliseconds, which, although Lisker and Abramson do not specifically point it out, is clearly audible under good acoustical conditions.[29]

Kim (1965) has described three phonemically contrastive sets of voiceless stops in Korean, which can be represented schematically as:

$t_1$: voiceless, unaspirated
$t_2$: voiceless, lightly aspirated
$t_3$: voiceless, heavily aspirated

Pressure measurements made by Kim indicate that $t_1$ and $t_3$, but not $t_2$, are produced with heightened subglottal pressure. Further, $t_1$

---

[28] Lisker and Abramson distinguish only three categories, collapsing (c) and (d). The reason for the four-way distinction made here will become apparent shortly.

[29] On the other hand, initial English *t* falls into category (d), while English *d* falls into category (b). Thus Spanish *t* and English *d* are in the same category. This would help to account for the fact that English speakers learning Spanish experience extreme difficulty in distinguishing (in isolation) pairs like *tos–dos*, *tía–día*, *Tezcoco–descoco*. For many years I have found it pedagogically helpful to call students' attention to the prevoicing of Spanish *d*.

falls into category (b), virtual coincidence of stop release and vocalic onset; $t_2$ falls into category (c), with moderate lag of onset; $t_3$ falls into category (d), with considerable lag of vocalic onset. Thus Korean $t_1$ and Spanish [t] are in the same category.

By an odd coincidence, there are Korean words that are phonetically identical to Spanish words (though, of course, different in meaning): for example, Korean $t_1al$, Spanish *tal*. The description "phonetically identical" was not used loosely: Mr. Kim accepts my pronunciation of Spanish *tal* as an absolutely native Korean pronunciation of $t_1al$; I find Mr. Kim's pronunciation of $t_1al$ utterly indistinguishable from a native Spanish pronunciation of *tal*. Thus it is possible—though hardly necessary—that Korean $t_1$ and Spanish [t] are produced with identical articulatory mechanisms and therefore should be assigned the same feature specifications in phonetic representations.

Largely on the basis of the investigations of Lisker and Abramson and of Kim, Chomsky and Halle (1968, Chapter Seven, Section 6.2) have proposed that Korean $t_1$, $t_2$, and $t_3$ be assigned the following feature specifications:

|  | $t_1$ | $t_2$ | $t_3$ |
|---|---|---|---|
| tense | + | − | + |
| voice | + | − | − |
| heightened subglottal pressure | + | − | + |
| glottal constriction | + | − | − |

I shall not summarize here the intricate argument that Chomsky and Halle give to support these specifications. The point most germane to the present discussion is the assignment of the feature [+voice] to "voiceless" $t_1$.[30] This feature is correlated with the nonspread position of the vocal cords appropriate for voicing; but $t_1$ is not "voiced" because of the tenseness of the supraglottal musculature ([+tense]) and glottal constriction. Onset of voicing of a following vowel is simultaneous with release of the glottal constriction, however, since

---

[30] Chomsky and Halle have proposed that the distinctive feature [voice], as opposed to the impressionistic terms "voiced" and "voiceless," be restricted such that [−voice] characterizes sounds produced with a glottal opening that is so wide that it prevents vocal vibration when air flows through the opening; [+voice] characterizes sounds produced with an aperture not so wide as to prevent vibration. In these terms, sounds that are [+voice] may or may not be "voiced." Vocal cord vibration will not result although the glottis is in [+voice] position if there is (a) closure in the supraglottal tract, and (b) sufficient tension in the supraglottal musculature to prevent expansion of the supraglottal cavity, such that the flow of air through the glottis is impeded: without air flow through the glottis there can be no vocal cord vibration.

the vocal cords are already in voicing position. In $t_2$, on the other hand, there is a moderate lag in the onset of vocal vibrations since the vocal cords are not in voicing position when the stop closure is released.

For the sake of argument, let us suppose that Spanish [t] has the same feature specifications as Korean $t_1$ and see what rules would be necessary to assign these specifications correctly. For completeness, we will consider all the rules in the grammar that play a role in specifying the features of the phonetic segments mentioned in (51), beginning with two early rules that will be discussed in more detail in Chapters 3 and 4.

The first of these rules is:

$$[+\text{obstr}] \quad \rightarrow \quad [+\text{tense}] \quad / \underline{\qquad} \begin{bmatrix} +\text{obstr} \\ +\text{tense} \end{bmatrix}$$

It is assumed that [−voice] is supplied to the output by marking convention (see Chomsky and Halle (1968), Chapter Nine). This rule is needed to account for the alternations illustrated by *describir–descripción* and *legible–lectura.*

Note that of the segments shown in (51), only /t/ and /d/ appear in systematic phonemic representations. Similarly, for labials and velars /p,b,k,g/ are systematic phonemes, while $[p^b,\beta,\beta^\phi,k^g,\gamma,\gamma^x]$ are not. Thus the effect of the tensing rule just given is to change some instances of underlying lax voiced /b,d,g/ to the tense voiceless segments [p,t,k].

The next relevant rule is:

$$[+\text{obstr}] \quad \rightarrow \quad [-\text{tense}] \quad / \text{V} \underline{\qquad} [-\text{obstr}] \quad (under\ certain\ conditions)$$

This accounts for alternations such as *natación–nadar, recipiente–recibir,* and *persecución–perseguir.* It is highly restricted, applying only to a small subset of the lexicon. In this case [+voice] is supplied to the output by marking convention.

So far the composition of the set of obstruents remains unaltered. Some tense voiceless segments have been changed to lax voiced ones and vice versa, but no new members have been added to the set. The next relevant rule, however, is the Spirantization rule discussed in the previous section, and this changes some instances of the lax voiced stops [b,d,g] to the lax voiced nonstrident continuants $[\beta,\delta,\gamma]$. Thus from underlying /p,t,k,b,d,g/ we now have [p,t,k,b,d,g,$\beta,\delta,\gamma$].

What remains to be accounted for are tense voiced $[t^d]$ and lax voiceless $[\delta^\theta]$ of (51) (and the corresponding labials and velars $[p^b,\beta^\phi,k^g,\gamma^x]$). Recall that we already have in the grammar rule (35), which voices *s* in certain environments. This rule is repeated here as (52):

(52)

$$s \rightarrow z \; / \; \underline{\quad\quad} (\#) \begin{bmatrix} +\text{cons} \\ +\text{voice} \end{bmatrix}$$

Clearly we must generalize (52) so that it will yield [$p^b, \beta^\phi, t^d, \delta^\theta$, $k^g, \gamma^x$] in the appropriate environments. But there is a problem. The segment $s$ voices before voiced obstruents (*des$^z$de, ras$^z$go*), nasals (*mis$^z$mo, as$^z$no*), and liquids (*is$^z$la, mus$^z$lo—s* does not occur before [r]); noncontinuant obstruents also voice before voiced obstruents (*coñak$^g$ bueno*—examples are hard to find since $p$, $t$, $k$ do not occur in this position in native words) and before nasals (*at$^d$mósfera, ték$^g$nico*), but they do not voice before liquids (*aplicar, aprecio, atleta, atroz, aclarar, acreditar*). Thus it would seem that to generalize rule (52) to account for the voicing assimilation of noncontinuant obstruents would be to sacrifice the simplicity implied in the present formulation.

But now recall that, *ex hypothesi*, we must specify the features of [p,t,k] more accurately, along the lines suggested by Chomsky and Halle's interpretation of Kim's data. Suppose, then, we insert rule (53) before rule (52):

(53)

$$\begin{bmatrix} -\text{cont} \\ +\text{tense} \end{bmatrix} \rightarrow \begin{bmatrix} +\text{voice} \\ +\text{h.s.press} \\ +\text{glott con} \end{bmatrix} \; / \; \underline{\quad\quad}(\#)\begin{bmatrix} -\text{obstr} \\ -\text{nasal} \end{bmatrix}$$

Rule (53) assigns the features [+voice, +heightened subglottal pressure, +glottal constriction] to [p,t,k] before vowels, glides, and liquids, but not before obstruents or nasal sonorants. That is, rule (53) applies to just those instances of [p,t,k] that do not become [$p^b, t^d, k^g$] by assimilation to a following voiced segment.

Now rule (52) may be generalized as in (54):

(54)

$$\begin{bmatrix} +\text{obstr} \\ -\text{h.s.press} \end{bmatrix} \rightarrow \begin{cases} [\alpha\text{voice}] \; / \; \underline{\quad\quad}(\#)\begin{bmatrix} +\text{cons} \\ \alpha\text{voice} \end{bmatrix} \\ [-\text{voice}] \; / \; \underline{\quad\quad}\| \end{cases}$$

In this form the rule will voice [p,t,k] as well as [s] and devoice [$\beta, \delta, \gamma$] before certain voiced and voiceless consonants. The second case of (54) will devoice [$\beta, \delta, \gamma$], as well as [$\gamma_1$] (see Section 2.4.2, especially rule (28$d$)) in absolute final position.

The incomplete specifications in (51) may now be replaced as follows:[31]

[31] I include also the specifications for the voiceless cognate of [$\gamma_1$] discussed in Section 2.4 and the "partially voiced" cognate of [s] discussed in Section 2.4.4.3. The fact that these are actually a voiceless lax segment and a voiced tense segment, respectively, was not insisted on in earlier sections so as not to complicate the exposition. The voiced counterpart of tense [s] is transcribed [s$^z$]; the symbol [x$_1$] is retained for the voiceless counterpart of [$\gamma_1$] because of typographical complications.

| | p | $p^b$ | b | $\beta$ | $\beta^\phi$ | | |
| | t | $t^d$ | d | $\delta$ | $\delta^\theta$ | s | $s^z$ |
| | k | $k^g$ | g | $\gamma$ | $\gamma^x$ | | |
| | | | | $\gamma_1$ | $x_1$ | | |
| continuant | − | − | − | + | + | + | + |
| tense | + | + | − | − | − | + | + |
| voice | + | + | + | + | − | − | + |
| heightened | | | | | | | |
| subglottal pressure | + | − | − | − | − | − | − |
| glottal constriction | + | − | − | − | − | − | − |

Let us now conclude with the following observations:

(a)  It was noted that the noncontinuant obstruents [p,t,k] become voiced in environments similar but not identical to the environments in which [s] becomes voiced. We are thus led, by motivation internal to the grammar of Spanish—namely, that of formulating a single, general obstruent voicing-assimilation rule—to postulate some entirely nonobvious feature that distinguishes those instances of [p,t,k] that do not voice in the same environments as [s] from those that do.

(b)  Attention to phonetic detail, in particular the simultaneity of voicing onset after [t], has suggested certain nonobvious feature specifications.

(c)  It turns out that the features suggested by (a) and (b) are consonant with theoretical observations arrived at independently of the present data. Specifically, it is tense noncontinuants that are assigned the features [+voice, +heightened subglottal pressure, +glottal constriction] in certain environments.

(d)  It is interesting that the occurrence of heightened subglottal pressure is coincident with syllable onset. For example, *atleta*, with [t], is syllabified *a-tle-ta*, while *atmósfera*, with [$t^d$], is *at-mós-fe-ra*.[32]

Any real judgment concerning the proposals made in this section must await instrumental investigation of the dialect under study. In any event, we have surely disclosed an area in which recent theoretical innovations may be confronted with a valuable body of empirical data.

---

[32] In many dialects, *atleta* is, rather, *at-le-ta*. I have not investigated these other dialects in terms of the range of data presented here. Mexican Spanish has, of course, many indigenous words with initial and final *tl* clusters: *tlaco, tlapalería, atlatl, Popocatépetl*. The influence these forms may have had on the syllabification of words of European origin represents an intriguing question.

## 2.6 Nonlateral liquids

It is well known that there is a phonemic contrast between the intervocalic segments spelled *r* and those spelled *rr*. Minimal pairs are plentiful: *pero–perro, caro–carro, amara–amarra, torero–torrero*, and perhaps hundreds more. For ease of discussion, we shall use the symbol [r] for the segment spelled *r* intervocalically and, temporarily, the noncommital symbol [R] for the segment spelled *rr*. (The graph *rr* is used only intervocalically. In other positions *r* is used for [R], as, for example, in word-initial position, where [r] does not occur. Thus [Roto] is spelled *roto*.)

Presumably, both [r] and [R] are liquids, distinguished from [l] (and from [λ] in dialects that have this palatal liquid) at least in being [−lateral]. In the theoretical framework assumed here, one must eventually determine what phonetic features fully characterize [r] and [R] and, concomitantly, distinguish [R] from [r]. This is, to my knowledge, completely unexplored territory, and the task does not promise to be a simple one. A principled approach to the problem demands that (a) acoustico-articulatory data, and (b) the rules that involve [r] and [R] be studied. In such a case as this, strong support is afforded a particular solution only when inferences from both (a) and (b) begin to converge on that solution.

### 2.6.1 *Acoustico-articulatory data*

The segment [r] is simply a voiced apicoalveolar single flap. We may confidently assign to it at least the features [+vocalic, +consonantal, −obstruent, +voice, +coronal, +anterior, −strident], and, with only slightly less confidence, [+continuant, −tense].

The specification of [R] is far less clear. As a first approximation let us say that [R] is a voiced apical trill, or multiple flap, where *multiple* means "greater than two." Note carefully that [r] is exactly one flap; anything more will be interpreted as [R] in any style of speech. It is safe to estimate that, on the average, the trill consists of three or four flaps. In highly emphatic speech, however, the trill is often quite prolonged and may, in extreme cases, reach as many as a dozen or so flaps.

In addition to this fully trilled phone, there also occur in the dialect under study the phones that will now be described, which we have subsumed under the symbol [R]:

(a) In nonenergetic speech, particularly at low volume, [R] followed by a vowel, either word-initially or intervocalically within a word, ceases to be a trill and becomes some sort of fricative. It seems that the articulatory phenomena involved are the following: the air stream does not act on the tongue with sufficient force to initiate or maintain a trill, for which considerable energy is required. This fricative is voiced and quite "strident" (using this as an impressionistic term). The tongue seems to be slightly retracted or retroflected. We will use the *ad hoc* symbol [ż] to distinguish this phone from fully trilled [R].

(b) In pre-pause but not pre-consonantal position, a voiceless apical fricative occurs erratically. This fricative will be represented as [ṣ], which is distinct from the normal alveolar [s]: *tomar*‖ [tomáṣ] versus *Tomás*‖ [tomás]. The phone [ṣ], like its voiced counterpart [ż], seems to be slightly retracted.

(c) The cluster *sr*, whether divided by a word boundary as in *los ricos* or within a word as in *Israel* (which, with its derivatives, is the unique example of morpheme-internal *sr*), has a number of pronunciations. Navarro Tomás (1965, pp. 109–123) states that just [R], with the *s* completely absorbed, is a normal Castilian pronunciation of the cluster. This pronunciation is not common, however, in the dialect under study; when it is heard, it is generally taken as an affectation. What does occur ranges from a voiced *s* followed by a trilled [R] to what seems to be a single phonetic segment which I will transcribe [ř] because it seems to be very much like the phone spelled *ř* in Czech. Now the question arises as to whether [ż] and [ř] are phonetically distinct. The closest I can come to minimal pairs are *irreal–Israel* and *irreligioso–es religioso*. When, on demand, native speakers pronounce these as [iżeál, iraél] and [iżelixyóso, éřelixyóso], they feel that [ż] and [ř] are different, but they do not seem objectively to hear any difference.

What inferences might we draw from these data about the features of the segments under discussion? First, [ṣ] and [ż] (= [ř]?) are surely strident, theoretically as well as impressionistically. Also, [r] and [R] should be distinguished by tenseness. Navarro (1965) states emphatically that "la tensión muscular es en [R] mucho mayor que en [r]" (p. 123). Thus [r] is [−tense] and [R] is [+tense].

The locutions "retracted" and "retroflected" were used in the preceding descriptive statements. I assume that in the segments under discussion "retractedness" should be characterized with the features [−anterior, −high] ([−high] being necessary to distinguish these segments from the alveolopalatals). However, neither my own kinesthetic sense nor Navarro's drawings and comments (1965, p. 121) are precise enough to warrant the categorical assertion that some of the segments under discussion should be specified as [−anterior, −high] and others not. It does seem a reasonable guess that [R] is [+anterior], since it seems to have the same point of articulation as [r], which is clearly alveolar, i.e., [+coronal, +anterior], as are the normal *n*, *l*, and *s*. On the other hand, [š] and [ž] (= [ř]?) seem to differ from [s] and [sᶻ] only in their slightly retroflected articulation; hence I will assume that the former are [−anterior, −high].

I give in (55) a first hypothesis, based on acoustico-articulatory data, concerning the feature specifications of relevant segments. (The specifications enclosed in parentheses are tentative.)

| (55) | r | R | ř | ž | š | z | s |
|---|---|---|---|---|---|---|---|
| vocalic | + | (+) | (−) | − | − | − | − |
| consonantal | + | + | + | + | + | + | + |
| obstruent | − | (−) | + | + | + | + | + |
| anterior | + | + | − | − | − | + | + |
| coronal | + | + | + | + | + | + | + |
| high | − | − | − | − | − | − | − |
| continuant | + | + | + | + | + | + | + |
| tense | − | + | + | + | + | + | + |
| voice | + | + | + | + | − | + | − |
| strident | − | − | + | + | + | + | + |

### 2.6.2 *Rules involving* [r], [R], *and related phones*

Let us now approach the problem of specifying the features of the segments in (55) from the other direction, that is, by examining the rules in which these segments are involved. For ease of exposition I shall make a bipartite stylistic split and consider more careful speech (Largo and Andante) separately from more casual speech (Allegretto and Presto). Further stylistic differentiation seems pointless here.

2.6.2.1. There follows a description of the distribution of flapped [r] and trilled [R] in careful speech. (I assume that [ž] (=[ř]?) and [š] occur only in casual speech.)

(a) Both [r] and [R] occur intervocalically, as illustrated by *pe*[r]*o–pe*[R]*o* and many other minimal pairs.

(b) Only [R] occurs word-initially: for example, *la ropa* is [laRopa], not *[laropa]. The phone [r] is also excluded from the indicated position in compounds such as *autorretrato*, "self-portrait" (*retrato*, "portrait"), *subrayar*, "to underline" (*raya*, "line"), *enrollar*, "to roll up" (*rollo*, "roll").[33]

(c)  Only [R] occurs after *l*, *n*, and *s*: *al*[R]*ededor, hon*[R]*a, Is*[R]*ael*.[34]

(d)  Only [r] occurs after consonants other than *l*, *n*, *s*: *b*[r]*azo, comp*[r]*a, f*[r]*ito, lad*[r]*ón, t*[r]*es, g*[r]*ito, c*[r]*ea*.

(e)  Only [R] occurs before [+consonantal] segments: *a*[R]*ma, a*[R]*te, a*[R]*de, á*[R]*bol, pe*[R]*la*.

(f)  In word-final position the distribution of [r] and [R] is determined by the initial segment of the following word: only [r] occurs before a vowel and only [R] occurs before a consonant or liquid. Thus we have, for example, *amo*[r] *eterno*, "eternal love," but *amo*[R] *paterno*, "paternal love."[35] In utterance-final position, only [R] occurs. This [R] devoices slightly if the final syllable is stressed and more so if the final syllable is unstressed.

In short, [r] and [R] contrast only in intervocalic position. In all other positions the distribution is determined by the environment.

2.6.2.2.  The distribution of [r] and [R] in casual speech is the same as in careful speech with the exception that [r] rather than [R] occurs before [+consonantal] segments both within a word and across word boundaries. Thus in casual speech *arma, amor paterno* are pronounced *a*[r]*ma, amo*[r] *paterno*, respectively, rather than *a*[R]*ma*,

---

[33] It is not clear what boundary is present between prefix and stem in these examples and others. In any event, we are still using # as a cover symbol, and we shall not concern ourselves at this point with the identity of the boundary in such cases.

[34] The following observations are also pertinent. First, in our dialect *alrededor* is the only example of *lr* within a word (disregarding obvious compounds such as *malrotar*, "to squander") and even this is historically two words—*al* (itself a contraction of *a*+*el*) and *rededor* (and this by metathesis from *derredor*, which in turn is also two words, *de* and *redor*, roughly). Thus there is no clear example of *lr* within a morpheme. Second, *honra*, "honor," plus the related *honrar, honrado*, and a handful of proper names such as *Enrique, Manrique* exhaust the instances of *nr*. Finally, as already mentioned, *Israel, israelita*, etc., are unique with *sr*. Thus these words are exceptional in the sense that there are very few of them. They are not exceptional, however, in the sense that they would be if there were forms with *l*[r], *n*[r], *s*[r] rather than *l*[R], *n*[R], *s*[R]. There are no such forms.

[35] Note the asymmetry in the distribution of [r] and [R] in word-initial and word-final positions. Only [R] occurs word-initially, regardless of the final segment of the previous word—*la* [R]*opa, sin* [R]*opa*—but word-finally either [r] or [R] may appear, depending upon the first segment of the following word.

*amo*[R] *paterno* as in more careful speech.[36] Before a vowel [ż] (= [ř]?) replaces [R] sporadically, and in utterance-final position [r] and [š] seem to vary freely.

2.6.2.3. We will now consider the question of the systematic phonemic representations of [r] and [R]. (The conclusions to be reached concerning [r] and [R] naturally carry over to the sporadically occurring [ż] (= [ř]?) and [š].)

In intervocalic position, and only in this position, [r] and [R] contrast phonemically. Here the underlying representations are apparently /r/ and /rr/, respectively. That is, *pe*[r]*o*, "but," and *pe*[R]*o*, "dog," are /pero/ and /perro/; *ca*[r]*o*, "expensive," and *ca*[R]*o*, "car," are /karo/ and /karro/; *to*[r]*e*[r]*o*, "bullfighter," and *to*[R]*e*[r]*o*, "lighthouse keeper," are /torero/ and /torrero/, and so on. The claim that /rr/ is the systematic phonemic representation of the single intervocalic phonetic segment [R] is based on only two arguments, but two highly convincing ones.

First, observe that the future tense forms of the verb *querer* are *que*[R]*é*, *que*[R]*ás*, *que*[R]*á*, *que*[R]*emos*, *que*[R]*án*, as opposed to the future forms of *hablar*, for example, which have [r] rather than [R]: *habla*[r]*é*, *habla*[r]*ás*, *habla*[r]*á*, etc. The difference can readily be accounted for by the fact that the *querer* forms are derived from the representations *quer*+*ré*, *quer*+*rás*, *quer*+*rá*, etc. (ignoring irrelevant details); that is, the future endings -*ré*, -*rás*, -*rá*, etc., are attached to the stem *quer*-, bringing together the final *r* of the stem and the initial *r* of the endings.[37] In the *hablar* forms, on the other hand, the endings are attached to the stem *habla*-, which does not end in *r*, and as a result the verb forms have only a single *r*.

For the second argument, consider the singular-plural pairs of nouns and adjectives given in (56):

[36] The occurrence of both [árma] and [áRma], for example, provides the basis for a devastating, though hardly unique, argument against the (taxonomic) phoneme as a perceptual unit. Since [r] and [R] contrast intervocalically, they must be phonemically distinct: /r/ and /R/ or /rr/. (The familiar and rather idle controversy over whether [R] should be phonemicized as geminate /rr/ or as a unit phoneme /R/ has no bearing on the issue at hand.) Now, if the phoneme is a perceptual unit, native speakers should be able to perceive immediately the difference between [árma] and [áRma], since these are phonemically /árma/ and /áRma/ (or /árrma/—these transcriptions are copied from the literature, not invented). In casual but often repeated experiments of mine, however, phonetically untrained native speakers consistently fail to perceive any difference, even under optimal acoustic conditions and after the difference has been specifically pointed out. On the other hand, native speakers of English usually hear the difference at once, even though this sort of phonetic contrast obviously plays

(56)  
    *a.*   *red–redes*      net  
         *pan–panes*      bread  
         *azul–azules*     blue  
         *amor–amores*    love  

    *b.*   *carne–carnes*    meat  
         *grande–grandes*   big  

    *c.*   *torre–torres*     tower  

*but r is not dental* (handwritten annotation)

It seems clear that the plural formative is *s* in all the pairs of (56) and that the singular forms all end in *e*. This *e* is deleted in the singular forms when preceded by a single (dental) consonant as in (56*a*), but not when preceded by more than one consonant as in (56*b*). The retention of the final *e* of *torre* [toRe], then, suggests that here the *e* is preceded by more than one consonant. (The rule that deletes final *e* will be formulated roughly in Section 3.4.3 and discussed in detail in Section 6.4.)

These two different sets of data—the future forms of *querer* and the retention of final *e* after [R]—seem to me to provide ample support for the claim that /rr/ is the systematic phonemic representation of intervocalic [R].

It was observed in Section 2.6.2.1 that [R], but not [r], occurs in the environments of (57):

(57)                #——  
                l——  
                n——  
                s——

One could postulate *rr* in these environments in systematic phonemic representations; alternatively one might postulate single *r*, with phonetic [R] then being predicted by rules. Upon closer examination, it becomes quite clear that the first alternative must be rejected in favor of the second. There are literally hundreds of words with initial [R] and none with initial [r]; there are a handful with [lR],[nR],[sR]

---

no role in English at all. If one took such facts seriously, one would be forced to the conclusion that, far from being alert to phonemic distinctions in their own language, Spanish speakers are actually deafened by the sound system they have acquired.

[37] It will be argued in Chapter 3 that the forms in question derive ultimately from representations that can be stated slightly more accurately as /ker+re+a+y/, /ker+re+a+s/, /ker+re+a+ɸ/, etc., but it would take us too far from the present discussion to justify these representations here. Note that the conditional forms *querría, querrías*, etc., are analogous to the future forms in that a suffix with initial *r* is attached to the stem with final *r*, giving *r+r*, which becomes phonetic [R].

and none with [1r],[nr],[sr]. Therefore some vague notion of simplicity might be invoked that would demand that the second alternative be selected as yielding a more highly valued grammar. More to the point, however, is the fact that if the first alternative is chosen, there is then no statement to the effect that nonoccurring *[#r],*[1r],*[nr], *[sr] are not merely accidental gaps in the lexicon.[38]

In Sections 2.6.2.1 and 2.6.2.2 it was indicated that the occurrence of [R] rather than [r] is predictable also in the environments ——[+consonantal], ——#[+consonantal], and —— ‖ in Andante (and that [R] → [š] varies with [r] in Allegretto). To show that the phonological representation must be /r/ in these cases, it is sufficient to point out that phonetically final [R] is, in the vast majority of cases, intervocalic r at a higher level of derivation, as in hundreds of singular-plural pairs: *amor–amores, honor–honores, tambor–tambores, pajar–pajares, alfiler–alfileres.*

Summarizing, we have seen that the distribution of [r] and [R] is predictable except in intervocalic position; that in this position [r] and [R] are represented underlyingly as /r/ and /rr/, respectively; and that in all other positions both [r] and [R] are represented as systematic phonemic /r/.

2.6.2.4. Let us now formulate rules that relate r with [r] and [R] and also with [ž] (=[ř]?) and [š]. We begin by examining the environments in (57) and comparing the sequences *lr, nr, sr*, which have [R], with the consonant clusters that have [r] as the second member: *pr, br, fr, tr, dr, kr, gr*.[39] The first member of each of the former sequences is [+coronal, +distributed], a characterization shared by none of the latter. Thus we may account for the occurrence of [R] in the environments of (57) with rule (58):

$$(58) \qquad r \;\rightarrow\; R \;\; / \left\{ \begin{array}{c} \# \\ \left[ \begin{array}{c} +\text{cor} \\ +\text{distr} \end{array} \right] \end{array} \right\} \underline{\quad} \begin{array}{c} a \\ \\ b \end{array}$$

---

[38] If it could be shown that *hon*[R]*a* and *hono*[r]*able* are related synchronically and share the formative that can be represented roughly as *honor*, this alone would be decisive evidence in favor of the second alternative. More specifically, the derivation of *hon*[R]*a* would have to contain the following steps: honor+a → honr+a → honR+a. However, the relationship between *hon*[R]*a* and *hono*[r]*able* is not clear enough to count as evidence for or against either alternative.

Some additional reason to reject underlying /rr/ in these cases is provided by the fact that geminate consonant clusters apparently occur only after vowels in lexical items. It would be odd, then, if *rr* were the only exception to this generalization.

[39] As far as I know, *xr* occurs only in *Jruschef* [xruščef]. Otherwise, the clusters listed are the only ones that occur.

Let us pause at this point to observe an intriguing possibility. Recall rule (47c), which is repeated here as (59):

(59)
$$\begin{bmatrix} -\text{voc} \\ -\text{cons} \end{bmatrix} \rightarrow [+\text{cons}] \ / \ \#\text{——}$$

*(turns glides into obstruents)*

Since r, the nonlateral liquid, is [+vocalic, +consonantal, −lateral], the first case of (58) could be collapsed with (59) as (60), provided that the X of (60) could be specified:

(60)
$$\begin{bmatrix} \alpha\text{voc} \\ \alpha\text{cons} \\ -\text{lat} \end{bmatrix} \rightarrow X \ / \ \#\text{——}$$

Since, however, the second case of (58) must still be given, it is not yet clear that (60) accomplishes anything. We return to this matter directly.

Now we must account for the occurrence of [R] rather than [r] in the environments ——[+consonantal], ——#[+consonantal], and —— ‖ in Andante. The obvious first approximation is (61):

(61)
$$r \ \rightarrow \ R \ / \ \text{——} \left\{ \begin{matrix} (\#) \ [+\text{cons}] \\ \| \end{matrix} \right\} \begin{matrix} a \\ b \end{matrix}$$

In order to account for the occasional occurrence of [R] or [š] in the environment —— ‖ in Allegretto, we simply make (61b) optional for Allegretto, as in (62):

(62)
$$r \ \rightarrow \ R \ / \ \text{——} \left\{ \begin{matrix} (\#)[+\text{cons}] \\ \| \end{matrix} \right\}$$
a. ANDANTE
b. ANDANTE: *obligatory*
   ALLEGRETTO: *optional*

One is again struck by the similarity of a rule changing r to R, rule (62), and one changing glides to obstruents, rule (47g), which is repeated here as (63):

(63)
$$\begin{bmatrix} -\text{voc} \\ -\text{cons} \end{bmatrix} \rightarrow [+\text{cons}] \ / \ V\text{——} \left\{ \begin{matrix} (\#)[-\text{cons}] \\ \| \end{matrix} \right\}$$
a. ANDANTE
b. ANDANTE:
   *obligatory*
   ALLEGRETTO:
   *optional*

Just as the first case of (58) might be collapsed with (47c) = (59) to give (60), so (62) and (47g) = (63) might be collapsed as (64):

(64)

$$
\begin{bmatrix} \alpha voc \\ \alpha cons \\ -lat \end{bmatrix} \rightarrow X \;/\; V\!\!-\!\!-\!\!\left\{ \begin{matrix} (\#)[\alpha cons] \\ \| \end{matrix} \right\}
\quad
\begin{matrix} a. \text{ ANDANTE} \\ b. \text{ ANDANTE}: \textit{obligatory} \\ \text{ALLEGRETTO}: \textit{optional} \end{matrix}
$$

The discovery of either (60) or (64) might be passed off as an odd coincidence, but the possibility of both (60) and (64) stretches the long arm of coincidence quite far. It seems that in at least two environments (one of which, (64), is rather unlikely), the glides and $r$ behave alike. It appears, then, that it would be worthwhile to attempt to determine $X$ in (60) and (64).

In approaching this problem, it is important to bear in mind that the formulation of $(47c) = (59)$ and $(47g) = (63)$ involves a certain amount of oversimplification. It was pointed out in Section 2.4.5.3— and illustrated in (46)—that the glides $y$ and $w$ differ from the obstruents $\gamma_1$ and $\gamma^w$, respectively, essentially in the major class feature [consonantal] and not in cavity (point-of-articulation) features. Thus only [+consonantal] was written on the right-hand side of the arrow in rules $(47c) = (59)$ and $(47g) = (63)$. Other features are involved, however, such as [+obstruent, +delayed release, −tense]. Thus the complete specification of the segments in question in these rules would involve at least the features in (65):

(65)

$$
\begin{bmatrix} -voc \\ -cons \end{bmatrix} \rightarrow \begin{bmatrix} +cons \\ +obstr \\ +del\ rel \\ -tense \end{bmatrix} \;/\; \dots
$$

It seems to me that some of these features should be supplied by marking conventions.[40] For example, [+delayed release] would presumably not have to be specified in a rule that converts glides into continuant obstruents. Thus it would be plausible to assume that the correct specification of the segment to the right of the arrow in (65) is [+obstruent, −tense]. This in turn suggests that the $X$ of rules (60) and (64) might be [−αobstruent, αtense]. With $X$ thus specified, (60) and (64) would convert $r$ into a segment that is [+tense]. Adding this to the unchanged specifications, the output of rules (60) and (64) when applied to $r$ would be some segment S* with the features [−obstruent, +vocalic, +consonantal, +anterior, +coronal, −high,

---

[40] None of the marking conventions proposed by Chomsky and Halle (1968, Chapter Nine, Section 2.1) would supply any of the features in the output of (65). Those conventions are, however, tentative and incomplete.

+continuant, +tense, +voice, −strident, −lateral], which is
distinct from all other segments of Spanish. Now note that S* has the
same features postulated for [R] in (55) (with the possible exception
of [vocalic]).

Even though the considerations concerning the specification of $X$
in the rules under discussion involve a good deal of speculation, the
identity of the set of features for S* and that postulated for [R] in
(55) is quite remarkable. The features of [R] in (55) were chosen
solely on the basis of impressionistic acoustico-articulatory data, with
absolutely no consideration of rules involving [R]; the features of S*
were arrived at solely on the basis of rule simplicity. It seems to me
that this convergence of conclusions reached by completely independent
paths allows us to state with some confidence that [R] is a tense
liquid (or a tense sonorant consonant).

2.6.2.5. Let us now tie up what loose ends we can. Returning to
rule (58), which changes $r$ to $R$ after # and after $l$, $s$, $n$, we recall that
we have tentatively transferred the first case to rule (60). The second
case might be restated as (66): *(see p.48 - only diff bet r+R is [tense])*

(66)
$$ r \rightarrow [+\text{tense}] \ / \ \begin{bmatrix} +\text{cor} \\ +\text{distr} \end{bmatrix} \underline{\qquad} $$

I do not know how to order rule (66) with respect to the other rules.
On the one hand, it might be combined with (60); on the other
hand, a case could be made for somehow combining (66) with rule
(49)-(50), Spirantization. The environment of (66) has quite a bit in
common with the environments in which $b$, $d$, $g$ *fail* to become the
nonstrident continuants $\beta$, $\delta$, $\gamma$ (see Section 2.5.1.1). Thus it seems
that $b$, $d$, $g$, and $r$ undergo some sort of "strengthening of articulation"
in some partially shared environments. (See the remarks at the end of
Section 2.3.) Attempts to write rules that capture these ideas, however,
have proved completely unilluminating. The conclusion that I draw
is that some crucial insight is missing either in the facts of Spanish or
in the nature of phonological processes in general.

Proceeding now to other details, we recall that underlying /rr/
in intervocalic position is realized phonetically as [R], indistinguishable
from the [R] that derives from single /r/ by (60), (64), or (66). Thus
a rule is needed with the effect of (67), which is ordered before (66):

(67)
$$ rr \Rightarrow R $$

Rule (67) is written as a one-step transformation since it would be
totally arbitrary to have to choose one of the two input $r$'s to become $R$,
the remaining $r$ then being deleted as a second step.

Since [R] is occasionally realized in Allegretto as [ż], and in some environments as [š], we apparently need a rule with the effect of (68):

(68)
$$R \rightarrow \begin{bmatrix} +\text{obstr} \\ -\text{ant} \end{bmatrix} \text{ ALLEGRETTO } (\textit{optional})$$

Other features are then supplied by convention. For example, of the marking conventions suggested by Chomsky and Halle (1968, Chapter Nine, Section 2.1), convention XXVI supplies [+delayed release] and XXVII supplies [+strident]. The [ż] resulting from (68) will be correctly devoiced to [š] in the environment ——‖ by rule (54).

## 2.7 Summary of rules

There follows a list of the rules proposed thus far, renumbered as (69) and placed in the proper order, insofar as this is known. In most cases the reasons for the ordering are obvious; in a few cases the ordering depends on considerations to be taken up in Chapters 3 and 4.

(69)

$a.\ \begin{Bmatrix} \acute{E} \\ _1\acute{O} \end{Bmatrix}_1 \rightarrow \begin{Bmatrix} y\acute{e} \\ _1w\acute{e} \end{Bmatrix}_1$  (*under certain conditions*)       (28*a*)

$b.\ g \rightarrow \phi\ /$ ——w       (29)

$c.\ rr \Rightarrow R$       (67)

$d.\ \begin{bmatrix} \alpha\text{voc} \\ \alpha\text{cons} \\ -\text{lat} \end{bmatrix} \rightarrow \begin{bmatrix} -\alpha\text{obstr} \\ \alpha\text{tense} \end{bmatrix}\ /\ \#$——     (28*b*), (44*a*), (47*c*), (58), (59), (60)

$e.\ r \rightarrow [+\text{tense}]\ /\ \begin{bmatrix} +\text{cor} \\ +\text{distr} \end{bmatrix}$——     (58), (66)

$f.\ \Bigg\{$

$[+\text{nasal}] \rightarrow \begin{bmatrix} \alpha\text{cor} \\ \beta\text{ant} \\ \gamma\text{back} \\ \delta\text{distr} \end{bmatrix}\ /$ —— $\begin{bmatrix} +\text{obstr} \\ \alpha\text{cor} \\ \beta\text{ant} \\ \gamma\text{back} \\ \delta\text{distr} \end{bmatrix}$  ANDANTE   (12)

$[+\text{nasal}] \rightarrow \begin{bmatrix} \alpha\text{cor} \\ \beta\text{ant} \\ \gamma\text{back} \\ \delta\text{distr} \end{bmatrix}\ /$ —— (#) $\begin{bmatrix} +\text{obstr} \\ \alpha\text{cor} \\ \beta\text{ant} \\ \gamma\text{back} \\ \delta\text{distr} \end{bmatrix}$  ALLEGRETTO   (14)

*(continued)*

(69 *continued*)

$$g.\begin{cases} 1 \rightarrow \begin{bmatrix} \alpha ant \\ \beta distr \end{bmatrix} \Big/ \underline{\hspace{1cm}} \begin{bmatrix} +obstr \\ +cor \\ \alpha ant \\ \beta distr \end{bmatrix} \text{ANDANTE} \hfill (19) \\\\ 1 \rightarrow \begin{bmatrix} \alpha ant \\ \beta distr \end{bmatrix} \Big/ \underline{\hspace{1cm}} (\#) \begin{bmatrix} +obstr \\ +cor \\ \alpha ant \\ \beta distr \end{bmatrix} \text{ALLEGRETTO} \hfill (20) \end{cases}$$

$$h.\begin{cases} \begin{bmatrix} +obstr \\ -tense \end{bmatrix} \rightarrow \begin{bmatrix} +cont \\ -strid \end{bmatrix} \Big/ \begin{Bmatrix} \begin{bmatrix} +obstr \\ +cont \end{bmatrix} \\ \langle[-\alpha cor]\rangle \end{Bmatrix} \begin{bmatrix} \underline{\hspace{0.7cm}} \\ \langle\alpha cor\rangle \end{bmatrix} \text{ANDANTE} \hfill (49) \\\\ \begin{bmatrix} +obstr \\ -tense \end{bmatrix} \rightarrow \begin{bmatrix} +cont \\ -strid \end{bmatrix} \Big/ \begin{Bmatrix} \begin{bmatrix} +obstr \\ +cont \end{bmatrix} \\ \langle[-\alpha cor]\rangle \end{Bmatrix} (\#) \begin{bmatrix} \underline{\hspace{0.7cm}} \\ \langle\alpha cor\rangle \end{bmatrix} \text{ALLEGRETTO} \hfill (50) \end{cases}$$

$$i.\begin{bmatrix} -cons \\ +high \\ -stress \end{bmatrix} \rightarrow [-voc] \Big/ \begin{Bmatrix} \underline{\hspace{0.6cm}}V \\ V\underline{\hspace{0.6cm}} \end{Bmatrix} \hfill (28c)$$

$$j.\begin{bmatrix} \alpha voc \\ \alpha cons \\ -lat \end{bmatrix} \rightarrow \begin{bmatrix} -\alpha obstr \\ \alpha tense \end{bmatrix} \Big/ V\underline{\hspace{0.5cm}} \begin{Bmatrix} (\#)[\alpha cons] \\ \| \end{Bmatrix} \begin{array}{l} \text{ANDANTE} \\ \text{ANDANTE: } obligatory \\ \text{ALLEGRETTO:} \\ optional \end{array}$$

$$\begin{array}{r} (28b), \\ (44b), (45), \\ (61), \\ (62), \\ (64) \end{array}$$

$$k. \; R \rightarrow \begin{bmatrix} +obstr \\ -ant \end{bmatrix} \text{ALLEGRETTO } (optional) \hfill (68)$$

$$l.\begin{bmatrix} -cont \\ +tense \end{bmatrix} \rightarrow \begin{bmatrix} +voice \\ +h.s.press \\ +glott \; con \end{bmatrix} \Big/ \underline{\hspace{0.6cm}} (\#) \begin{bmatrix} -obstr \\ -nasal \end{bmatrix} \hfill (53)$$

$$m.\begin{bmatrix} +obstr \\ -h.s.press \end{bmatrix} \rightarrow \begin{Bmatrix} [\alpha voice] \; / \underline{\hspace{0.5cm}} (\#) \begin{bmatrix} +cons \\ \alpha voice \end{bmatrix} \\ [-voice] \; / \underline{\hspace{0.5cm}} \| \end{Bmatrix}$$

$$\begin{array}{r} (28d), (35), \\ (52), (54) \end{array}$$

$$n.\begin{Bmatrix} \gamma_1 \\ {}_1\tilde{\gamma}^w \end{Bmatrix}_1 \rightarrow \begin{Bmatrix} y \\ {}_1 w \end{Bmatrix}_1 \text{ALLEGRETTO} \hfill (31)$$

## 2.8 Observations on boundaries

### 2.8.1 *The boundary symbol #*

The sequence of rules (69) has the following properties, among others:

(a)  Rules *a–e* are shared by Andante and Allegretto.

(b)  Rules *f–h* are identical in Andante and Allegretto except for the optional occurrence of # in the environment of the Allegretto version of each.

(c)  In Andante, *i* is the last rule that may be blocked by the presence of # in a string of units. That is, after *i* all rules that apply in Andante have an optional # in the environment.[41]

(d)  In Allegretto, no rule from *f* on is blocked by # (ignoring rule *i*). That is, after *f* all rules have an optional # in the environment or apply in all environments.

Thus, from rule *j* on in Andante and from rule *f* on in Allegretto (except for rule *i*—see note 41), the presence of the boundary symbol # in strings of phonological units is simply irrelevant to the applicability of the phonological rules. Clearly the formulation of the rules in (69) does not properly reflect this fact: if we write rules with parenthesized boundaries, we do not recognize the fact that the boundaries are irrelevant (since we must mention them in the rules), and their irrelevance does not give us simpler rules. What this suggests is that one of the formal correlates of the stylistic distinction between Andante and Allegretto is not the appearance of optional boundary elements in the rules of one style but not of the other, but rather the deletion of these elements from phonological representations at a higher level of derivation in Allegretto than in Andante. Specifically, boundary elements are deleted before the application of rule *f* in Allegretto but before rule *j* in Andante, and no rule need then specify optional boundary elements in its environment.

Chomsky and Halle (1968, Appendix to Chapter Eight) have proposed that by convention the features of boundary elements are deleted from phonological representations at the end of a sequence of phonological rules. The observations made in this section suggest that this proposal must be refined in some way.

Actually, much more than just the single boundary # is involved, as has already been observed. In particular, in Sections 2.2.3 and 2.5.1, examples were given in which the term "word boundary" was

---

[41] Recall, however, the discussion in Section 2.4.5.1 concerning the somewhat dubious status of (69*i*) = (28*c*).

associated with configurations of boundaries more complex than $\#$, and in the sets of rules given thus far the distinction between $=$ and $\#$ has been ignored. I simply do not have enough well-organized evidence to say anything further about $=$. As for "word boundaries," what is involved is the notion "terminus," as developed by Chomsky and Halle (1968, Chapter One, Section 5.3; Chapter Three, Section 1.3.1; and Chapter Eight, Section 6, especially 6.2). In terms of this notion my proposal is that at a certain point in a sequence of rules some or all termini are removed from the representations to which subsequent rules apply, the point at which termini are removed varying from one style of speech to another.[42] It seems that after the removal of termini (and presumably all other boundary symbols as well), all subsequent rules apply "across the board": an entire utterance is scanned and each rule $R_i$ is applied wherever applicable; then the entire utterance is again scanned for applicability of $R_{i+1}$, and so on.

It must be kept in mind, however, that (69) is only a fragment of the total set of phonological rules of the dialect under study. Furthermore, looking ahead to the entire set of rules to be proposed in this investigation, various suggestions could be made concerning the erasure of termini and other boundaries, but it is not yet clear what empirical evidence might have a bearing on the correctness of such suggestions. I shall therefore not pursue the matter further at this point.

### 2.8.2 *The symbol* ‖

The *ad hoc* symbol ‖, which represents silence—that is, total lack of phonation—appears in rules (69*j*) and (69*m*). The phonological theory of Chomsky and Halle (1968), however, makes no provision for the incorporation of such a symbol. The purpose of this section is to present evidence that suggests that some such provision must be made.

Note first that it would be possible to avoid mention of ‖ by some artifice such as replacing rules of the form (70) by sequences of rules of the form (71):

(70)          *a.*    $A \rightarrow B \ / \ \text{\_\_\_}‖$

                *b.*    $A \rightarrow B \ / \ ‖\text{\_\_\_}$

---

[42] This can be stated intuitively as follows: the less carefully one speaks, the more one ignores word boundaries. As is well known, syllable boundaries need not coincide at all with word boundaries in casual speech. For example, in (a) below, space indicates (orthographic) word divisions, and in (b), space indicates phonetic syllable divisions:

        (a) los otros están en el (h)otel

        (b) lo so tro ses tá ne ne l(h)o tel

(71)  $\left\{\begin{array}{l} a. \quad \begin{array}{l} A \rightarrow B \\ B \rightarrow A \end{array} \ / \ \text{———}[+\text{segment}] \\ \\ b. \quad \begin{array}{l} A \rightarrow B \\ B \rightarrow A \end{array} \ / \ [+\text{segment}]\text{———} \end{array}\right.$

The incorrectness of such an artifice is surely obvious and merely underscores the theoretical inadequacy under discussion.

It might be thought that the symbol ‖ is equivalent to the $J$(uncture) $P$(oint) proposed by Stockwell (1960), which marks the end point of intonational contours, or to the boundary symbol $0\#$ proposed by Bierwisch (1966). This, however, is not the case: ‖ refers quite literally to silence, nonphonation, while $JP$ and $0\#$ are associated with intonational phenomena such as retardation in tempo and rapid rise or fall in pitch. For example, a two-sentence utterance such as *Los dos. Dámelos,* "Both of them. Give them to me," may have either of the pronunciations illustrated in (72):

(72)  a.  *Los dos. Dámelos.*  [los$^z$ðós$^z$↓dámelos↓]

b.  *Los dos.‖Dámelos.*  [los$^z$ðós ↓dámelos↓]

The symbol ↓ in (72) subsumes all the phonetic properties of the (falling) intonational contours of both sentences of *Los dos. Dámelos*; (72*a*) and (72*b*) are to be interpreted as having identical contours. The boundary ‖, then, may or may not accompany a terminal intonation. The voicing assimilation of *s* is broken only by the total absence of phonational activity, as in (72*b*), as opposed to the spirantization of *d*, for example, which may be blocked by the occurrence of (inaudible) # (see Section 2.5.1.1). Thus (72) shows clearly that the domain of phonological processes such as voicing assimilation is not limited to the boundaries of "phonological phrases" or "Phrasierungseinheiten," as has generally been believed.

## 2.9 Concluding remarks

In this chapter we have been concerned largely, but not exclusively, with rather fine phonetic detail. As will be seen when the set of phonological rules for (this dialect of) Spanish is extended in the following chapters, most of the rules of (69) are quite late in the ordering. In fact, the explicit formulation of rules that account for phonetic detail has been pushed further here than in any other study of generative phonology known to me, with the exception of Chomsky and Halle's (1968) treatment of stress contours in English and Sledd's (1966) study of southern American English. The results are open to question at several points, as has been indicated, and it may well be that further study of phonetic detail in Spanish and in other languages will lead to considerable modification both in the interpretation of data and in the content of universal phonological theory. Certain suggestions have been made here concerning the possible direction of such modification; additional investigation may reveal the need for change in ways that are unsuspected at present. The important point to be made here is that, as Chomsky (1957) has stated:

> precisely constructed models for linguistic structure can play an important role, both negative and positive, in the process of discovery itself. By pushing a precise but inadequate formulation to an unacceptable conclusion, we can often expose the exact source of this inadequacy and, consequently, gain a deeper understanding of the linguistic data (p. 5).

# 3. Verb Forms:
# Regular Verbs

## 3.1 Preliminary remarks

The Spanish verb is highly inflected. As an example, the complete set of inflectional paradigms of the regular verb *amar*, "to love," is shown in (1). (Following traditional practice, infinitives are used as citation forms throughout this chapter.)

The following comments are to be made about (1) before we begin the actual discussion of verb forms.

(a) The labels in (1) are fairly close to traditional terminology:

| | |
|---|---|
| [−finite, −participle] *amar* | = infinitive |
| [+participle, −past] *amando* | = present participle |
| [+participle, +past] *amado* | = past participle |
| [−imperative, −past] *ame*, etc. | = present subjunctive |
| [−imperative, +past] *amara*, etc. | = imperfect subjunctive |
| [+imperative] *ama*, etc. | = imperative |
| [+indicative, −past, −future] *amo*, etc. | = present indicative |
| [+indicative, −past, +future] *amaré*, etc. | = future |
| [−perfective, −future] *amaba*, etc. | = imperfect |
| [−perfective, +future] *amaría*, etc. | = conditional |
| [+perfective] *amé*, etc. | = preterit |

As used in (1) these labels are purely illustrative, but it could no doubt be shown that they have syntactic as well as morphological significance. For example, the forms of (1) seem to

(1)
finite
(marked for person-number)

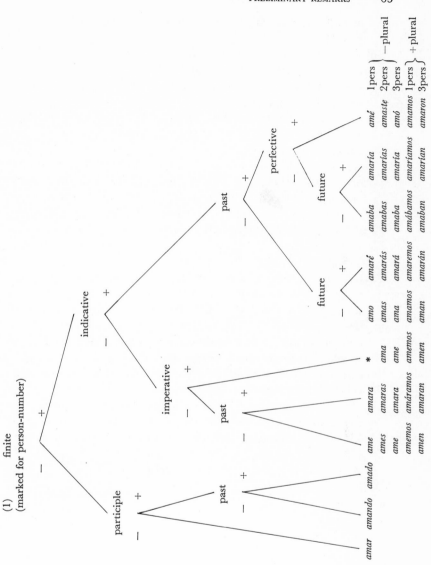

cross-classify syntactically such that the illustrative labels also function as syntactic features available for independent reference in a number of syntactic rules. In this phonological study I shall not attempt to justify these speculations but rather refer the interested reader to Lenz (1944, pp. 424–473), Bull (1960), and Stockwell, Bowen, and Martin (1965, pp. 132–165) for extended discussion of verbal syntax. (See also note 12 of this chapter.)

(b) All of the forms illustrated in (1) are in current use in the spoken language; that is, none is a "literary" form like the *passé simple* and past subjunctive in French. There is an alternative set of past subjunctive forms in which *-se-* appears in place of *-ra-*: *amase, amases, amásemos, amasen*. The *-ra-* and *-se-* forms are almost, but not quite, interchangeable syntactically. I have omitted the *-se-* forms from this study because of certain syntactic complexities and because they are possibly somewhat obsolescent—though by no means obsolete—in the spoken language. Their inclusion, however, would entail only minimal complication of the rules to be given. The "future subjunctive" *amare, amares, amare, amáremos, amaren* is also excluded as it is now totally obsolete even in the literary language, except in a few petrified formulas.

(c) Second person plural forms (*vosotros amáis*) occur only marginally in the dialect under investigation. Educated speakers learn them in school, encounter them in literature, and occasionally use them—often incorrectly—in religious and other types of stylized discourse. That is, these forms have in Mexican Spanish roughly the same status as that of "thou" and "ye" forms in standard American English. I therefore see no reason to include them in this study.

(d) *Tú*, "you (familiar)," takes second person singular verb forms while *usted*, "you (formal)," takes third person singular forms. The plural of both *tú* and *usted* is *ustedes*, which takes third person plural forms. See also note 30 of this chapter.

Traditional grammarians and structural linguists have, in general, considered Spanish verb forms to consist of strings of morphemes.[1] In some of the inflected forms of a given verb, it is possible to "locate" in a fairly straightforward way each of the inflectional morphemes in a particular isolable fragment of the phonetic form. For example, consider the following forms of the verb *comer*, "to eat":

imperfect    *com+í+a+mos*
preterit     *com+i    +mos*

In the imperfect *comíamos*, *com* can be called the stem, *í* the past tense morpheme, *a* the imperfective aspect morpheme, and *mos* the person-number morpheme. In contrast, preterit *comimos* lacks the aspectual

---

[1] See, for example, Hall (1945), Hockett (1947, pp. 238–239), Nida (1948, pp. 256–257), Bull (1949; 1960), Saporta (1956b; 1959a; 1959b).

morpheme, or has a zero allomorph of the morpheme of perfective aspect. This kind of segmentation and classification process is reasonably successful in the two forms illustrated, but problems arise when other forms are considered. For example, *como* must somehow be described as first person singular present indicative. *Com* is obviously the stem; hence all the inflectional categories must reside elsewhere. Are they all located in the portmanteau *o*? Or are there zeros? If so, how many and where? Problems of this sort are, of course, familiar, and the lack of a principled way of answering such questions within structural linguistic theory did not go unnoticed in careful structuralist studies.[2]

The transformational generative approach of Foley (undated; 1965) is essentially the same as that of traditional grammarians and structural linguists in that he considers Spanish verb forms (more accurately, the underlying or systematic phonemic representations of verb forms) to consist of strings of morphemes. Foley's approach differs in two respects, however. First, Foley postulates separate morphemes for person and number where structuralists had one portmanteau person-number morpheme. Second, Foley disallows allomorphs; that is, he seeks to construct for each morpheme a single underlying representation that will be mapped by general phonological rules into the variety of actually occurring phonetic shapes.[3] These two methodological considerations lead to the postulation of underlying forms of extraordinary abstractness and complexity. For example, for two-segment phonetic [és] the underlying representation is four-segment /s+ə+t^we/; for three-segment phonetic [amó] the underlying representation is seven-segment /am+a+ə+m+t^we/. Foley's efforts fall short in a number of crucial ways: syntax is ignored entirely; there is no indication of what the complete set of verb inflection morphemes might be; only the preterit receives extensive consideration, and even here derivations are given with steps mediated by "rules not yet discovered" (1965, pp. 94–95); in fact, not even the present indicative of regular verbs—presumably

---

[2] See Saporta (1959a, p. 615).

Furthermore, as has been stated repeatedly in recent years, structuralist phonological theory is at the root of another defect in the analysis of Spanish verb forms, namely, that generalizations are missed when predictable alternations in the phonetic shape of morphemes must be listed just as though they were suppletive. For example, in Saporta (1959b) the predictable alternation /pwéd- ~ pod-/ in present *puedo* and imperfect *podía* is listed alongside the suppletive /s- ~ fw-/ in present *soy* and preterit *fui*.

[3] Suppletive alternants are obvious exceptions, but Foley does attempt to construct underlying representations that would automatically yield phonetic forms that, in a number of cases, traditional grammarians and structural linguists alike considered to be suppletive.

the simplest of all cases—can be generated. Many of the difficulties that plague Foley's work seem to be simply the result of a priori assumptions. For example, it is assumed, with no discernible motivation, that verb forms must include separate morphemes for person and number and that each of these morphemes must have the same underlying shape in all occurrences. The "rules not yet discovered" would, if discovered, serve no purpose other than to delete the segments that were postulated solely to implement these arbitrary assumptions. It should be pointed out, however, that Foley's work was begun before the role of syntactic features had really received serious attention. It now seems obvious that features—for instance, those suggested by the labels of (1)—play a role not only in the syntax of the Spanish verb but in the phonology as well, in ways that will be elaborated on in this chapter.[4]

There is good reason for choosing the study of verb forms to begin our analysis of higher-level phonological phenomena after the phonetically detailed studies of Chapter 2. The data of Spanish verb inflection are both rich and clear—rich in the sense that this highly inflected system offers many phonological alternations for study (most of which are quite general, occurring also in categories other than verbs), and clear in the sense that vexing questions of morphological relatedness rarely arise. It is often difficult to determine whether some noun is related to some verb or adjective, and so on, and consequently whether systematic phonemic representations and rules must be postulated so as to account for the putative relationship. In the case of verb forms, however, paradigmatic evidence settles the matter in the vast majority of instances. On the other hand, the facts have so far resisted insightful analysis in any linguistic theory, even though they are readily available in school grammars. Given the existence of both relatively clear data and a host of unanswered questions about these data, verb forms represent a fertile ground for investigation within our theoretical framework.

[4] Hazarding some premature psychological speculation, it seems that from the point of view of the language learner there is no really compelling reason to analyze verb forms at all. Since the set of verbs in the lexicon and the set of verbal inflections are both finite, every form of every verb could, in principle, be learned as a separate item; and since new coinages are invariably completely regular, some weak theory of analogy could presumably handle these. Still, there are syntactic and phonological regularities that must be accounted for. (It is surely no accident that every form of every verb is not in fact suppletive.) Since syntactic regularities must apparently be expressed with the help of syntactic features, it is natural that morphological regularities (and, ultimately, phonetic representations) should be accounted for, in part, with the help of the same features.

## 3.2 Present indicative

### 3.2.1 *First conjugation*

The five forms of the present indicative of regular first conjugation verbs are illustrated in (2) with *amar*, "to love."

(2)
|  | SINGULAR | PLURAL |
|---|---|---|
| 1st person | *ámo* | *amámos* |
| 2nd person | *ámas* | |
| 3rd person | *áma* | *áman* |

The root is *am*; the vowel that follows the root in all forms except *ámo* is traditionally called the "theme vowel." (The root plus the theme vowel is often referred to as the "stem.") The "first conjugation" is defined as consisting of those verbs whose theme vowel is *a*. However, the theme vowel does not appear phonetically in first person singular *amo*. This may be accounted for, and the paradigm regularized, by postulating for *amo* the systematic phonemic representation /am+a+o/. Thematic *a* is then deleted from this form by rule (3) (which will be generalized and given independent motivation as the discussion proceeds):

(3)          $V \rightarrow \phi / + \underline{\hspace{1cm}} + o$

Thus the forms of (2) consist of the root, followed by the theme vowel, followed by one of the person-number endings *o, s, φ, mos, n.* For the moment these endings can be thought of as being supplied by rules with the effect of (4):

(4)

$$a. \quad [1\text{pers}] \rightarrow \begin{cases} o & / \left[ \underline{\hspace{1cm}} \atop -\text{plural} \right] \\ \text{mos} & / \left[ \underline{\hspace{1cm}} \atop +\text{plural} \right] \end{cases}$$

$$b. \quad [2\text{pers}] \rightarrow s$$

$$c. \quad [3\text{pers}] \rightarrow n / \left[ \underline{\hspace{1cm}} \atop +\text{plural} \right]$$

Since the feature complex [3rd person, −plural] is here represented by phonological null, there need be no corresponding rule.[5]

---

[5] We will return to rules of this sort at various points in the chapter. With only the minimal illustration provided by (4), however, an enormous descriptive advantage is already apparent over the analysis of inflections into strings of morphemes: features are independently available for mention either as the input or as the environment of a rule, and phonologically irrelevant features need not be mentioned at all. It is thus possible to capture a vast number of generalizations when the full set of such rules is considered, generalizations that are unstatable in terms of ordered strings of morphemes.

All the forms of (2) are stressed on the phonetically penultimate vowel. Thus we may state, as a first approximation, that stress is assigned to verbs by rule (5), which is ordered after rule (3):

(5)    $V \rightarrow$ [1stress] $/ \underline{\quad\quad} C_0VC_0\#]_V$

The derivation of the forms of (2) is therefore as shown in (6).

### 3.2.2 *Second conjugation*

The present indicative of regular second conjugation verbs is illustrated in (7) with *comer*, "to eat." (The forms are arrayed as in (2).)

(7)    *cómo    comémos*
       *cómes*
       *cóme    cómen*

The root is *com*; the theme vowel of the second conjugation is *e* (by definition). Otherwise the present tense of the second conjugation is just like that of the first conjugation.

### 3.2.3 *Third conjugation*

The present indicative of regular third conjugation verbs is displayed in (8) with *unir*, "to unite."

(8)    *úno    unímos*
       *únes*
       *úne    únen*

The stem is *un*; the person-number endings are the same as in the first and second conjugations, but the theme vowel alternates between stressed *i* and unstressed *e*. A few exceptions aside, no Spanish word has an unstressed high vowel in the final syllable.[6] Therefore we may account for the theme vowel alternation by postulating underlying thematic *i* and the very general rule (9):

(9)    $\begin{bmatrix} V \\ -\text{stress} \end{bmatrix} \rightarrow$ [−high] $/ \underline{\quad\quad} C_0\#$

*(this rule has to be ordered after stress placement)*

The derivation of the forms of (8) will then be as shown in (10):

---

[6] The apparent exceptions include the clitics *su, tu, mi*, and *casi* (if the last is in fact a clitic). The real exceptions include a few words of Greek origin such as *énfasis, dosis*, the three Latin words *espíritu, tribu, ímpetu*, affective words such as *mami, papi*, and a few miscellaneous others such as *fuchi* (used to indicate that something is nasty or foul smelling).

(6)

| | | | | | |
|---|---|---|---|---|---|
| | $am + a + \begin{bmatrix} 1pers \\ -plu \end{bmatrix}$ | $am + a + \begin{bmatrix} 2pers \\ -plu \end{bmatrix}$ | $am + a + \begin{bmatrix} 3pers \\ -plu \end{bmatrix}$ | $am + a + \begin{bmatrix} 1pers \\ +plu \end{bmatrix}$ | $am + a + \begin{bmatrix} 3pers \\ +plu \end{bmatrix}$ |
| (4) | o | s | | mos | n |
| (3) | φ | | | | |
| (5) | á | á | á | á | á |
| | *ámo* | *ámas* | *áma* | *amámos* | *áman* |

(10)

| un+i+o | un+i+s | un+i | un+i+mos | un+i+n | |
|--------|--------|------|----------|--------|-----|
| φ | | | | | (3) |
| ú | ú | ú | í | ú | (5) |
| | e | e | | e | (9) |
| *úno* | *únes* | *úne* | *unímos* | *únen* | |

## 3.3 Present subjunctive

The forms of the present subjunctive of regular verbs are illustrated with *amar, comer,* and *unir* in (11):

(11)

| | | | |
|------|--------|--------|--------|
| *áme* | *amémos* | *cóma* | *comámos* |
| *ámes* | | *cómas* | |
| *áme* | *ámen* | *cóma* | *cóman* |

| | |
|------|--------|
| *úna* | *unámos* |
| *únas* | |
| *úna* | *únan* |

Let us take care of the simplest things first. Throughout (11) the person-number marker for first person singular is null, rather than *o* as in the present indicative. It seems then that rule (4a) should be replaced by (12):

(12)
$$[\text{1pers}] \quad \rightarrow \quad \left\{ \begin{array}{l} \text{o} \quad / \quad [+\text{indicative}] \left[ \overline{\phantom{xx}} \atop -\text{plu} \right] \\ \text{mos} \quad / \quad \left[ \overline{\phantom{xx}} \atop +\text{plu} \right] \end{array} \right\}$$

Thus the extension of data can be accounted for at the cost of one additional feature. As in the case of third person singular indicative and subjunctive, nothing must be added to the grammar to state that the first person singular marker is phonologically null in the present subjunctive: rather, the additional feature in (12) is needed to account for the indicative form.

Before we attempt to account for what appears to be thematic *e* rather than *a* in the first conjugation, and *a* rather than *e* and *i* in the second and third conjugations, consider the consonantal alternations illustrated in (13):

(13)   *a.*

| | |
|---|---|
| *opa*[k]*o–opa*[s]*idad* | opaque–opacity |
| *sue*[k]*o–Sue*[s]*ia* | Swedish–Sweden |
| *místi*[k]*o–misti*[s]*ismo* | mystic(al)–mysticism |
| *Costa Ri*[k]*a–costarri*[s]*ense* | Costa Rica–Costa Rican |

*(continued)*

*(13 continued)*

b.  *Bel[g]a–bél[x]ico*          Belgium–Belgian
    *análo[g]o–analo[x]ía*       analogous–analogy
    *conyu[g]al–cónyu[x]e*       conjugal–spouse
    *larin[g]oscopio–larin[x]e*  laryngoscope–larynx

The examples in (13) show that Spanish must have rules with the effect of (14). (Rule (14) has only illustrative value for the present discussion. It will be revised in Section 6.3.2.)

(14) $$\left\{ \begin{matrix} k \\ {}_1g \end{matrix} \right\}_1 \rightarrow \left\{ \begin{matrix} s \\ {}_1x \end{matrix} \right\}_1 \Big/ \underline{\qquad} \left[ \begin{matrix} -\text{cons} \\ -\text{back} \end{matrix} \right]$$

Now observe in (15) that the alternations illustrated in (13) do not occur in regular verbs:

(15)

|  |  | INDICATIVE | SUBJUNCTIVE |
|---|---|---|---|
| *sa[k]ar:* | | *sa[k]o* | *sa[k]e (\*sa[s]e)* |
| | | *sa[k]as* | *sa[k]es* |
| *pa[g]ar:* | | *pa[g]o* | *pa[g]e (\*pa[x]e)* |
| | | *pa[g]as* | *pa[g]es* |
| *prote[x]er:* | | *prote[x]o (\*prote[g]o)* | *prote[x]a (\*prote[g]a)* |
| | | *prote[x]es* | *prote[x]as* |
| *diri[x]ir:* | | *diri[x]o (\*diri[g]o)* | *diri[x]a (\*diri[g]a)* |
| | | *diri[x]es* | *diri[x]as* |

Thus, at the point in the derivation of the forms of (15) at which rule (14) is reached, the vowel following the stem cannot be the vowel of the phonetic form in every case since the incorrect forms *\*sa[s]e*, *\*pa[x]e*, *\*prote[g]o*, etc., would result. (It will be shown in Section 5.2.3.4 that the root-final consonant of *prote[x]er* and *diri[x]ir* is /g/.) The correct root-final phonetic segments can be derived, however, if at the time rule (14) is reached these consonants are followed by the same theme vowels as in the indicative.

It is quite clear on syntactic grounds that the subjunctive, that is, the feature [−indicative], is introduced transformationally. Therefore it is natural to suppose that subjunctive forms are in some way more complex than indicative forms (the latter being "unmarked"). I propose that the subjunctive forms have *e* for the first conjugation and *a* for the second and third between the theme vowel and the person-number endings in all forms. Rule (14) will then apply to the appropriate occurrences of /k/ and /g/, after which the theme vowel is deleted by a simplification of rule (3). Illustrative derivations are given in (16):

(16)

| SUBJ | SUBJ | INDIC | SUBJ | |
|------|------|-------|------|---|
| sak+a+e+ϕ | pag+a+e+ϕ | proteg+e+o | dirig+i+a+ϕ | |
| — | — | x | x | (14) |
| ϕ | ϕ | ϕ | ϕ | (3) |
| á | á | é | í | (5) |
| sáke | páge | protéxo | diríxa | |

The simplification of rule (3) referred to may be stated for the time being as (17):

(17)                 $V \rightarrow \phi \ / +\text{------}+V$

There is no doubt that alternative proposals for deriving the correct post-root vowels in subjunctive forms may be easily imagined. Perhaps the most plausible is the following. The feature [−indicative] is added transformationally to the complex symbol of the verb. Instead of a subjunctive formative being "spelled out," as just suggested, the forms remain with the person-number endings directly following the theme vowels (*a, e,* and *i*). Then, after rule (14) is passed in the ordering, the theme vowels are subject to rule (18):

(18)
$$
\begin{bmatrix} V \\ \alpha\text{low} \end{bmatrix} \rightarrow \begin{bmatrix} -\alpha\text{low} \\ -\alpha\text{back} \\ -\text{high} \end{bmatrix} \ / \ \begin{bmatrix} \text{------} \\ -\text{indic} \end{bmatrix}
$$

Rule (18) changes first conjugation thematic *a* to *e* and second and third conjugation *e* and *i* to *a*, as desired. Although this proposal may seem attractive, there are several things that argue against it. First, (18) must be restricted so that it will apply only in the case of the *present* subjunctive. (The past subjunctive will be discussed in Section 3.6.) Second, rule (18) is added to the grammar for the sole purpose of deriving the correct phonetic forms of the vowels in question. On the other hand, rule (17), which is needed to implement the first proposal, is merely a generalization (simplification) of a rule already in the grammar. Third, rule (17) but not rule (18) may possibly allow for a simple account of a few irregular forms. For example, the present subjunctive forms of *ser,* "to be," and *ver,* "to see," are *sea, seas, sea, seamos, sean* and *vea, veas, vea, veamos, vean,* respectively, instead of the expected *\*sa, \*sas,* etc., and *\*va, \*vas,* etc. The correct forms could be accounted for quite simply by proposing that their irregularity consists in their being exceptions to rule (17). Given the alternative proposal with rule (18), these forms would be much more difficult to explain.

## 3.4 Participles and infinitives

### 3.4.1 *Past participles*

The term "past participle" is traditionally used in Spanish just as in English, namely, for the verb form that co-occurs in the perfect tenses with the auxiliary "have," *haber* in Spanish. Unlike French and Italian, in the perfect tenses Spanish never uses "be" as the auxiliary and never has gender or number agreement between the subject and a past participle.

Examples of the past participle in the first, second, and third conjugations are *amádo*, *comído*, and *unído*, respectively. Note that the theme vowel *e* of the second conjugation appears as *i*. We will account for this with rule (19), which in Section 3.5.2 will be shown to be somewhat less *ad hoc* than it now appears.

$$(19) \qquad \begin{bmatrix} V \\ -\text{low} \end{bmatrix} \rightarrow [+\text{high}] \quad / \underline{\quad} \begin{bmatrix} +\text{part} \\ +\text{past} \end{bmatrix}$$

The past participle ending seems to be *-do*. However, we note that in a few irregular verbs in which the participial ending is attached directly to the root, without an intervening theme vowel, the ending appears as *-to*: *abierto, cubierto, muerto, vuelto, puesto*.[7] Furthermore, we observed in Section 2.5.2 that to account for alternations such as *natación–nadar*, a rule is needed that laxes *t* to *d*. This rule, which will be discussed further at a number of points in the following chapters, is repeated here as (20):

$$(20) \quad [+\text{obstr}] \rightarrow [-\text{tense}] \quad / \text{ V}\underline{\quad}[-\text{obstr}] \quad (\textit{under certain conditions})$$

Given the past participle forms just cited and the independent need for rule (20), we may say that the past participle ending is always *-to*, the *t* being laxed to *d* by rule (20) in the appropriate forms.

### 3.4.2 *Present participles*

What has traditionally been called the "present participle" in Spanish corresponds morphologically (and in part syntactically) to

---

[7] None of the forms called "irregular past participles" by Foley (undated, pp. 87–88; 1965, pp. 17, 22–23, 25) is in fact a past participle. Those forms that actually exist—not all are in current use or even listed in the *Vox Diccionario general ilustrado de la lengua española*—are adjectives or nouns. Although Foley's phonological analysis of these forms is perhaps roughly correct, the motivation for it—namely, to demonstrate the relationship of the forms to regular past participles—is based on confusion. For a brief discussion of the irregular past participles *dicho* and *hecho* of *decir* and *hacer*, see Chapter 6, note 8.

the "present participle," or "-ing form," in English.[8] Illustrative forms
for each of the three conjugations are *amándo, comyéndo, unyéndo.* These
forms are invariable: there is never any number or gender agreement
of any sort. The ending of the present participle is *-ndo.* To account for
the vowels that appear between the root and this ending, we must first
gather up a few loose ends.

At several points in Chapter 2 we referred to a rule, (2:69*a*), which
diphthongizes *é* and *ó* to *yé* and *wé* under certain conditions. We used
the notational device of representing as upper-case *E* and *O* those
instances of *e* and *o* that diphthongize under stress (reserving lower-case
*e* and *o* for those that do not diphthongize when stressed). For expository
purposes, let us hypothesize an *ad hoc* feature [D], mnemonic for
"diphthongization," such that [e, +D] = *E* and [o, +D] = *O*, and so on.[9]

Now note that the theme vowel of the second conjugation must be *e,*
rather than *E,* since it does not diphthongize when stressed: *comémos,*
not *\*comyémos.* (The first conjugation subjunctive marker must also be
*e,* not *E: amémos,* not *\*amyémos.*) Since, however, the present participles
of the second and third conjugations are *comyéndo* and *unyéndo,* respectively, we must postulate rule (21), which applies before the
diphthongization rule (2:69*a*):

$$(21) \qquad \begin{bmatrix} V \\ +\text{stress} \end{bmatrix} \rightarrow \begin{bmatrix} -\text{high} \\ +\text{D} \end{bmatrix} \; / \; \text{---} +\text{ndo}$$

It will be shown that rule (21) is considerably more general. Note
that it will assign the feature [+D] to thematic *a* of the first conjugation
as well as to the theme vowels of the second and third conjugations.
This will have no effect on the phonetic representation of first conjugation forms, however, since they are not subject to any further
relevant rules.

The derivation of present participles is illustrated in (22):

| (22) | am+a+ndo | com+e+ndo | un+i+ndo | |
|------|----------|-----------|----------|------|
| | á | é | í | (5) |
| | Á | É | É | (21) |
| | | yé | yé | (2:69*a*) |
| | *amándo* | *comyéndo* | *unyéndo* | |

### 3.4.3 *Infinitives*

Infinitives of the three conjugations have already been illustrated:
*amár, comér, unír.* Note, however, the final stressed syllable, an apparent

---

[8] For further discussion see Section 3.8.

[9] The identification of [D] is discussed in Section 4.2.

exception to penultimate stress for verbs, assigned by rule (5). In Section 2.6.2.3, some evidence was given for a rule that deletes final *e* after zero or one dental consonant. The coincidence of two facts suggests that the systematic phonemic representation of infinitives has a final *e*: (a) infinitives will have regular penultimate stress if there is a final vowel when rule (5), stress assignment, is reached, and (b) precisely *e* actually occurs phonetically in the plural of nominalized infinitives: *andares*, "walks," "goings about"; *amaneceres* "dawns," "dawnings"; *decires*, "sayings." We must make one clarification, however. The final *e* of infinitives must be *E*—that is, [e, +D]—since neither second conjugation thematic [e] nor first conjugation subjunctive [e], both of which are known *not* to be *E*, is deleted in word-final position after a single dental consonant: *cede, quiere, suele* (second conjugation indicative); *mude, mire, suene* (first conjugation subjunctive). Therefore, as a first approximation, we state the rule for final *e* deletion as (23):

(23)
$$\begin{bmatrix} e \\ +D \end{bmatrix} \rightarrow \phi \ / \ V \begin{bmatrix} +\text{cor} \\ +\text{ant} \end{bmatrix}_0^1 —\#$$

This rule will be discussed at some length and refined in Section 6.4.

## 3.5 Imperfect

The "imperfect" is one of the simple past tenses of Spanish; the "preterit" is the other. The difference between the imperfect and the preterit is one of "aspect," in the familiar sense: the imperfect is past tense, imperfective aspect; the preterit is past tense, perfective aspect. We assume that the phonological segments of the imperfect and preterit endings are supplied by "spell-out" rules for feature bundles that contain the features [+past] and [±perfective].

### 3.5.1 *First conjugation*

(24)      *amába      amábamos*
          *amábas*
          *amába      amában*

Given the systematic phonemic representations *am+a+ba,* *am+a+ba+s, am+a+ba, am+a+ba+mos, am+a+ba+n,* where *ba* is the realization of the feature complex [+past, −perfective], the only part of (24) that requires comment is the antepenultimate rather than penultimate stress of *amábamos*. To accommodate this form (and the remainder of (24)), we will provisionally replace rule (5) by (25) (where [−perf] stands for the imperfective marker *ba*):[10]

(25)       $V \rightarrow$ [1stress] / ―― $([-\text{perf}]) C_0 V C_0 \#]_V$

### 3.5.2 *Second and third conjugations*

(26)      
| *comía* | *comíamos* | | *unía* | *uníamos* |
|---------|-----------|---|--------|-----------|
| *comías* | | | *unías* | |
| *comía* | *comían* | | *unía* | *unían* |

The examples in (26) present two problems: the theme vowel of the second conjugation and the form of the imperfect marker. We may handle the theme vowel with a rule already in the grammar, namely, rule (19), which was proposed to account for the same phenomenon in the second conjugation past participle. By simply removing the feature [+participle] from the environment, we generalize the rule to (27), which will apply also to the relevant imperfect forms:

(27)       $\begin{bmatrix} V \\ -\text{low} \end{bmatrix} \rightarrow$ [+high] / ――[+past]

We will return to rule (27) in Section 4.1.2.2.

In the first conjugation, the imperfect marker is *ba*; in the second and third conjugations it seems to be just *a*. Let us assume *ba* for all three conjugations and postulate the following rule, which deletes the *b* in the second and third conjugations:

(28)       $b \rightarrow \phi$ / $i+$――

The motivation for (28) is admittedly rather slim. Although there are many instances of historical loss of intervocalic *b*, I am not aware of any clear synchronic evidence aside from the imperfect forms. Consider, however, the implications of this evidence alone: (a) if rule (28) were not in the grammar, ordered after rule (17), which deletes vowels in the environment $+$――$+V$, we would have to find

---

[10] The familiar Latin stress rule was mentioned in Section 2.4.5.1, in connection with words like *láudano*, *áureo*, and will be discussed further in Section 3.9 and in Section 4.3. In the present connection it is interesting to note that the imperfect (penultimate) *a* was long (tense) in Latin *amabāmus* and the Spanish reflex was stressed *amabámos* for a number of centuries. Subsequently the stress shifted to *amábamos*, as it is today, for no discernible reason (see Menéndez Pidal (1962, p. 276)). I can find no motivation for believing that this stress shift is to be accounted for by an unexplained laxing of the penultimate *a* rather than by an equally unexplained change in the stress rule itself.

some way to account for the fact that (17) does not delete the theme vowel in *com+i+a*, *com+i+a+s*, etc.; (b) the irregular imperfect forms of *ir*, "to go" *(iba, ibas, iba, íbamos, iban* rather than the expected *\*ía, \*ías*, etc.) can be accounted for quite naturally by simply making *ir* an exception to rule (28), and the same is true of a few substandard forms such as *creíba* for standard *creía*, the imperfect of *creer*; and (c) *ceteris paribus*, the "spell-out" rule for the imperfect marker will be simpler if it is the same for all three conjugations.

## 3.6 Past subjunctive

It was noted in Section 3.5 that Spanish has two sets of indicative "past tense" forms, the "imperfect" and the "preterit," which contrast aspectually. In the subjunctive, on the other hand, there is only one set of "past tense" forms and hence no aspectual contrast. I will tentatively assume that the past subjunctive is in fact imperfective in aspect (the term "imperfect subjunctive" is used at least as often as "past subjunctive"), although the facts do not seem to me to be entirely clear.[11] If this assumption is correct, then the complex symbol of the forms in question, like those of the imperfect indicative, contains the feature [−perfective].[12] The relevance of these remarks will become obvious directly.

### 3.6.1 *First conjugation*

(29)           *amára*    *amáramos*
                *amáras*
                *amára*    *amáran*

I assume that the marker of the past subjunctive is given phonological shape by a rule with the effect of [+past, −indicative]→*ra*. Thus the forms of (29) consist of the root, followed by the theme vowel *a*, followed by *ra*, followed by the familiar person-number

---

[11] Although many grammarians mention verbal aspect, and sometimes discuss it at considerable length, few commit themselves explicitly as to the aspect of indicative forms other than the preterit and imperfect, and even fewer bring the subjunctive into the discussion at all. (See Lenz (1944, pp. 447–472), Bull (1960), Gili y Gaya (1964, pp. 147–154), Stockwell, Bowen, and Martin (1965, Chapter Six).)

[12] It should be noted that the tree diagram (1) does not reflect this. However, this is hardly a matter that can appropriately be taken up here. In any event (1) is only illustrative, and a two-dimensional tree diagram is not the proper formal representation for categories that involve cross-classification: note that [past] and [future] are repeated in (1) as it stands (see Chomsky (1965, Chapter Two, Section 2.3.2)).

endings. The stress contours of the examples in (29) are the same as those of the imperfect indicative examples in (24) and (26). If, then, the past subjunctive marker is assigned the feature [ −perfective] as was the imperfect marker *ba*, stress will be correctly assigned by the revised stress rule (25).[13]

### 3.6.2 *Second and third conjugations*

(30)     comyéra    comyéramos        unyéra    unyéramos
         comyéras                     unyéras
         comyéra    comyéran          unyéra    unyéran

The phonetic representations of the inflections for the past subjunctive are the same in the second and third conjugations, just as they were for the imperfect indicative and both past and present participles. The person-number endings are the familiar ones, and they are immediately preceded by the past subjunctive marker *ra*, as in the first conjugation forms. What remains to be accounted for is the diphthong *ye* that appears to have replaced the theme vowels *e* and *i*. Recall that we have rule (2:69a), which will give the diphthong from *É*, and we also have rule (21), which gives *É* from *e* or *i* before the present participle ending *-ndo*. Thus the forms of (30) can be accounted for with only one minor modification of independently motivated rules. We now replace (21) with (31) (which will be further motivated and simplified as we proceed):

(31)     $$\begin{bmatrix} V \\ +\text{stress} \end{bmatrix} \rightarrow \begin{bmatrix} -\text{high} \\ +D \end{bmatrix} \ / \ \text{---} + \begin{Bmatrix} \text{ndo} \\ \text{ra} \end{Bmatrix}$$

Thus the derivation of the forms of (30) is as illustrated in (32):

(32)   com+e+ra+s         un+i+ra+mos
         i                                      (27)
         í                  í                    (25)
         É                  É                    (31)
         yé                 yé                   (2:69a)
       comyéras           unyéramos

---

[13] If this treatment of stress assignment for Spanish verbs is correct, it provides yet another example of the relevance of syntactic information to phonology. The striking thing is that stress placement is affected by such an intuitively insignificant syntactic feature as "imperfective aspect." Incidentally, the history of the stress of *amáramos* is parallel to that of *amábamos* (see note 10).

## 3.7 Preterit

The forms of the preterit diverge considerably from those of the paradigms surveyed up to this point:[14]

(33)  *amé*    *amámos*       *comí*    *comímos*      *uní*    *unímos*
    *amáste*           *comíste*           *uníste*
    *amó*    *amáron*       *comyó*    *comyéron*      *unyó*    *unyéron*

In spite of the apparent complexity of these forms, which has been a serious stumbling block for all previous analyses known to me (see Section 3.1), I hope to be able to show that the phonetic representations can be derived with almost no *ad hoc* machinery, that is, almost exclusively with the help of rules that would have to be in the grammar even if the preterit forms did not exist. The demonstration involves a large number of details, and we will proceed slowly.

### 3.7.1 *Theme vowels*

In first conjugation *amaste, amamos, amaron* and third conjugation *uní, uniste, unimos,* the theme vowels of the phonetic forms are the usual first conjugation *a* and third conjugation *i*. Thus they presumably pose no problem. The same is true for thematic [i] in second conjugation *comí, comiste, comimos:* we already have rule (27) in the grammar, which converts thematic /e/ into [i] in any form that has the feature [+past], as preterit forms obviously do.

The [y] of *comyó, unyó* can also be accounted for immediately. First, thematic /e/ of *comyó* is converted to *i* by rule (27), as observed in the preceding paragraph. Then rule (2:69*i*) applies to the unstressed high front vowels of *com+i+ó* and *un+i+ó*, giving *comyó* and *unyó* as desired. (Final [ó] will be discussed directly.)

The diphthongs of *comyeron* and *unyeron* can be derived with rules already in the grammar. Rule (31) must be modified slightly, but the modification is a simplification, not a complication: the environment ——+*ra* is simplified to ——+*r*V. We thus replace (31) by (34):[15]

---

[14] This is hardly surprising in view of the history of the preterit forms. They are the reflexes of the Latin perfect forms, a paradigm already quite different from other Latin paradigms. Many points in the historical development of the Spanish preterit forms are not at all well understood by philologists. (See García de Diego (1961, pp. 229 f.), Menéndez Pidal (1962, pp. 308 ff.).)

[15] Rule (34) must not apply to second and third conjugation infinitives (the phonetic forms being *comér, unír,* not *\*comyér, \*unyér*), which at an early level of derivation are *comere, unire.* All that need be done is to order rule (34) after rule (23), which deletes final *e,* so that thematic *e, i* of the infinitives are no longer in the environment ——*r*V when (34) is reached. Rule (34) will be simplified still further in Section 4.1.3.

(34)
$$\begin{bmatrix} V \\ +\text{stress} \end{bmatrix} \rightarrow \begin{bmatrix} -\text{high} \\ +D \end{bmatrix} / \underline{\phantom{xx}} + \begin{Bmatrix} \text{ndo} \\ \text{rV} \end{Bmatrix}$$

*Comyeron* and *unyeron* may now be derived as in (35):

(35)          com+e+ron          un+i+ron
                    i                                              (27)
                    í                        í                    (25)
                    É                        É                    (34)
                    yé                      yé                   (2:69*a*)
              *comyeron*            *unyeron*

It thus seems that the usual theme vowels are present in the systematic phonemic representations of thirteen out of the fifteen forms of (33) and that the phonetic realizations of these vowels are predicted by independently motivated rules. If this is correct, then it is surely the case that the underlying representations of the remaining two forms also contain the usual theme vowels: *amé* and *amó* must be /am+a+X/ and /am+a+Y/, where $X$ and $Y$ are the person-number endings of the first and third persons singular, respectively. What remain to be accounted for are the phonetic shapes of the final vowels of *amé*, *amó* and, more generally, the systematic phonemic representations of all the person-number endings in the preterit.

### 3.7.2 *Person-number endings*

I see no alternative to postulating person-number endings for the preterit whose systematic phonemic representations are different (except for first person plural *mos*) from those of the other paradigms.[16] In other words, the "spell-out" rules for person-number endings must provide a set of endings for the preterit that is distinct from the set for other paradigms. I will attempt to show that underlying representations incorporating the endings to be proposed will yield the correct phonetic forms through the application of phonological rules that are required in the grammar in any event. Demonstration of the incorrectness of this approach therefore demands the discovery of a more general set of phonemic representations and phonological rules: in other words, it would have to be shown that the representations proposed here fail to capture some significant generalization about Spanish. The implicit background of these remarks is of course

---

[16] The only attempt known to me to derive the preterit forms with the same set of underlying person-number endings as in the other tenses is Foley's (undated; 1965, Chapter Six). It seems to me that Foley's unsuccessful efforts along these lines provide a strong *reductio ad absurdum* argument against his own proposals. See also note 14.

the "naturalness condition," formulated most clearly by Postal (1968, pp. 53–77).

We begin by postulating /ste/ for the second person singular and /ron/ for the third person plural. These are also the forms that occur phonetically, and there seems to be nothing more of immediate relevance to say about them.

We are now left with the task of accounting for first person singular *amé, comí, uní* and third person singular *amó, comyó, unyó*.

3.7.2.1. Let us first consider the third person singular forms. Ideally, the systematic phonemic representations would be /am+a+V*/, /com+e+V*/, and /un+i+V*/, where V* is some vowel such that:

(a) Rule (17), which deletes vowels in the environment +——+V, *why?* fails to delete the theme vowels preceding V*.

(b) In *amó*, *á*+V* is converted into [ó].

(c) In *comyó, unyó*, stress assigned to the penultimate theme vowels of *com*+*i*+V*, *un*+*i*+V* is shifted onto V* (the unstressed high theme vowels then being changed to *y* by (2:69*i*)).

(d) In *comyó, unyó*, V́* is realized as [ó].

Several independent lines of argument converge on the identification of V* as *u*, more precisely, as *U*, that is, [u, +D]. We will take points (a)–(d) in order and see what support is lent by each to the identification of V* as *U* = [u, +D].

In order for (b)–(d) to be carried out, rule (17) must not delete the theme vowels of *am*+*a*+V*, *com*+*e*+V*, *un*+*i*+V*. Recall that (17) must apply before stress is assigned, as was illustrated a number of times in Sections 3.2 and 3.3. If the theme vowels in question here were deleted before stress assignment, then stress would be assigned incorrectly to the root vowel. Furthermore, without the theme vowels there would be no source for the [y] of *comyó, unyó*. Let us approach the problem by reviewing certain of the cases where (17) *must* apply, to see what clarification is afforded. In the first conjugation present subjunctive /am+a+e/, /am+a+e+s/, /am+a+e+mos/, /am+a+e+n/, rule (17) must delete *a* in the environment +——+e. We noted in Section 3.4.2 that the *e* in the position after the theme vowel must in fact be [e, −D] rather than *E* = [e, +D] since it does not diphthongize when stressed in *amémos*. (Further evidence that first conjugation subjunctive *e* cannot be *E* was given in Section 3.4.3, where it was noted that this *e* is not deleted in forms like *mude, mire*.) Since first conjugation subjunctive *e* is known to be [e, −D] and since no cases are known to me where a vowel must be deleted in the environment +——+[V, +D], it is natural to

assume that rule (17) deletes vowels only in the environment
$+$———$+$[V, $-$D]. Rule (17) is therefore replaced by rule (36):[17]

(36)
$$V \rightarrow \phi \ / +\!\!-\!\!-\!\!-\!\!+ \begin{bmatrix} V \\ -D \end{bmatrix}$$

If, then, the theme vowels are not to be deleted in $am+a+$V*,
$com+e+$V*, $un+i+$V*, V* must be some vowel with the feature
[$+$D].

We next turn to the problem of converting $á+$V into [ó] to yield
$amó$. Note that there are a number of pairs of presumably related
words that show an alternation between $au$ and $o$:

(37)

| | |
|---|---|
| *auca–oca* | wild goose–goose |
| *audible–oíble* | audible–audible |
| *auricular–oreja* | pertaining to the ear–ear |
| *aurífero–oro* | bearing gold–gold |
| *taurino–toro* | pertaining to bulls–bull |

There are no known alternations between $a$V and $o$ where V is not $u$
(or the cognate glide $w$). To account for the alternation illustrated in
(37), there must be rules with the effect of (38):[18]

(38)
$$\begin{Bmatrix} au \\ aw \end{Bmatrix} \Rightarrow o \quad \textit{(under certain conditions)}$$

Actually, (38) must be broken down into two steps. The first of
these changes $a$ to $o$ in the environment ———[u,w] as in (39) (where it
is assumed that [$+$round] is supplied by the marking conventions):

(39)
$$\begin{bmatrix} V \\ +low \end{bmatrix} \rightarrow [-low] \ / \ -\!\!-\!\!- \begin{bmatrix} -cons \\ +high \\ +back \end{bmatrix} \quad \begin{array}{l} \textit{(under certain} \\ \textit{conditions)} \end{array}$$

The second step involved in (38) is the deletion of unstressed $u$
or $w$ after $o$. The rule that effects this change is actually much more

---

[17] Rule (36) will later be combined with another rule that deletes vowels in other
environments. There are data from derivational morphology, however, that suggest
that (36) may need further refinement. Consider, for example, the proper names
*María, Sofía* and the derivatives *Marista* [marísta], "Marist," and *Sofiíta* [sofiíta],
diminutive of *Sofía*. The underlying representations of the derived forms are presumably
/mari$+$ista/ and /sofi$+$ita/. It is not clear why stem-final /i/ is deleted in the former
case but not in the latter.

[18] Because of the existence of forms like the left-hand members of the pairs in (37),
rule (38) must obviously be restricted in some way. This is discussed in Section 4.4.

general, for there are in fact no sequences within a word consisting
of a nonlow vowel followed by an unstressed high vowel or glide that
agrees with the first vowel in backness: *$ii$, *$iy$, *$ei$, *$ey$, *$uu$, *$uw$, *$ou$,
*$ow$.[19] We may thus formulate the second step of (38) as the completely
general rule (40):

(40)
$$\begin{bmatrix} -\text{cons} \\ -\text{stress} \\ +\text{high} \\ \alpha\text{back} \end{bmatrix} \rightarrow \phi \;/\; \begin{bmatrix} \text{V} \\ -\text{low} \\ \alpha\text{back} \end{bmatrix}\underline{\phantom{xxx}}$$

Further motivation for rules (39) and (40) will be given in Section
3.7.2.2.

The existence of (36), (39), and (40), in which preterit forms in no
way figure, strongly suggests that *amó* be derived as in (41):

(41)
$$
\begin{array}{ll}
\text{am}+\text{a}+\text{U} & \\
\quad- & (36) \\
\quad\text{á} & (25) \\
\quad\text{ó} & (39) \\
\qquad\phi & (40) \\
\text{amó} &
\end{array}
$$

In *comyó*, *unyó*, stress must be shifted from the penultimate theme
vowel to the final vowel. Let us act upon the arguments presented
thus far and assume that this final vowel is $U = [\text{u}, +\text{D}]$. First we may
observe that with a few exceptions such as *muy* (which seems to be
realized as either [muy] or [mwi], the former certainly being more
common), there are no instances within a word of *$uy$ or *$iw$, although
the sequences *wi* and *yu* do occur. Since we already have in the
grammar rule (2:69$i$), which turns unstressed high vowels into glides
before vowels, the general rule (42) may be proposed to account for
the absence of *$uy$ and *$iw$:

(42)
$$\begin{bmatrix} \text{V} \\ +\text{high} \\ +\text{stress} \end{bmatrix}\begin{bmatrix} \text{V} \\ +\text{high} \end{bmatrix} \Rightarrow [-\text{stress}]\;[+\text{stress}]$$
$$\quad\;\;1\qquad\quad\;2\qquad\qquad\;\;1\qquad\quad\;2$$

All sequences of *úi* and *íu* are converted by rule (42) into *uí* and *iú*,

---

[19] There are a few exceptional occurrences of *ey*, as in *peine*, *aceite*, and perhaps only
one of *ow*, in the proper name *Bousoño*. (Some dialects also use the Catalan loan word
*bou*.)

respectively. Rule (2:69$i$) then converts $uí$ and $iú$ into $wí$ and $yú$, respectively. Given the necessity of having rule (42) in the grammar, the derivations of *comyó* and *unyó* can be accounted for to the extent shown in (43):

(43)         com$+$e$+$U     un$+$i$+$U

|  |  |  |
|---|---|---|
| i |  | (27) |
| í | í | (25) |
| i   Ú | i   Ú | (42) |
| y | y | (2:69$i$) |

Final $Ú$ must still be converted into $ó$. (Note, incidentally, that disregarding the feature [D], $u$ and $o$ differ only in the feature [high]. It is worth observing that the systematic phoneme /U/, which differs so little from its phonetic realization, was actually selected without regard for the fact that it is realized as $o$ in *comyó* and *unyó*. Such convergence certainly increases the plausibility of the correctness of this choice.) Recall that we already have a rule that lowers high vowels under certain conditions. This is rule (9), which is repeated for convenience here as (44):

(44)
$$\begin{bmatrix} V \\ -\text{stress} \end{bmatrix} \rightarrow [-\text{high}] \ / \ \text{---}C_0\#$$

This rule may now be pressed into service in the derivation of *comyó* and *unyó* by the addition of only one feature, as in (45):

(45)
$$V \rightarrow [-\text{high}] \ / \ \left\{ \begin{array}{ll} \begin{bmatrix} \underline{\quad} \\ -\text{stress} \end{bmatrix} C_0\# & a \\ \begin{bmatrix} \underline{\quad} \\ +\text{D} \end{bmatrix} & b \end{array} \right. \quad \begin{array}{l} \\ \textit{(under certain} \\ \textit{conditions)} \end{array}$$

Case (*a*) of (45) changes unstressed $u$, $U$ to $o$ (and $i$, $I$ to $e$) in final syllables; case (*b*) changes $U$ (and $I$), stressed or unstressed, to $o$ (and $e$). The case we have just added, case (*b*), is apparently needed independently of the preterit forms in question. However, the complete justification of (45*b*)—which involves alternations such as *cometer*, "to commit," *comisión*, "commission"—requires much discussion, and it will be carried out little by little, beginning with Section 4.1.1 and continuing through Section 5.2.5.2. Assuming that (45*b*) is independently justifiable, the complete derivations of *comyó* and *unyó* are effected, still without *ad hoc* additions to the grammar, as in (46):

(46)          com+e+U     un+i+U
                  i                              (27)
                  í               í              (25)
                  i   Ú           i   Ú          (42)
                      ó               ó          (45)
                  y               y              (2:69i)
          comyó           unyó

3.7.2.2. The first person singular preterit forms must be /am+a+V'/, /com+e+V'/, and /un+i+V'/, where V' is some vowel other than U with the feature [+D]. For first conjugation amé, a+V' must become [e], but second conjugation (e→)i+V' and third conjugation i+V' remain [i]. We shall see that if V' is identified as I = [i, +D], the correct phonetic forms are derived by a simple generalization of an already existing rule.

Let us begin with comí and uní. The derivations are quite simple, as shown in (47):

(47)          com+e+I     un+i+I
                  i                              (27)
                  í               í              (25)
                      φ               φ          (40)
          comí            uní

(Some motivation is seen in (47) for breaking (38) into the two steps (39) and (40) since (40) must apply to i+I. Note also that (40) must be ordered before (42), which shifts stress to the second of a sequence of two high vowels.)

If comí and uní are /com+e+I/ and /un+i+I/, then amé must be /am+a+I/, and a+I must be converted into [e]. This can be done by generalizing rule (39) so that it converts a to e before i (or y) as well as to o before u (or w). We replace (39) by (48):[20]

$$(48) \quad \begin{bmatrix} V \\ +\text{low} \end{bmatrix} \rightarrow \begin{bmatrix} -\text{low} \\ \alpha\text{back} \end{bmatrix} \bigg/ \underline{\quad} \begin{bmatrix} -\text{cons} \\ +\text{high} \\ \alpha\text{back} \end{bmatrix} \quad \textit{(under certain conditions)}$$

The derivation of amé is now as shown in (49):

[20] Additional evidence for rule (48) may be found in Section 6.3.1.4 and Chapter 6, note 16.

Examples such as *naipe, baile, gaita*, and many others indicate that this generalization of (39) must also be restricted (see note 18).

(49)                              am+a+I
                                    á        (25)
                                    é        (48)
                                         φ   (40)
                         *amé*

### 3.7.3 *Concluding remarks*

The survey of regular preterit forms is now complete. We have
seen that with the postulation of systematic phonemic representations
for the preterit person-number endings that are distinct (except for
*mos*) from those of the other paradigms, the correct phonetic representations of these apparently highly idiosyncratic forms can be derived
totally without recourse to *ad hoc* apparatus. Note, furthermore, that
the endings proposed could hardly be less complex (/ste/, /mos/, and
/ron/ are identical to their phonetic realizations; /U/ differs from [o]
only in the feature [high]), and that the longest derivation contains
five steps. There is no doubt, then, that the solution proposed here is a
highly plausible one.

It should perhaps be observed that a thorough investigation of the
fairly large number of irregular preterits, which I have not studied
carefully, might lead to some further insight. In any event, it seems to
me that the present analysis of the regular preterit forms embodies
one crucial observation that has not been made in previous analyses,
namely, that the idiosyncrasies of preterit forms lie solely in the
person-number endings, not in the set of phonological rules that these
forms undergo.

One additional comment. Aside from the question of person-
number endings, perhaps the most striking difference between the
analysis of preterit forms presented here and that of Foley (undated;
1965, Chapter Six) is the following. In my analysis there is no
"preterit marker." In Foley's analysis all preterit forms contain the
"preterit morpheme" /s/, which is assumed to be the source of the [s]
in second person singular *-ste* and of the [r] of third person plural *-ron*
(via rhotacism in intervocalic position) but which is deleted in the
other forms. The difficulty with Foley's proposal is that it doesn't
work. The effort to get rid of preterit /s/ where it is not manifested
phonetically and to account for the remainder of the endings (including
the *te* of *-ste*) leads only to "rules not yet discovered." Furthermore,
the role of rhotacism as a phonological process of Spanish is dubious
and at best extremely marginal: there exist at least as many clear
examples where rhotacism as formulated by Foley must fail as examples
where it might work.

### 3.8 Syntactic excursus

This is a study of the phonology of a particular dialect of Mexican Spanish. It is not intended as a contribution to syntactic theory in any sense. There are, however, points that have been glossed over in the exposition thus far, as well as matters to be examined in subsequent sections, where any clarification depends crucially on a certain amount of discussion of syntax. Given both the stated scope of this study and the extremely unsettled state of syntactic theory at this writing, I will try to be as neutral as possible on controversial points. I will present a set of data relevant to the phonology of verb forms that any descriptively adequate syntax of Spanish must have the machinery to handle, but I will remain silent about the exact nature of this machinery. A familiarity with recent work in syntax by Chomsky, Lakoff, Postal, Rosenbaum, and Ross is assumed throughout the discussion in this section.

We note first that there can be little doubt that the principles of "noun phrase complementation" and "verb phrase complementation," in the sense of Rosenbaum (1967a; 1967b), are quite similar in Spanish and English. Thus we may say that the *-rE* infinitival ending in Spanish (see Section 3.4.3) is syntactically analogous to the "to" in "for-to" complements in English. For example, the sentence *Juan quiere comer*, "John wants to eat," has, at an early stage of derivation, roughly the structure shown in (50) (where *rE* stands for a bundle of syntactic features):

(50)

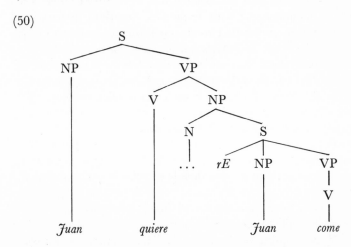

Several transformations, among them "equi-NP deletion" (which deletes one of the instances of *Juan*), "complementizer placement"

(which places the infinitival complementizer *rE* to the right of the verb stem *come*), and "person-number agreement" (which attaches the person and number features of the subject *Juan* onto the main verb *quiere*) then map (50) onto the derived tree (51). (I hold no brief for any particular detail of this derived structure.)

(51)

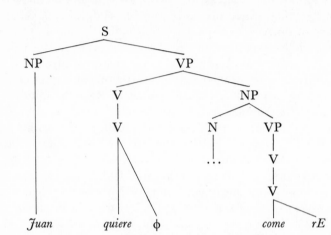

English "-ing" complements are matched, roughly, by *-ndo* complements in Spanish: *Juan sigue comiendo*, "John keeps on eating," "John continues to eat." I know of no reason to treat Spanish *está--ndo* ("be -ing") complement structures differently from any other *-ndo* complement: *estar* does not behave differently from other verbs that take *-ndo* complements with respect to negation, interrogative formation, or anything else that might be considered motivation for claiming that "be -ing" is different from, say, "insist on -ing," in English. I assume, then, that all verbs that take *-ndo* complements, including *estar*, are main verbs in some underlying sentence, just as are all verbs that take infinitival complements. The sentence *Juan está comiendo*, "John is eating," thus has at an early stage of derivation roughly the structure shown in (52*a*), where *ndo*, like *rE*, stands for a bundle of syntactic features. The structure (52*b*) is then derived from (52*a*) in essentially the same way that (51) is derived from (50). (Again, the correctness of all the details of (52) is irrelevant to the present discussion.)

There seems to be no motivation in Spanish for distinguishing a class of "modals." There simply is no class of verbs that, like the class of "modals" in English or German, has inflectional peculiarities, cannot occur in the perfect tenses, behaves differently in negation, interrogative formation, and imperatives, and whose members exclude

(52)

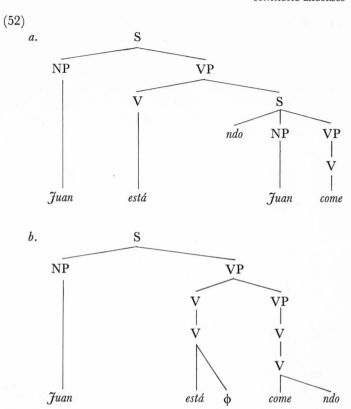

one another. If there are no modals and if it is correct to treat *estar* always as a full verb, then we are left with, at most, *haber*, "have," as an auxiliary verb in Spanish.[21] We will not argue at this point that even *haber* should be a main verb in deep structures, the past participial ending *to* falling in with *rE* and *ndo* as a complementizer. Note, however, that the "perfect auxiliary" *haber* must somehow be categorized as a verb since (a) *haber* takes the full gamut of verbal inflections, and (b) if it does not belong to the category *V*, then an unknown but presumably large number of transformations must be complicated to the extent of mentioning *haber* (and only *haber*) in the same term of their structural description as *V*.

Now let us look more closely at the constituent structure of verb forms themselves. It seems clear enough that the inflectional features

[21] *Haber* never means "have" in the sense of "possess," "own"; this is *tener*. Spanish is thus excluded from the large number of languages in which "have" and the perfect auxiliary are the same (see Allen (1964)).

for person, number, tense, etc., and the features representing the complementizers *rE, ndo,* and the past participial *to* (whether or not this is also a complementizer) all come under the domination of *V* by transformation. We have assumed in (51) and (52*b*) that such feature complexes are "Chomsky-adjoined" to the node *V,* as illustrated.[22] If this is correct, then after the relevant transformations have applied, there will be such configurations as (53*a*) and the equivalent linear representation (53*b*):

(53)  *a.*

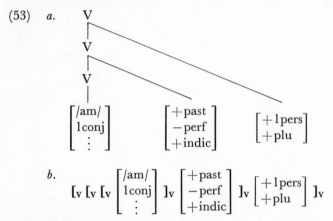

$$b. \quad [_V [_V [_V \begin{bmatrix} /am/ \\ 1conj \\ \vdots \end{bmatrix} ]_V \begin{bmatrix} +past \\ -perf \\ +indic \end{bmatrix} ]_V \begin{bmatrix} +1pers \\ +plu \end{bmatrix} ]_V$$

On the theory of universal insertion of the boundary $\#$ presented in Chomsky and Halle (1968, Chapter One, Section 5.3), (53) is automatically converted into (54):

$$(54) \quad [_V\# [_V\# [_V\# \begin{bmatrix} /am/ \\ 1conj \\ \vdots \end{bmatrix} \#]_V \begin{bmatrix} +past \\ -perf \\ +indic \end{bmatrix} \#]_V \begin{bmatrix} +1pers \\ +plu \end{bmatrix} \#]_V$$

A set of "readjustment rules"[23] will give a phonological representation to the complexes of syntactic features of (54), as illustrated in (55):

$$(55) \qquad [_V\# [_V\# [_V\#am+a\#]_V ba\#]_V mos\#]_V$$

The set of readjustment rules must apparently also contain devices that simplify structures such as (54) or (55) to representations such as (56):

$$(56) \qquad [_V\#am+a+ba+mos\#]_V$$

Now suppose that, rather than being Chomsky-adjoined, inflectional features and features of complementizers are added to the complex

---

[22] There seems to be no other commonly used term for this type of adjunction.
[23] For discussion see Chomsky and Halle (1968, Chapter One, Section 5.1).

symbol of the verb stem. In this case, after application of the relevant
agreement and/or affix transformations, there will be "segmentaliza-
tion rules" that map the expanded complex symbol dominated by $V$
into a sequence of formatives like that of (56). However, this and other
alternatives relating to the constituent structure of verb forms will not
be discussed further, because of the present lack of empirical evidence,
syntactic or phonological, that might have a bearing on the issues
involved.

The immediate relevance of this discussion of syntax will become
obvious in the following section.

## 3.9 Future and conditional[24]

### 3.9.1 *Future endings*

All verbs, without exception, take the same future endings. These
are illustrated in (57):

(57)

|        | *amaré*  | *amarémos* |        | *comeré*  | *comerémos* |
|--------|----------|------------|--------|-----------|-------------|
|        | *amarás* |            |        | *comerás* |             |
|        | *amará*  | *amarán*   |        | *comerá*  | *comerán*   |

|        | *uniré*  | *unirémos* |
|--------|----------|------------|
|        | *unirás* |            |
|        | *unirá*  | *unirán*   |

It has long been noted, and stated in every school grammar, that
the future endings have the same phonetic shape as the present
indicative of the highly irregular "auxiliary" *haber*,[25] the forms of
which are given in (58):

(58)

|  *he* [é]  | *hemos* [émos] |
|------------|----------------|
|  *has* [ás] |                |
|  *ha* [á]  | *han* [án]     |

The traditional statement is that the future is formed by adding
the present indicative forms of *haber* to the infinitive of a verb. To my
knowledge, not a scintilla of synchronic evidence has ever been
presented to show that this is anything but a good mnemonic device.

[24] The entire discussion of the future carries over with only minor modifications
to the verb forms traditionally called "conditional," which will not be discussed
separately.

[25] This is not quite true for dialects that use the second person plural. This form
of *haber* is *habéis*, but the corresponding form of the future is, for example, *amaréis*,
not *\*amarabéis*.

However, one would like to think that more than mere chance is involved in the identical irregularities of the future endings and *haber* and in the appearance of the same form as the future stem and the infinitive.[26] Note that the latter is true even in suppletive verbs such as *ir:* present indicative *voy, vas, va,* etc.; preterit *fui, fuiste, fue,* etc.; but future *iré, irás,* etc. When the relevant data are examined closely, it seems to me that one does indeed find substantial synchronic syntactic evidence for the traditional analysis of future forms, in addition to the suggestive coincidences just mentioned.

Consider first the following sentences, in which *haber* is rather clearly a main verb (obviously not the perfect auxiliary) and in which the construction *haber de verbar* (*verbar* = an arbitrary infinitive) expresses a plausible conjecture:

(59)  *a.  ha de estar aquí ahora*
           be   here now      = he's probably here now

      *b.  ha de tener como 40 años*
           have like    years = he must be about 40 years old

It is also common in Spanish for a future verb form to be used to express a conjecture about the present:

(60)  *a.  estará aquí ahora*
           will be               = he's probably here now

      *b.  ¿estará aquí ahora?*  = $\begin{cases}\text{I wonder if he's here now}\\\text{do you suppose he's here now?}\end{cases}$

      *c.  tendrá como 40 años*
           will have             = he's probably about 40 years old

In (59) and (60) *ha* (*he, has,* etc.) *de verbar* is synonymous with *verbará* (*verbaré, verbarás,* etc.) There are, however, other instances of these two expressions that do not seem to be entirely synonymous:

(61)  *a.  Juan ha de cantar mañana*  John is to sing tomorrow

      *b.  Juan cantará mañana*       John will sing tomorrow

There appears to be the same difference between Spanish *ha de verbar* and *verbará* in sentences such as (61) as there is between English "is to verb" and "will verb," whatever this difference is.

---

[26] It is of course well known that the traditional explanation is correct historically. Until the seventeenth century the future was expressed by the infinitive followed by the present of *haber*. These were written as two separate words, and object pronouns could come between them (as is still the case in modern Portuguese): for example, seventeenth century *dar me lo has* versus modern *me lo darás,* "you will give it to me." However, historical facts such as these do not constitute synchronic evidence.

However one feels about (61), there can be no doubt about the facts presented in (62):

(62)   a.   The future endings are phonetically identical to the present indicative forms of *haber*, a wild coincidence of idiosyncratic forms.

b.   In cases of suppletion the infinitive and the future stem are the same.

c.   The final stressed syllables in the future forms are anomalous.

d.   *Haber* is a main verb in some sentences.

e.   *Haber* can take an *rE* (infinitival) complementizer.

f.   In conjectural sentences, *ha* (*he*, etc.) *de verbar* = *verbará* (*verbaré*, etc.)

The conjunction of these six facts makes a very strong case for saying that *verbará* is simply *ha de verbar* with the forms of *haber* permuted to the right of the infinitive and the *de* deleted.

*[handwritten marginal note: a de amar / amará]*

Let us pause to compare the merits of this vaguely stated proposal with those of two plausible alternatives. First, there is the possibility that the future has nothing to do with *haber*. The future endings *ré, rás, rá, rémos, rán* are simply the phonological shapes given to the syntactic feature [+future] plus the person-number features. These endings are then attached to the same base as the other inflectional endings. Even without looking closely at syntax, it is easily seen that this alternative poses several problems:

(a)   *Ad hoc* phonological rules are required to derive the correct phonetic shape of the endings. In other words, one cannot take advantage of the fact that the grammar must in any event handle the irregularities of *haber*.

(b)   One claims, in effect, that in cases of suppletion it is fortuitous that the infinitive and the future have identical stems.

(c)   Some *ad hoc* device is needed to assign stress to the final syllable of four of the five future forms.

(d)   One must claim that in conjectural sentences the synonymy of *ha de verbar* and *verbará* is lexical synonymy or that it is fortuitous.

We now turn to the second alternative, suggested by Stockwell, Bowen, and Martin (1965, Chapter 6).[27] They propose that the future

---

[27] The purpose of the work cited is pedagogical, and it must be judged on the basis of its pedagogical value, which, in my opinion, is outstanding. Still, the theoretical apparatus within which the pedagogical exposition is framed is quite clear, and its appropriateness can also be evaluated.

endings are in fact the present indicative forms of *haber*, which is dominated by *Aux* (rather than by *V*) and which is permuted to the right of the main verb in the future forms. What they fail to account for is that the future endings (= *haber*) must be attached to the infinitive, not to the stem that the other tense-mode-aspect formatives are attached to. "Morphophonemic" rules are said to exist that, the authors claim, give the correct phonetic forms. Significantly, however, such rules are never given, either in the work under discussion or in the companion volume, Stockwell and Bowen (1965). Thus, in this analysis, either one must introduce *ad hoc* phonological rules to insert /r/ in the correct position of the future forms or one must introduce as an expansion of *Aux* not only (*habe–past part*), but also (*habe–rE*), and then somehow get everything in the right place. But this is an otiose duplication of machinery: *haber* as a main verb must be allowed in any event and *rE* complementizers must be in the grammar in any event.

Returning now to the analysis proposed here, let us be slightly more precise and see if we can take account of the facts listed in (62) and at the same time avoid the difficulties encountered by the alternatives just described. The derivation of a sentence such as *Juan comerá*, "John will eat," will include the structure that can be represented roughly as in (63). (Oversimplifying slightly, I disregard the origin and subsequent deletion of *de*, which poses no problem in principle.)

(63)

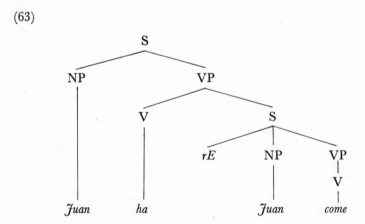

The derivation of *Juan comerá* must apparently yield the surface structure that can be represented roughly as in (64):

(64)

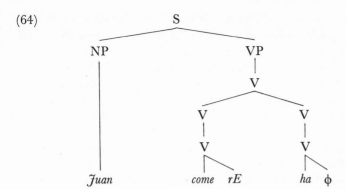

The insertion of # and the application of "readjustment rules" of the sort referred to in Section 3.8 convert the configuration dominated by the uppermost $V$ node in (64) into the configuration that can be represented as in (65):

(65)          $[_V\# \ [_V\#com+e+rE\#]_V \ [_V\#a\#]_V \ \#]_V$

The stress rule (25) (appropriately adjusted to apply to mono-syllabic verb forms—see rule (4:24)) applies twice to (65), assigning stress to both $[_V\#com+e+rE\#]_V$ and $[_V\#a\#]_V$. Thus, when the outermost paired brackets are reached, (65) will have been converted into (66), roughly:

(66)          $[_V\#com+\acute{e}+r\#\acute{a}\#]_V$

In order to derive the correctly stressed phonetic form *comĕrá*, a rule is needed that can be stated informally as (67):

(67)          Erase all stresses but the rightmost in a word.

It is not obvious at this point why two stresses, one of which is subsequently deleted, must be assigned to *comerá*. It would seem plausible to assign a larger role to the readjustment rules so that (65) is converted into, say, (68) before stress is assigned:

(68)          $[_V\#com+e+rE\#a\#]_V$

In (68) the internal # would prevent stress from being assigned farther to the left than the final syllable, and it would also retain the correct environment ( . . .———#) for the deletion of $E$ by rule (23). There are, however, several arguments against this alternative proposal. Consider, for example, the future forms of *oír*, "to hear," which are [oiré], [oirás], [oirá], [oirémos], [oirán], not *[oyré], *[oyrás], *[oyrá], etc. What must be explained in these forms is why rule (2:69*i*), which converts unstressed high vowels into glides when adjacent to another vowel, does not change the unstressed theme vowel [i] of [oiré], etc., to [y]. This is quite easily accounted for if stress is assigned, as proposed originally, to [#[#o+í+rE#] [#é#]#], etc., the leftmost stress then being deleted by rule (67) after rule (2:69*i*) has been passed in the sequence of rules. An entirely different kind of argument that also supports the original proposal will be presented in Section 4.1.2.3. Furthermore, evidence for rule (67) independent of any future forms will be given in Section 4.3.4.

Thus we see that in addition to the kinds of evidence summarized in (62) which suggest that future forms are composed of the infinitive plus *haber*, there is also considerable phonological evidence that future forms are composite in the obvious sense. In other words a fairly wide range of syntactic, morphological, phonological, and even detailed phonetic evidence is relevant to the correct description of Spanish future verb forms. It seems to me that the proposal presented here must be quite close to the correct account, since all of the various kinds of facts converge on this solution, which furthermore involves only a small and perhaps irreducible number of *ad hoc* statements.

The proposal just outlined cannot be made more precise at this time because of the lack of a sufficiently clear syntactic theory in terms of which certain nontrivial questions can be answered. Thus the discussion in this section is offered primarily to present, in as much detail as is presently feasible, certain syntactic and phonological data that must be considered in assessing the descriptive adequacy of any grammar of Spanish.[28]

### 3.9.2 *Future stems*

There are twelve verbs in which the stem of the future forms differs in some way from the infinitive. These verbs are listed in (69):

(69)

|     | INFINITIVE | FUTURE STEM |             |
|-----|------------|-------------|-------------|
| *a.* | *poder*   | *podr-*     |             |
|     | *saber*    | *sabr-*     |             |
|     | *caber*    | *cabr-*     |             |
|     | *querer*   | *querr-*    |             |
|     | *haber*    | *habr-*     | *(continued)* |

---

[28] The range of relevant data is actually wider than that presented here. For example, the rules that govern the placement of clitic object pronouns in surface structures are relevant to the correctness of structures such as (64). For a recent study of these rules see Perlmutter (1968).

*(69 continued)*

|     | | |
|-----|-----------|-----------|
| *b.* | *salir*   | *saldr-*  |
|     | *tener*   | *tendr-*  |
|     | *poner*   | *pondr-*  |
|     | *venir*   | *vendr-*  |
|     | *valer*   | *valdr-*  |
| *c.* | *hacer*   | *har-*    |
|     | *decir*   | *dir-*    |

The stems in (69) can be described as follows: those in (69*a*) consist of the infinitive minus the theme vowel; those in (69*b*) have a *d* inserted in the place of the theme vowel of the infinitive; those in (69*c*) consist of the infinitive minus the theme vowel and also minus the final root consonant (the *e* in the infinitive *decir* is the result of a rule to be given in Section 4.1.2.3). In short, in order to handle these forms, we apparently need rules that (a) delete the theme vowel in all three groups, (b) insert *d* in the second group, and (c) delete the final root consonant in idiosyncratic *hacer* and *decir*.

It is an interesting fact that all the verbs in (69) have some irregularity in addition to the future stem. For example, *poder* has the irregular preterit *pude, pudiste, pudo*, etc.; *saber* has the irregular first person singular present indicative *sé* and the irregular preterit *supe, supiste, supo*, etc.; *haber* is completely idiosyncratic; all the verbs in groups (69*b*) and (69*c*) have irregular imperatives and irregular first person singular present indicative forms (*valgo* for *valer* versus regular *muelo* for *moler*; *hago* for *hacer* versus regular *mezo* [méso] for *mecer* [mesér]).[29] One would like to find some general property shared by these verbs in terms of which their several irregularities might be at least in part

---

[29] Let us dispose once and for all of the fiction that the present indicative of *hacer* and *decir* is regular. (See Foley (1965), McCawley (1967, p. 111).) The forms of *hacer* are *hago, haces, hace, hacemos, hacen* (orthographic *c* = [s]). The putative "regular" derivation goes essentially as follows:

|hako| |hakes|
    s      (14)
  g        (20)

This would seem plausible enough if one had no prior notion of what a "regular" verb is like in Spanish and if one were willing to apply a couple of well-known rules at random. It has been shown in some detail in Section 3.3 why the irregularities of *hacer* and *decir* cannot be "explained" away as in the above simple but impossible derivation. If *hacer* and *decir* are regular (contrary to all grammarians), then *mecer* (*me*[s]*o, me*[s]*es*), *cocer* (*cue*[s]*o, cue*[s]*es*), *vencer* (*ven*[s]*o, ven*[s]*es*), *torcer* (*tuer*[s]*o, tuer*[s]*es*), to mention only a few of the huge number of relevant examples, cannot be.

accounted for. It does not seem, however, that this expectation can be fulfilled at the present stage of our knowledge. Instead, the rule that deletes the theme vowels in these twelve irregular future stems apparently must apply only to specially marked formatives. Let us state this rule as in (70), as a first approximation:

(70)
$$V \rightarrow \phi \ / \ + \left[ \overline{\phantom{xxx}} \atop +\text{irreg} \right] + r\#[+\text{fut}]$$

There seems to be no reason why (70) cannot be amalgamated with (36), which deletes vowels in a similar environment, although the motivation for doing so is not overwhelming. (The resulting reformulation is given in (78c).)

A more satisfactory rule can be given for the insertion of $d$ in the stems of group (69b). The final root consonants in this group are $n$ and $l$, which form a class that can be characterized by [+consonantal, −obstruent, −continuant]. None of the verbs in groups (69a) and (69c) have root-final $n$ or $l$. Thus we may order rule (71) after (70):

(71)
$$\phi \rightarrow d \ / \ \left[ \begin{array}{c} +\text{cons} \\ -\text{obstr} \\ -\text{cont} \end{array} \right] + \text{———} r$$

*[handwritten: does this ever apply anywhere else?]*

We are now left with *hacer* and *decir*. These verbs are so wildly idiosyncratic throughout their paradigms that little purpose would be served by examining them further at this point.

## 3.10 Further remarks

### 3.10.1 *Conjugational classes and theme vowels*

*[handwritten: do you learn in root?]*

The conjugational class of a verb is unpredictable, that is, it must be listed as a lexical property of each verb stem in the dictionary. We may reasonably assume, then, that one of the features [1conjugation], [2conjugation], [3conjugation] is a lexical feature of every verb stem. These features also play a role in derivational morphology, as shown by the following sets of related forms: first conjugation *tolerar*, "tolerate," *tolerancia*, "tolerance," *tolerable*, "tolerable," *tolerante*, "tolerant"; second conjugation *creer*, "believe," *creencia*, "belief," *creíble*, "credible," *creyente*, "believer."

It has been assumed all along in this study (see in particular the discussion of readjustment rules toward the end of Section 3.8) that theme vowels do not appear as such in the lexicon. Rather, they are "spelled out" by a readjustment rule with the effect of (72):

(72)
$$\phi \rightarrow \begin{Bmatrix} a & / & [\text{1conj}] \\ e & / & [\text{2conj}] \\ i & / & [\text{3conj}] \end{Bmatrix} + \text{———} \#]_v$$

The results of (72) are illustrated in (73):

(73)
$$[_v\# \begin{bmatrix} /\text{am}/ \\ 1\text{conj} \end{bmatrix} \#]_v \qquad\qquad [_v\# \begin{bmatrix} /\text{com}/ \\ 2\text{conj} \end{bmatrix} \#]_v$$

$$[_v\#\text{am}+\text{a}\#]_v \qquad\qquad [_v\#\text{com}+\text{e}\#]_v \qquad (72)$$

The formulation of (72) leaves much to be desired. For instance, it is interesting that *a*, the least marked vowel, is the theme vowel of the least marked conjugational class, namely, the first (which is the largest class by far, the most regular, and the only productive one, with all new verbs invariably being assigned to it). One has no clear intuition about which of the two remaining conjugations is the more heavily marked. Possibly, then, a hierarchy among the conjugations exists that can be stated as [+Verb]→[±1conjugation], [−1conjugation]→ [±3conjugation], where [−3conjugation] corresponds to [2conjugation]. In terms of markedness, each verb stem could be listed in the lexicon with one of the features [*u* conjugation], [+3conjugation], [−3conjugation], where [*u* conjugation] means no mark at all. By marking convention, stems unmarked for conjugational class would be assigned the features [+1conjugation, −3conjugation], verbs marked [+3conjugation] or [−3conjugation] would be assigned [−1conjugation]. Thus verb stems of the first conjugational class, that is, the vast bulk of verb stems in the lexicon, would require no mention of conjugational class features in their lexical entry. Then (72) could be replaced by (74):

(74)
$$\phi \rightarrow \begin{bmatrix} +\text{voc} \\ \alpha\text{low} \\ \alpha\text{back} \\ \beta\text{high} \end{bmatrix} / \begin{bmatrix} \alpha1\text{conj} \\ \beta3\text{conj} \end{bmatrix} + \text{———} \#]_v$$

The content of the preceding paragraph is of course sheer speculation, and (74) approaches phonological legerdemain. There are, however, substantive issues involved. It is clear at least that theme vowels must be supplied by rule, rather than being fully specified in the lexicon. To support this assertion, one can give, in addition to vague claims involving some notion of "simplicity," the following argument. There are just three conjugational classes and hence three different theme vowels. This fact is not captured if each theme vowel is fully specified in the lexicon. That is, if theme vowels are fully specified lexically, then it is a lexical idiosyncrasy of each verb stem that its theme vowel is not /u/ or /o/. This is simply wrong.

### 3.10.2 *Inflectional categories*

The systematic phonemic representations that have been proposed for the various person-number endings are summarized in chart form in (75).[30] Only those categories that have some phonological manifestation are shown.

(75)

| PERSON | NUMBER | |
| --- | --- | --- |
| | SINGULAR | PLURAL |
| 1 | *o* (pres indic) *I* (pret) | *mos* |
| 2 | *s* *ste* (pret) | * |
| 3 | *U* (pret) | *n* *ron* (pret) |

Similarly, the phonological representations of the categories traditionally referred to as "tense," "mood," "aspect," etc., are summarized in chart (76).

(76)

| ASPECT | NONFINITE | FINITE | |
| --- | --- | --- | --- |
| | | INDICATIVE | SUBJUNCTIVE |
| unmarked | *rE* | | *e* ([+1conj]) *a* ([−1conj]) |
| imperfective | *ndo* | *ba* | *ra* |
| perfective | *to* | | * |

[30] Closer scrutiny of syntax might reveal that the features [1person], [2person], [3person] should be replaced by the binary features [±1person], [±2person], [±3person]. For example, the "familiar" second person singular pronoun *tú* might be characterized as [−1person, +2person, −3person], and the "formal" counterpart *usted* as [−1person, +2person, +3person]. *Usted*, in spite of its second person reference, requires third person agreement in every instance in which agreement for person shows up in the language (verb inflections, possessive adjectives, direct and indirect object pronouns, reflexive pronouns, and so on). Similarly, since it is fairly easy to show that the "inclusive-exclusive" contrast is relevant to Spanish syntax, "inclusive" first person plural *nosotros* might be characterized as [+1person, +2person, −3person] and "exclusive" *nosotros* as [+1person, −2person, +3person].

*what exactly are "spell-out rules"?*

It is not intended that any theoretical import be attached to either of these charts. They are simply convenient ways to present information. As has been suggested a number of times in preceding sections, however, it is a relatively straightforward matter to write rules of the familiar sort that state the same data as the charts. For example, (75) might be restated as (77), among other possibilities:[31]

(77)

a.　[1pers] → $\left\{ \begin{array}{l} \left\{ {0 \atop {}_1\mathrm{I}} \right\}_1 \quad / \quad \left\{ \begin{array}{l} \left[ \begin{array}{l} -\mathrm{past} \\ +\mathrm{indic} \\ {}_1[+\mathrm{perf}] \end{array} \right] \end{array} \right\}_1 + \left[ \underline{\phantom{xx}} \atop -\mathrm{plu} \right] \\ \\ \mathrm{mos} \quad / \quad \left[ \underline{\phantom{xx}} \atop +\mathrm{plu} \right] \end{array} \right\}$

b.　[2pers] → s⟨te⟩　/ ⟨[+perf]⟩+——

c.　[3pers] → $\left\{ {⟨\mathrm{U}⟩ \atop {}_1⟨\mathrm{ro}⟩\mathrm{n}} \right\}_1$ / ⟨ [+perf]⟩+$\left\{ \begin{array}{l} \left[ \underline{\phantom{xx}} \atop -\mathrm{plu} \right] \\ {}_1\left[ \underline{\phantom{xx}} \atop +\mathrm{plu} \right] \end{array} \right\}_1$

One of the attractive properties of rules like (77) that "spell out" bundles of syntactic features is that no otiose machinery need be added to a grammar to indicate that a given feature has no phonological realization. Furthermore, generalizations can be captured by making appropriate use of the usual notational conventions. Still it is not clear that rules like (77) are the proper formal device for specifying the kind of information in question. The formal properties of syntactic and phonological rules (in the usual sense) are dictated on empirical grounds, but it is far from obvious what empirical support can be found for preferring, say, (77) over (75). It seems that much more investigation of complex inflectional systems is needed to clarify the issues involved here.

## 3.11 Summary of rules

All the phonological rules proposed in this chapter will now be listed, renumbered as (78). Certain of the rules discussed in Chapter 2 which played a role in the discussion here are also included. The rules are

---

[31] The formalism of (77) is to be taken with a grain of salt, but it should be noted that (a) subcases of rules are ordered, (b) paired angled brackets mean that either both members or neither member of the pair must be present, and (c) angled brackets impose disjunctive ordering just as parentheses do (see Chomsky and Halle (1968), Chapter Two, Section 5)).

given in the correct order, to the extent that this can be determined by the data presented up to this point. It must be stressed that several of the rules of (78) are not yet in their final form.

(78)

*a.* $\begin{bmatrix} V \\ -\text{low} \end{bmatrix} \rightarrow [+\text{high}] \quad / \quad \underline{\quad\quad}[+\text{past}]$        (19),(27)

*b.* $\begin{Bmatrix} k \\ {}_1g {}_1 \end{Bmatrix} \rightarrow \begin{Bmatrix} s \\ {}_1x {}_1 \end{Bmatrix} \quad / \quad \underline{\quad\quad} \begin{bmatrix} -\text{cons} \\ -\text{back} \end{bmatrix}$        (14)

*c.* $V \rightarrow \phi \quad / + \begin{bmatrix} \underline{\quad\quad\quad} \\ \langle +\text{irreg} \rangle \end{bmatrix} + \begin{Bmatrix} \begin{bmatrix} V \\ -D \end{bmatrix} \\ \langle r\#[+\text{fut}] \rangle \end{Bmatrix}$        (3),(17) (36),(70)

*d.* $\phi \rightarrow d \quad / \begin{bmatrix} +\text{cons} \\ -\text{obstr} \\ -\text{cont} \end{bmatrix} + \underline{\quad\quad} r$        (71)

*e.* $b \rightarrow \phi \quad / \; i + \underline{\quad\quad}$        (28)

*f.* $V \rightarrow [\text{1stress}] \quad / \quad \underline{\quad\quad}([-\text{perf}]) \, C_0VC_0\#]_V$        (5),(25)

*g.* $\begin{bmatrix} V \\ +\text{low} \end{bmatrix} \rightarrow \begin{bmatrix} -\text{low} \\ \alpha\text{back} \end{bmatrix} \quad / \quad \underline{\quad\quad} \begin{bmatrix} -\text{cons} \\ +\text{high} \\ \alpha\text{back} \end{bmatrix}$ *(under certain conditions)*    (38), (39),(48)

*h.* $[+\text{obstr}] \rightarrow [-\text{tense}] \quad / \; V\underline{\quad\quad}[-\text{obstr}]$ *(under certain conditions)*    (20)

*i.* $\begin{bmatrix} e \\ +D \end{bmatrix} \rightarrow \phi \quad / \; V\begin{bmatrix} +\text{cor} \\ +\text{ant} \end{bmatrix}_0^1 \underline{\quad\quad}\#$        (23)

*j.* $\begin{bmatrix} -\text{cons} \\ -\text{stress} \\ +\text{high} \\ \alpha\text{back} \end{bmatrix} \rightarrow \phi \quad / \begin{bmatrix} V \\ -\text{low} \\ \alpha\text{back} \end{bmatrix}\underline{\quad\quad}$        (38),(40)

*k.* $\begin{bmatrix} V \\ +\text{stress} \end{bmatrix} \rightarrow \begin{bmatrix} -\text{high} \\ +D \end{bmatrix} \quad / \quad \underline{\quad\quad} + \begin{Bmatrix} \text{ndo} \\ \text{rV} \end{Bmatrix}$        (21),(31), (34)

*(continued)*

*(78 continued)*

*l.* $\begin{Bmatrix} \acute{E} \\ {}_1\acute{O} \end{Bmatrix}_1 \rightarrow \begin{Bmatrix} y\acute{e} \\ {}_1w\acute{e} \end{Bmatrix}_1$   *(under certain conditions)*      (2:69a)

*m.* $\begin{bmatrix} V \\ +\text{high} \\ +\text{stress} \end{bmatrix} \begin{bmatrix} V \\ +\text{high} \end{bmatrix} \Rightarrow [-\text{stress}]\ [+\text{stress}]$      (42)

       1       2          1       2

*n.* $V \rightarrow [-\text{high}] \bigg/ \left\{ \begin{matrix} \begin{bmatrix} \underline{\phantom{xx}} \\ -\text{stress} \end{bmatrix} C_0\# \\[4pt] \begin{bmatrix} \underline{\phantom{xx}} \\ +D \end{bmatrix} \end{matrix} \right\}$   *(under certain conditions)*      (9),(44), (45)

*o.* $\begin{bmatrix} -\text{cons} \\ +\text{high} \\ -\text{stress} \end{bmatrix} \rightarrow [-\text{voc}] \bigg/ \left\{ \begin{matrix} \underline{\phantom{xx}}V \\ V\underline{\phantom{xx}} \end{matrix} \right\}$      (2:69i)

*p.* Erase all stresses but the rightmost in a word.      (67)

# 4. Verb Forms: Further Details

## 4.1 Vowel alternations in third conjugation verb stems

The only vowel alternations that occur in the stems of otherwise regular first and second conjugation verbs are $\breve{e} \sim y\acute{e}$ and $\breve{o} \sim w\acute{e}$: first conjugation $p[\breve{e}]ns\acute{a}mos$, $p[y\acute{e}]nsa$; $c[\breve{o}]nt\acute{a}mos$, $c[w\acute{e}]nta$; second conjugation $p[\breve{e}]rd\acute{e}mos$, $p[y\acute{e}]rde$; $m[\breve{o}]v\acute{e}mos$, $m[w\acute{e}]ve$. These alternations have been accounted for by a diphthongization rule tentatively formulated as $(3:78l)$. In third conjugation stems, on the other hand, there are other alternations, which will be examined in this section. Third conjugation verbs whose stems have consonantal alternations traditionally considered to be irregular will not be taken into account.

### 4.1.1 *Stems with back vowels*

It is a striking fact that in third conjugation verbs with back stem vowels,[1] there are just a few forms with stem $a$ and only two forms with stem $o$. All other verbs have the vowel $u$ in the stem.[2] In the few third conjugation verbs with stem $a$ (e.g., *abrir*, *partir*), the vowel never

---

[1] The term "stem vowel" will be used to refer to the only vowel of monosyllabic stems and to the *final* vowel of polysyllabic stems, not counting the "theme vowel." Polysyllabic stems frequently consist of a monosyllabic root with a prefix.

[2] There are surprisingly few marginal or only apparent exceptions. *Oír*, "to hear" (which is not studied here because of irregular consonantal alternations—but see discussion following rule $(3:67)$), is presumably only apparently an exception to the

alternates with another vowel; hence these verbs need not be considered further. The two verbs with stem *o*, *dormir* and *morir*, will be discussed directly. First let us examine the forms with the vowel *u* in the stem. These are listed in (1), which is close to exhaustive for the dialect under study.

(1)

| | | | | |
|---|---|---|---|---|
| *huir* | *urgir* | *enfurtir* | *aducir* | *fundir* |
| *fruncir* | *gruñir* | *infurtir* | *conducir* | *confundir* |
| *nutrir* | *cumplir* | | *producir* | *difundir* |
| *urdir* | *luir* | *incumbir* | *reducir* | *infundir* |
| *rugir* | *tullir* | *sucumbir* | *traducir* | |
| *lucir* | *mullir* | | | *acudir* |
| *unir* | *surtir* | *fluir* | *sumir* | *percudir* |
| *cundir* | *esculpir* | *influir* | *asumir* | *recudir* |
| *embutir* | *aturdir* | | *consumir* | *sacudir* |
| *uncir* | *suplir* | *interrumpir* | *presumir* | |
| *aburrir* | *deglutir* | *prorrumpir* | *resumir* | *curtir* |
| *zurrir* | *muñir* | | | *encurtir* |
| *engullir* | *sufrir* | *tupir* | *cubrir* | |
| *bruñir* | *gruir* | *entupir* | *descubrir* | *concurrir* |
| *hundir* | *derruir* | | *encubrir* | *escurrir* |
| *bullir* | *zurcir* | *aludir* | | *incurrir* |
| *ungir* | | *coludir* | | *ocurrir* |
| *escupir* | *tundir* | *eludir* | *pungir* | *recurrir* |
| *subir* | *contundir* | | *compungir* | |
| *crujir* | *retundir* | | | |

The verbs in (1) are largely regular, that is, they are conjugated as *unir* is throughout Chapter 3. There are, of course, a few irregularities here and there: for example, the past participle of (*des/en*)*cubrir* is (*des/en*)*cubierto*, the preterit of *a-*, *con-*, *pro-*, *re-*, *tra-ducir* is *-duje*, *-dujiste*, *-dujo*, *-dujimos*, *-dujeron*. In any event, the only stem vowel that occurs in any form, regular or irregular, is *u*.

Although crystal-clear cases are hard to find, there seem to be a few nonverbs in which certain of the stems of (1) appear with some vowel other than *u*. For example, the stem of *mullir*, "to soften," apparently occurs also in the adjective *m*[wé]*lle*, "soft," and in the noun *m*[o]*lície*,

---

generalization in question: the stem may well be /awd-/ (cf. *audición*, "audition," "hearing"). *Abolir*, "to abolish," is defective, and there seems to be no consensus concerning what forms are in use or what their shapes are. The infinitives *podrir* and *pudrir*, "to rot," are in free variation for some speakers, as are the past participles *podrido* and *pudrido*, but all finite forms have *pudr-*.

"softness." This suggests that the systematic phonemic representation of the stem is /mO11/. In the noun, /O/ is realized as [o], in the adjective it is diphthongized under stress to [we] by rule (3:78*l*), and in the verb it is changed to *u*. The stem of *hundir*, "to sink," "to submerge," may conceivably be the same as that of the adjective *hondo*, "deep," suggesting that the systematic phonemic representation is /hUnd/ or /hond/. If it is the former, then /U/ is lowered to [o] in the adjective by rule (3:78*n*) but changed to *u* in the verb; if it is the latter, then /o/ is raised to *u* in the verb but not in the adjective. Whether or not these suggestions are correct, it is surely no accident that only *u* appears in all the stems of (1). Clearly, then, a rule is needed with the effect of (2) (in which the final V of the environment represents the theme vowel):

$$(2) \qquad \begin{bmatrix} V \\ +\text{back} \\ -\text{low} \end{bmatrix} \rightarrow u \ / \ \left[\overline{\underset{3\text{conj}}{\phantom{xxx}}}\right] C_0 V]_V$$

We now turn to the two verbs with stem *o* rather than *u*: *dormir*, "to sleep," and *morir*, "to die." Only *dormir* need be dealt with since the same alternations occur in both verbs, except for the irregular past participle *muerto* of *morir*. The forms of *dormir* are given in (3):

(3)

| INFINITIVE | PAST PARTICIPLE | PRESENT PARTICIPLE |
|---|---|---|
| d[o]rmír | d[o]rmído | d[u]rmiéndo |

PRESENT

| INDICATIVE | | | SUBJUNCTIVE | |
|---|---|---|---|---|
| d[wé]rmo | d[o]rmímos | | d[wé]rma | d[u]rmámos |
| d[wé]rmes | | | d[wé]rmas | |
| d[wé]rme | d[wé]rmen | | d[wé]rma | d[wé]rman |

IMPERFECT

| INDICATIVE | | | SUBJUNCTIVE | |
|---|---|---|---|---|
| d[o]rmía | d[o]rmíamos | | d[u]rmiéra | d[u]rmiéramos |
| d[o]rmías | | | d[u]rmiéras | |
| d[o]rmía | d[o]rmían | | d[u]rmiéra | d[u]rmiéran |

PRETERIT

| | | |
|---|---|---|
| d[o]rmí | d[o]rmímos | |
| d[o]rmíste | | |
| d[u]rmió | d[u]rmiéron | |

The simplest statement of the distribution of [u], [o], and [we] seems to be the following:

$$\text{STRESSED:} \quad \text{we}$$

$$\text{UNSTRESSED:} \quad \left\{ \begin{array}{ll} \text{o} & / \ \underline{\qquad} C_0\text{í} \\ \text{u} & \textit{elsewhere} \end{array} \right\}$$

We already have in the grammar part of the machinery to account for this distribution. To begin with, rule (2) will apply to all the forms of *dormir* and *morir*. Nothing more is required for the forms in which phonetic [u] occurs. With regard to the forms with phonetic [wé], recall that we already have a rule, (3:78*k*), which in certain environments lowers stressed high vowels to mid vowels and supplies the feature [+D]. One of the environments is precisely that in which the stem vowel of *morir* occurs, namely, ——*r*V. Furthermore, it will be proposed in Section 4.1.3 that the other environment in which (3:78*k*) applies, namely, ——*ndo*, can be generalized to include the environment of the stem vowel of *dormir*, namely, ——*rm*. Thus the independently motivated rule (3:78*k*) will convert /u/, when stressed, to [O], and the diphthongization rule (3:78*l*) will then apply to yield [we], as desired.

Finally, to account for the occurrences of unstressed [o] in forms of *dormir* and *morir*, a rule is needed with the effect of (4):

$$(4) \qquad\qquad \text{u} \ \rightarrow \ \text{o} \ / \ \underline{\qquad} C_0\text{í}$$

Since (4) applies to none of the verbs in (1), it must be restricted in some way.[3] This will be clarified in Section 4.1.3, after analogous alternations among front vowels have been examined.

The derivations of representative forms of *dormir* are given in (5). (Words like *dormitorio* suggest that the underlying stem vowel is /o/.)

(5)

| dorm+i+rE | dorm+i+o | dorm+ i+a+mos | |
|---|---|---|---|
| u | u | u | (2) |
| | φ | φ | (3:78*c*) |
| í | ú | á | (3:78*f*) |
| φ | | | (3:78*i*) |
| | Ó | | (3:78*k*) |
| | wé | | (3:78*l*) |
| o | | | (4) |
| *dormír* | *dwérmo* | *durmámos* | |

[3] It is an interesting fact that at an earlier stage of the language many of the verbs in (1) had phonetic *o* rather than *u* in the environment of (4). Menéndez Pidal (1962, p. 273) mentions older *ordir, complir, cobrir, sofrir, somir,* and *adocir* for modern *urdir, cumplir, cubrir, sufrir, sumir,* and *aducir*.

## 4.1.2 *Stems with front vowels*

Third conjugation verbs with front stem vowels may be grouped into several subclasses:

  (a)  those with stem *i* in all verb forms, and stem *i* also in nominalizations—for example, *inscribir*, "to inscribe," *inscripción*, "inscription"

  (b)  those with stem *i* in all verb forms but stem *e* in nominalizations—for example, *recibir*, "to receive," *recepción*, "receipt"

  (c)  those with stem *i* alternating with *e*—for example, *pedir*, "to request," *pido*, " I request"

  (d)  those with *e*, *i*, and *ye*—for example, *herir*, "to wound," *hiriendo* (present participle), *hiero* (first person singular present indicative)

We will consider each of these subclasses in turn.

4.1.2.1. The following stems have *i* in all verb forms and also in -*ión* nominalizations:

(6)

| | | |
|---|---|---|
| *esgrimir* | *escribir* | *exigir* |
| *vivir* | *describir (descripción)* | *transigir* |
| *fingir* | *inscribir (inscripción)* | |
| *refringir* | *prescribir (prescripción)* | *presidir* |
| *definir (definición)* | *proscribir (proscripción)* | *residir* |
| *elidir (elisión* | *su(b)scribir (su(b)scripción)* | |
| *dividir (división)* | *transcribir (transcripción)* | *asistir* |
| | | *consistir* |
| *cohibir (cohibición)* | *afligir (aflicción)* | *desistir* |
| *exhibir (exhibición)* | *infligir (inflicción)* | *existir* |
| *inhibir (inhibición)* | | *insistir* |
| *prohibir (prohibición)* | *coincidir* | *persistir* |
| | *decidir (decisión)* | *resistir* |
| *admitir (admisión)* | | *subsistir* |
| *dimitir (dimisión)* | *astringir (astricción)* | |
| *emitir (emisión)* | *constringir (constricción)* | *prescindir* |
| *omitir (omisión)* | *restringir (restricción)* | *rescindir* |
| *permitir* | | |
| *remitir (remisión)* | *distinguir (distinción)* | |
| *transmitir (transmisión)* | *extinguir (extinción)* | |

From the data of (6) one can only assume that these stems have the underlying vowel /i/.

4.1.2.2. The stems represented in (7) have *i* in all verb forms but *e* in *-ión* nominalizations, agentive nouns and adjectives in *-tor/-sor*, and adjectives in *-to :*

(7)  *apercibir (apercepción)*             *comprimir (compresión, compresor)*
     *percibir (percepción, perceptor)*    *deprimir (depresión)*
     *recibir (recepción, receptor)*       *imprimir (impresión, impresor)*
                                           *oprimir (opresión, opresor)*
     *eximir (exención, exento)*           *reprimir (represión, represor)*
     *redimir (redención, redentor)*       *suprimir (supresión, supresor)*

     *dirigir (dirección, director)*
     *erigir (erección, erector)*

We may account for these vowel alternations by postulating underlying /e/ in the stems of (7). In all verb forms, but not in nouns and adjectives, this /e/ is raised to [i]. To achieve the desired results we need only simplify rule (2) so that it converts nonlow front vowels to *i* as well as nonlow back vowels to *u* in third conjugation forms. That is, (2) can be restated as

$$\begin{bmatrix} V \\ -\text{low} \end{bmatrix} \rightarrow \begin{bmatrix} +\text{high} \\ -D \end{bmatrix} \ / \ \cdots$$

We now note that we already have in the grammar a rule that raises nonlow vowels to high vowels in another environment, namely, rule (3:78a). There seems to be no reason why rule (2), as just revised, and rule (3:78a) cannot be combined as (8):

(8)
$$\begin{bmatrix} V \\ -\text{low} \end{bmatrix} \rightarrow \begin{bmatrix} +\text{high} \\ -D \end{bmatrix} \ / \ \begin{cases} \text{——} [+\text{past}] & a \\ \begin{bmatrix} \text{——} \\ \text{3conj} \end{bmatrix} C_0 V]_V & b \end{cases}$$

The feature $[-D]$ in the output of (8) is not necessary for case (*a*) since the only vowels to which this case applies are second and third conjugation thematic /e/ and /i/, which are already $[-D]$ (see Section 3.5.2). This feature is apparently necessary, however, for case (*b*), since some of the stem vowels to which it applies are $[+D]$ (cf. *muelle, mullir*, Section 4.1.1).

Further investigation might very well reveal that other cases should be added to (8). For example, second conjugation thematic *e* appears as *i* before the derivational affixes *-ble* and *-miento : mover,* "to move," *movible, movimiento* (cf. first conjugation *tratar,* "to treat," *tratable, tratamiento*). It is quite possible that the various cases of (8) could be generalized, but I have not investigated the matter further at this point.

4.1.2.3. The verbs in (9) show a stem vowel alternation between *i* and *e*:

(9)
| | | | |
|---|---|---|---|
| *pedir* | *medir* | *seguir* | *regir* |
| *despedir* | *gemir* | *conseguir* | *corregir* |
| *impedir* | *freír* | *perseguir* | |
| | | *proseguir* | *derretir* |
| *competir* | *colegir* | | *concebir* |
| *repetir* | *elegir* | *reír* | |
| | | *sonreír* | |

The forms of this class are illustrated in (10) with *pedir:*

(10)
| INFINITIVE | PAST PARTICIPLE | PRESENT PARTICIPLE |
|---|---|---|
| *p*[e]*dír* | *p*[e]*dído* | *p*[i]*diéndo* |

PRESENT

| INDICATIVE | | SUBJUNCTIVE | |
|---|---|---|---|
| *p*[i]*do* | *p*[e]*dímos* | *p*[i]*da* | *p*[i]*dámos* |
| *p*[i]*des* | | *p*[i]*das* | |
| *p*[i]*de* | *p*[i]*den* | *p*[i]*da* | *p*[i]*dan* |

IMPERFECT

| INDICATIVE | | SUBJUNCTIVE | |
|---|---|---|---|
| *p*[e]*día* | *p*[e]*díamos* | *p*[i]*diéra* | *p*[i]*diéramos* |
| *p*[e]*días* | | *p*[i]*diéras* | |
| *p*[e]*día* | *p*[e]*dían* | *p*[i]*diéra* | *p*[i]*diéran* |

PRETERIT

| | |
|---|---|
| *p*[e]*dí* | *p*[e]*dímos* |
| *p*[e]*díste* | |
| *p*[i]*dió* | *p*[i]*diéron* |

Examination of (10) shows that the distribution of stem *e* and *i* is not fully determined by stress: only *i* occurs when the stem is stressed, but both *e* and *i* occur when the stem is unstressed. We find, however, that there is a generalization to be made independent of stem stress: *e* occurs just in the environment ——*dí*; *i* occurs elsewhere. Since we already have rule (4) which lowers *u* to *o* in the environment ——$C_0 i$, which includes ——*dí*, and since we have found no reason to restrict rule (8), which raises all nonlow third conjugation stem vowels, all of the forms of *pedir* (and of the other verbs of (9)) may be accounted for. Rule (8) applies (perhaps vacuously, as we shall see) to all forms, giving stem *i;* this *i* is lowered to *e* in the appropriate forms by the simplification of rule (4) given in (11):

(11)                    $V \rightarrow [-\text{high}] \ / \ \text{---}C_0 \text{í}$

The future forms of *pedir* are *pediré, pedirás, pedirá, pediremos, pedirán*, as follows from the rule of thumb for regular futures: "Add *-é, -ás, -á, -emos, -án* to the infinitive." Note, however, that the stem vowel in these forms is *e*, not *i*, even though this vowel does not seem to occur in the environment of rule (11). But this is no problem, given the analysis of future forms presented in Section 3.9. In this analysis, as will be recalled, stress is assigned both to the infinitive and to the attached forms of *haber*. Thus rule (11) applies to *pidíré*, converting it to *pedíré*, as desired. Subsequently, *pedíré* is changed to *pedíré* by rule (3:78*p*), which erases all stresses but the rightmost in a word.

Rule (11) must still be restricted in some way so that it does not apply to the forms of (1), (6), or (7) but does apply to the appropriate forms of (3) and (9). One would hope to be able to find some general property of the stems in question that would determine the applicability of rule (11). In view of contrasts like the following, however, this seems unlikely:

| e | i |
|---|---|
| (*con*)*cebir* (9) | (*re*)*cibir* (7) |
| (*cor*)*regir* (9) | (*di*)*rigir* (7) |
| *gemir* (9) | *oprimir* (7) |

We are thus left with no alternative but to indicate the applicability of rule (11) by some lexical subcategorization. This will be discussed further in Section 4.1.3.

Given the existence of rule (8), which raises and assigns the feature $[-D]$ to all nonlow stem vowels in third conjugation verbs, the underlying stem vowel of the verbs in (9) could be any nonlow front vowel. Some of these stems, however, participate in alternations such as in (12):

(12)

| VERB | NOUN | ADJECTIVE |
|---|---|---|
| *concibo* | $\left\{ \begin{array}{l} concepción \\ concepto \end{array} \right\}$ | |
| *corrijo* | *corrección* | *correcto* |
| *elijo* | $\left\{ \begin{array}{l} elección \\ elector \end{array} \right\}$ | *electo* |
| *consigo* | *consecución* | |

It can be seen from (12) that such stems have underlying *e* or *E* which is changed to *i* by rule (8) in verb forms but not in other categories (and subsequently changed back to *e* in forms to which rule (11) applies). For the stems in (9) that show no such alternations, we make the simplest assumption, namely, that the underlying stem vowel is *i*.

The verbs in (13) are also conjugated like *pedir*, that is, they have stem *e* in the environment ——$C_0 i$ and stem *i* elsewhere:

(13)

| | | | |
|---|---|---|---|
| *servir* | *vestir* | *teñir* | *astreñir* |
| *embestir* | *investir* | *ceñir* | *estreñir* |
| *rendir* | *revestir* | *heñir* | *constreñir* |
| *henchir* | | *reñir* | |

The verbs of (13) have been separated from those of (9) on the following basis: the stem vowels in (9) are immediately followed by at most one consonant; those of (13) are followed by a consonant cluster or by *ñ*, which may come from a consonant cluster at an early level of derivation.[4] The significance of this division will become apparent in Section 4.1.3.

Only a few of the stems in (13) show alternations in categories other than verbs which might indicate what the underlying stem vowels are. The forms in (14) illustrate what seem to be the clearest cases:

(14)

| VERB | NOUN |
|---|---|
| *teñir* | *tinte, tintura* |
| *ceñir* | *cinto, cintura* |
| *heñir* | *hintero* |
| *reñir* | *riña* |

The simplest assumption for the forms in (14) is that the underlying stem vowel is *i*, which is lowered to *e* by rule (11) in the environment ——$C_0 i$, which happens to occur only in the verb forms.

There are other, less clear cases. For example, the noun *siervo*, which means "slave" or, in a highly specialized religious sense, "servant," may be related to the verb *servir*, "to serve." If this is correct, then the stem is /sErv/, and the forms are derived as in (15):

(15)

| NOUN | VERB | VERB | |
|---|---|---|---|
| sErv+o | sErv+i | sErv+i+mos | |
| – | i | i | (8) |
| É | í | í | (3:78*f*) |
| yé | | | (3:78*l*) |
| | e | | (3:78*n*) |
| | | e | (11) |
| *syérvo* | *sírve* | *servímos* | |

4.1.2.4. The stems of the verbs in (16) show the alternations *e* ~ *i* ~ *ye*:

---

[4] In these cases, the underlying cluster is probably *ng* or *gn*. See Foley (1965, pp. 9–15) for discussion.

(16)                   *herir*            *conferir*
                       *adherir*          *deferir*
                                          *diferir*
                       *digerir*          *inferir*
                       *ingerir*          *preferir*
                       *sugerir*          *proferir*
                                          *referir*
                       *requerir*         *transferir*

The forms of these verbs are illustrated in (17) with *herir:*

(17)     INFINITIVE          PAST PARTICIPLE          PRESENT PARTICIPLE
         *h*[e]*rír*           *h*[e]*rído*              *h*[i]*riéndo*

                                  PRESENT
         INDICATIVE                                    SUBJUNCTIVE
 *h*[yé]*ro*   *h*[e]*rímos*                    *h*[yé]*ra*   *h*[i]*rámos*
 *h*[yé]*res*                                   *h*[yé]*ras*
 *h*[yé]*re*   *h*[yé]*ren*                     *h*[yé]*ra*   *h*[yé]*ran*

                                 IMPERFECT
         INDICATIVE                                    SUBJUNCTIVE
 *h*[e]*ría*   *h*[e]*ríamos*                   *h*[i]*riéra*   *h*[i]*riéramos*
 *h*[e]*rías*                                   *h*[i]*riéras*
 *h*[e]*ría*   *h*[e]*rían*                     *h*[i]*riéra*   *h*[i]*riéran*

                                 PRETERIT
                         *h*[e]*rí*   *h*[e]*rímos*
                         *h*[e]*ríste*
                         *h*[i]*rió*   *h*[i]*riéron*

Examination of (17) reveals that the distribution of [ye], [e],
and [i] exactly parallels that of [we], [o], and [u] in the forms of
*dormir* and *morir:* only [ye] occurs under stress, [e] occurs in the
environment ——C₀*i*, and [i] occurs elsewhere. Thus nothing must
be added to the grammar to account for all the forms of *herir* and of
the other verbs of (16). Sample derivations are given in (18):

(18)     her+i+rE        her+i+o        her+i+a+mos
          i               i              i               (8)
                           φ              φ               (3:78*c*)
              í           í                   á          (3:78*f*)
                  φ                                      (3:78*i*)
                          É                              (3:78*k*)
                          yé                             (3:78*l*)
          e                                              (11)
        *herír*         *hyéro*         *hirámos*

The verbs in (19) are also conjugated like *herir:*

| (19) | | |
|---|---|---|
| | *sentir* | *advertir* |
| | *asentir* | *convertir* |
| | *consentir* | *controvertir* |
| | *disentir* | *divertir* |
| | *presentir* | *invertir* |
| | *resentir* | *pervertir* |
| | *mentir* | *hervir* |
| | *arrepentir* | |

The verbs of (19) have been separated from those of (16) on the following basis: the stem vowels in (16) are followed by *r;* those in (19) are followed by consonant clusters, namely, *nt, rt,* and *rv.* The reason for distinguishing these two groups of verbs, and also the verbs in (9) versus (13), will become obvious in Section 4.1.3.

4.1.2.5. To conclude this survey of third conjugation verbs with front stem vowels, I will make the following brief comments about a few highly idiosyncratic verbs.

*Divergir* and *sumergir* have no alternations at all: the stem vowel is *e* in all forms. Apparently these verbs undergo neither rule (8) nor the generalized version of rule (3:78*k*) mentioned in Section 4.1.1 with regard to *dormir.*

*Discernir* and *concernir* are defective, and native speakers are unsure of the forms. According to the *Vox* dictionary the only forms of *concernir* in use are the infinitive, third person singular present indicative *concierne,* imperfect indicative *concernía,* and the present participle *concerniendo.* This last form shows the verb to be an exception to rule (8) (*\*concirniendo*).

*Agredir* and *aguerrir* are defective, and there is no consensus concerning which forms are in use.

*Erguir,* about which speakers are uncertain, has, according to the authorities, two sets of forms, one set belonging to the class of (19) (*yergo, yergues,* etc.), the other belonging to the class of (13) (*irgo, irgues,* etc.) Presumably the first set undergoes rule (3:78*k*) while the second does not, or, perhaps, the first set fails to undergo (8).

The stem *-quirir,* occurring only in *adquirir* and *inquirir* (cf. *requerir* of (16)), is unique in that it undergoes rule (3:78*k*) (*adquiéro, adquiéres,* etc.) but not rule (11) (*adquirímos, adquiría, adquiríste,* etc.)

### 4.1.3 *Concluding remarks*

We have seen that third conjugation vowel alternations, which have long puzzled scholars (see Malkiel (1966)), can be accounted for quite naturally by subcategorizing stems with respect to whether or not they undergo just three ordered rules, even in highly idiosyncratic and unique cases. Of these three rules, one, (3:78$k$), must be in the grammar in some form in any case. Another, rule (8), is quite general, applying to all third conjugation stems except idiosyncratic *divergir, sumergir,* and defective *concernir.* The third rule, (11), as was observed in Section 4.1.2.3, apparently applies only to lexically marked stems. Since rule (11) does *not* apply to the majority of third conjugation stems, it will be designated a "minor rule" in the sense of Lakoff (1965).[5] There seems to be no reason why (11) cannot be combined with rule (3:78$n$) as (20):

(20)

$$V \rightarrow [-\text{high}] \; / \; \left\{ \begin{array}{l} \left[ \begin{array}{c} \overline{\phantom{+D}} \\ +D \end{array} \right] \\ \left[ \begin{array}{c} \overline{\phantom{-\text{stress}}} \\ -\text{stress} \end{array} \right] C_0 \left\{ \begin{array}{c} \# \\ i \end{array} \right\} \end{array} \right\} \quad \begin{array}{l} a \quad \text{\textit{(under certain}} \\ \quad \text{\textit{conditions)}} \\ \; \\ b \\ c \quad \text{MINOR} \end{array}$$

We are left, then, with the task of clarifying in exactly what environments and under what conditions rule (3:78$k$) applies. A statement of the special conditions of application of this rule will have to be postponed until Section 4.4, where further data will be presented, but the question of the environments can be settled now.

In addition to the environments detailed in Chapter 3, rule (3:78$k$) must apply to the stem vowels, when stressed, of the following classes of verbs:

(a)  (16) plus *morir,* i.e., in the environment ——$r$V

(b)  (19) plus *dormir,* i.e., in the environments ——$rm$, ——$rt$, ——$rv$, and ——$nt$

The environment of (a), ——$r$V, is already stated in the rule as formulated in Chapter 3. Now we must state the set of environments in (b) so as to include the environment ——$nd(o)$ of previous formulations. This is done in (21):

(21)

$$\text{——} \left[ \begin{array}{c} +\text{cons} \\ -\text{obstr} \end{array} \right] \left[ \begin{array}{c} -\text{voc} \\ +\text{ant} \end{array} \right]$$

Let us assume for the moment, then, that (3:78$k$) can be replaced by (22):[6]

---

[5] This rule was apparently more general at an earlier stage of the language. For example, modern *escribir* and *vivir* were once *escrebir* and *vevir.* See also note 3.

[6] Note that the $+$ has been removed from the environment of this rule. It must now be restricted in some way so as not to apply to words like *brindo, lindo, rindo, tamarindo, fecundo, fundo, mundo, segundo, vagabundo* and *admiro, ira, mentira, giro, tiro, cintura, cura, locura, procure, duro, muro, futuro,* as well as the verb forms to be mentioned directly. To reflect this fact, "under certain conditions" has been added to the rule temporarily. This statement will be clarified in Section 4.4.

(22)

$$\begin{bmatrix} V \\ +\text{stress} \end{bmatrix} \rightarrow \begin{bmatrix} -\text{high} \\ +D \end{bmatrix} \Big/ \underline{\quad} \begin{cases} rV & a \\ \begin{bmatrix} +\text{cons} \\ -\text{obstr} \end{bmatrix} \begin{bmatrix} -\text{voc} \\ +\text{ant} \end{bmatrix} & b \end{cases} \quad \begin{array}{l} (under \\ certain \\ conditions) \end{array}$$

Scanning the classes of verbs to which (22) must *not* apply, we find the following cases where the rule will apply incorrectly if not restricted:

(a)  none in the environment ——*r*V

(b)  ——*nc* (*fruncir, uncir*),  ——*nd* (*cundir, hundir, -tundir, -fundir, -scindir, rendir*),  ——*mpl* (*cumplir*),  ——*mb* (*-cumbir*),  ——*mp* (*-(r)rumpir*),  ——*rd* (*urdir, aturdir*),  ——*rt* (*surtir, -furtir, -curtir*),  ——*rc* (*zurcir*),  ——*rv* (*servir*)

When the restrictions on (22)—and on all rules now marked "under certain conditions"—are clarified in Section 4.4, it will be seen that the exclusion of these stems from the domain of (22) is by no means *ad hoc*.

## 4.2 The feature [D] versus tense and lax vowels

I have postulated an unidentified feature [D], mnemonic for "diphthongization," which distinguishes otherwise identical vowels. This feature appears in a number of the rules that have been proposed here up to this point, namely, rules (3:78*c*), (3:78*i*), (8), (20), and (22). Thus it is obvious that [D] is essential to certain generalizations about Spanish. At this point in the exposition we have accumulated sufficient data to allow us to examine this feature more closely and to attempt at least a tentative identification.

Anyone reasonably familiar with the history of Spanish will have recognized that several of the rules presented here are similar to historical rules and that, given this similarity, [αD] corresponds to [−αtense], that is, [+D] vowels are historically "short" or "lax" and [−D] vowels are historically "long" or "tense." For example, the vowels that diphthongize when stressed are reflexes of Latin lax vowels, and it is the reflex of lax *e* that is deleted word-finally after a single dental consonant. However, I have not yet taken the step of identifying [+D] as [−tense] and [−D] as [+tense] in the synchronic grammar being developed here because I do not believe that this can be justified exclusively on the basis of synchronic data. I will suggest, though, that general theoretical considerations may conceivably provide sufficient motivation for making such an identification.

The only careful discussion known to me of the distribution of tense and lax vowels in phonetic representations is that of Navarro Tomás (1965, pp. 35 ff.) for Castilian. Navarro's description, however, does not carry over to any Latin American dialect I have ever heard. King's (1952) study of a Mexican dialect essentially identical to the one studied in the present investigation contains, in effect, the statement that phonetically tense and lax vowels are in free variation. King takes some pains to press the point, perhaps because his description is so much at variance with Navarro's well-known and highly respected work. He has oversimplified slightly, but in any event it seems to me that a detailed study of phonetically tense and lax vowels in Mexican Spanish would be most unrewarding. This is apparently the position taken in Stockwell, Bowen, and Silva-Fuenzalida's (1956) extremely detailed study of another dialect, where discussion of tense and lax vowels is limited to the single statement that "we have been unable to classify the distribution of lax [E] and tense [e] and similar data well enough to include them here, except to assert that they exist . . . " (p. 408).

Navarro (1965, pp. 35 *passim*) is careful to point out that although tenser and laxer vowel allophones ("vocales más cerradas, más abiertas" in his terminology) can be distinguished in Castilian, the differences are not so marked as in other languages, for example French, Italian, and German. That is, Castilian tense vowels are less tense—"no suele[n] llegar al grado de tensión y estrechez"—and Castilian lax vowels are less lax, with the result that the Castilian variants are confined to "un timbre medio entre las diversas variantes abiertas y cerradas que en otros idiomas se conocen" (p. 41). In Navarro Tomás (1968, Chapter III) twelve pages are devoted almost exclusively to insistence on the semi-open and semi-close character of Castilian vowels.

Although the *distribution* of tense and lax vowel allophones given by Navarro for Castilian does not seem to carry over to Mexican Spanish, the description of the medial quality of such allophones does carry over, perhaps to all major Latin American dialects.[7]

Navarro (1965, pp. 41–42) also points out that there is absolutely no correlation between historically tense and lax vowels and phonetically tense and lax vowels in modern Castilian. For example, Castilian

[7] A number of Latin Americans I have known—some with phonetic training and some without—are able to make quite fine discriminations among consonantal allophones with no difficulty (for example, [s] versus [sᶻ] versus [z], [β] versus [βᶲ] versus [ɸ]), both in their own speech and in the speech of others. However, they are completely unable to consistently identify tenser and laxer vowel allophones under the same conditions.

*sol,* with lax *o,* comes from Latin *sōle,* with tense *o,* while Castilian *pecho,* with tense *e,* comes from Latin *pectu,* with lax *e.*

It goes without saying that this last observation of Navarro's also carries over to Mexican Spanish. What is more important for the present synchronic study is the fact that there is also no correlation between the specification with respect to the feature [D] of vowels in systematic phonemic representations and tenseness and laxness of vowels in phonetic representations. Consider, for example, *poder,* "to be able," *puedo,* "I can," and *podemos,* "we can." As has already been argued at many points, the systematic phonemic representations of these forms must be, ignoring irrelevant details, /pOder/, /pOdo/, and /pOdemos/, respectively. The phonetic forms are, however, [poδÉr], [pweδo], and [poδémos], where /O/ appears as [o], [wé], and /e/ appears as [É], [é]. Therefore, the identification of [D]—in terms of which distinctions are made that are necessary to capture generalizations about the language—is wholly arbitrary unless general theoretical constraints can be found to justify a decision.

The familiar Latin stress rule mentioned previously does apparently play a role in assigning stress in Spanish, as we shall see. If this is correct, then it is perhaps from this rule that the most cogent theoretical argument can be adduced for the synchronic identification of [αD] as [−αtense] since "vowel quantity," i.e., the tense-lax distinction, and the derivative notions "strong" and "weak" syllable figure crucially in the rule. Let us turn, now, to the question of stress assignment and leave the identification of [D] for the moment.

Having gotten this extended caveat into the record, I will henceforth use the feature [tense] rather than [D], but only to reduce terminological strangeness.

## 4.3 More on stress assignment

### 4.3.1 *The Latin stress rule*

Foley (undated; 1965, pp. 80–87; 1967) presents interesting and, I believe, essentially valid arguments for stress assignment in Spanish by the Latin stress rule (hereafter "LSR"), which, roughly, assigns stress to the penultimate syllable of polysyllabic words if that syllable is "strong" (contains a tense vowel, or a lax vowel followed by two or more consonants) and to the antepenultimate syllable if the penultimate is "weak" (contains a lax vowel followed by at most one consonant). What is emphasized by Foley is that stress *can* be assigned by this rule. Complementary arguments at least as strong can be given on the basis of the stress contours that are *excluded* by the LSR in polysyllabic words. These are as follows:

(a) Stress on the final syllable. It was seen in Sections 3.7 and 3.9 that some forms with stress on the final syllable in phonetic representations, namely, certain preterits (*amé, amó, comí*, etc.) and futures (*amaré, amarás*, etc.) are only apparent exceptions to the LSR. Foley accounts for other apparent exceptions, e.g., *después*, in a similar fashion. There is left, then, only a residue of exceptions that includes proper names such as *Cantú, Jehová*, foreign loans such as *ballét, debút*, and a few absolute exceptions such as *mamá, papá*.

(b) Stress four syllables from the end. The only class of apparent exceptions to the LSR of this sort known to me are those discussed in Section 2.4.5.1, e.g., *láudano, ventrílocuo*. Such forms are not exceptions, however, if stress is assigned to representations such as /lawdAno/, /ventrilOk^wo/, as suggested in the section referred to. Forms like *dándonoslos* are not exceptions since they are composite: ##*dándo*#*nos*#*los*##, "giving-us-them" = "giving them to us."

(c) Antepenultimate stress in words with a "strong" penultimate syllable. A hypothetical example of an exception of this sort would be something like *tánampo*. I have searched carefully through all the antepenultimately stressed words in a fairly large rhyming dictionary but have not found a single such exception to the LSR, however marginal.

(d) Stress on a penultimate lax vowel in a "weak" syllable. Here there are problems. It is not obvious how the LSR can assign stress in nouns like the following, in which diphthongization indicates an underlying lax vowel and this lax vowel is followed by a single consonant: *Venez*[wé]*la* (cf. *venez*[ŏ]*láno*), *ag*[wé]*ro* (cf. *ag*[ŏ]*rár*), *trop*[yé]*zo* (cf. *trop*[ĕ]*zár*), *ab*[wé]*lo* (cf. *ab*[ŏ]*léngo*). Further examples of this sort can be found easily. In most cases the historical reason for the apparently aberrant placement of stress is known, but there seems to be no residue that would provide a synchronic explanation. With a little ingenuity one could, of course, incorporate into the synchronic grammar relevant aspects of the historical development of these forms. However, without independent synchronic motivation, that is, without evidence for the underlying representations and rules postulated aside from stress placement, such a move would be totally *ad hoc*, and any "explanation" provided thereby would be illusory.

If stress were "phonemic" in Spanish, that is, if stress could occur on any syllable in complete independence of the segmental phonemes, then the almost total absence of forms mentioned in (a)-(c) could be attributed only to coincidence. But surely it is no accident that just the stress patterns excluded by the LSR are those that are missing in Spanish (assuming that some explanation can be found for the forms of paragraph (d)). Until a more detailed investigation of stress assignment in Spanish has been carried out, I will accept the LSR as a first approximation to the stress assignment rule for categories other than verbs.

Let us now examine verb stress more carefully. First, consider the paired examples in (23), where antepenultimate stress appears in the noun or adjective but penultimate stress occurs in the verb, which presumably has the same stem:

(23)

| NOUN, ADJECTIVE | VERB | NOUN, ADJECTIVE | VERB |
|---|---|---|---|
| *contínuo* | *continúo* | *práctica* | *practíca* |
| *náufrago* | *naufrágo* | *trámite* | *tramíte* |
| *tráfago* | *trafágo* | *tránsito* | *transíto* |
| *ánimo* | *anímo* | *catálogo* | *catalógo* |
| *fábrica* | *fabríca* | *plática* | *platíca* |
| *válido* | *valído* | *triángulo* | *triangúlo* |
| *lágrima* | *lagríma* | *cálculo* | *calcúlo* |
| *página* | *pagína* | *coágulo* | *coagúlo* |
| *círculo* | *circúlo* | *intérprete* | *interpréte* |
| *crédito* | *(a)credíto* | *doméstico* | *domestíco* |
| *íntegra* | *intégra* | *(in)édito* | *edíto* |
| *legítima* | *legitíma* | *réplica* | *replíca* |
| *solícito* | *solicíto* | *crítica* | *critíca* |
| *recíproco* | *recipróco* | *líquido* | *liquído* |
| *estímulo* | *estimúlo* | *partícipe* | *participe* |
| *vínculo* | *vincúlo* | *equívoco* | *equivóco* |
| *próspero* | *prospéro* | *síncope* | *sincópe* |
| *próximo* | *(a)proxímo* | *título* | *(en)titúlo* |
| *óxido* | *oxído* | *óvalo* | *oválo* |
| *vómito* | *vomíto* | *pródigo* | *prodígo* |
| *fórmula* | *formúla* | *depósito* | *deposíto* |
| *cómputo* | *compúto* | *oxígeno* | *oxigéno* |
| *público* | *publíco* | *cómodo* | *(a)comódo* |
| *júbilo* | *jubílo* | *rótulo* | *rotúlo* |
| *súplica* | *suplíca* | *número* | *numéro* |
| *cárcel* | *(en)carcélo* | | |

It is clear from (23) (which is not exhaustive) that in order for the

LSR to assign stress to the antepenultimate vowel in a noun or adjective, the penultimate vowel must be lax, but this same lax penultimate vowel is stressed in the corresponding verb. Therefore, either (a) verbs cannot be stressed by the same rule as nouns and adjectives, or (b) the stressed vowel in verbs is antepenultimate at the time stress is assigned. I know of no reason to suppose that (b) is correct. Let us, then, make the following assumptions and see where they lead us: (a) the identification of [αD] as [−αtense] is theoretically justifiable; (b) stress is assigned to nouns and adjectives by the LSR; and (c) stress is assigned to verbs by rule $(3:78f)$. Then case $(a)$ of (24) is just the LSR, and case $(b)$ is $(3:78f)$:

(24)
$$V \rightarrow [1\text{stress}] \quad / \quad \underline{\hspace{1cm}} \left\{ \begin{array}{l} (C_0(\check{V}C_0^1(L))V)C_0\#]_{N,A} \\ (([−\text{perf}])C_0V)C_0\#]_V \end{array} \right\} \begin{array}{l} a \\ \\ b \end{array}$$

There are a number of unclarities in (24), but just two comments will suffice for the moment. First, the outermost set of parentheses in both cases is to allow stress to be assigned to monosyllabic nouns and verbs such as *té* and *va*. Second, the parenthesized L in case $(a)$ is intended to express the fact that a consonant plus liquid cluster is "weak," as is shown by *íntegro, múltiple*, and many other clear examples.

One might entertain the idea of attempting to achieve somewhat greater generality in the assignment of stress, which would be reflected in a simplification of (24), perhaps along the following lines. Let us assume that the vowel in the [−perfective] markers *ba* (indicative) and *ra* (subjunctive) is in fact lax /A/. Then we might try to collapse the two cases of (24) by somehow letting the $\check{V}$ in case $(a)$ and the imperfective /A/ fall together, thereby eliminating case $(b)$. This will not work, however, as is shown by pairs like *náufrAgo* (noun) but *naufrÁgo* (verb), *tráfAgo* (noun) but *trafÁgo* (verb). Thus, although (24) can undoubtedly be refined slightly, I see no alternative to assigning stress to verbs by one rule and to nouns and adjectives by another, and, furthermore, to assigning verb stress in fixed positions, without regard for the "strong" and "weak" syllables in terms of which stress is assigned by the LSR.[8]

---

[8] The situation described here arose historically in two steps. The first took place some time after the thirteenth century. Menéndez Pidal (1962) states that "los verbos cultos dislocaron el acento latino para hacer llanas [penultimately stressed] las formas latinas esdrújulas [antepenultimately stressed]: así [Spanish] *recupéro, colóco, vigíla* y otros muchos; compárense las formas españolas de [Latin] *súpplico, imágino, detérmino, hábito, árrogo, ággrego, élevo, íntimo, fructí-, amplí-, notí-fico* [which are *suplíco, imagíno, determíno*, etc., in Spanish]. El cambio de acento latino no lo hacían aún los cultismos

One final observation needs to be made here. The careful reader will have noted a number of apparent contradictions between statements in this section and those of previous sections. For example, in the antepenultimately stressed nouns *intérprEte* and *catálOgo*, the penultimate vowels must be lax, and yet these lax vowels do not diphthongize when stressed in the verbs *interprÉte* (*\*interpr*[yé]*te*) and *catalÓgo* (*\*catal*[wé]*go*). Also, in the antepenultimately stressed adjective *contínUo* and the similarly stressed noun *ánImo*, to choose only two out of many possible examples, the penultimate vowels must be lax, as indicated. We have a rule, (20*a*), which lowers lax high vowels in any environment, but the forms in question are not *\*contín*[o]*o*, *\*án*[e]*mo*. These apparent contradictions, and others, will be resolved in Section 4.4.

### 4.3.2 Cambiar *versus* ampliar

We have hypothesized that verbs are always stressed penultimately, except for the first person plural of the imperfect indicative and subjunctive. (Henceforth, when "penultimate verb stress" is mentioned, the exceptions just made will be assumed to be understood.) There are clearly no verb forms with unstressed penultimate *a*, *e*, *o*. However, there is a large class of verbs, numbering at least 150, which might be taken to have unstressed penultimate *i*. Consider, for example, the nonfinite and present indicative and subjunctive forms of *cambiar*, "to change," which are typical of the verbs of this class:[9]

(25)    INFINITIVE       PAST PARTICIPLE       PRESENT PARTICIPLE
       *camb*[y]*ár*         *camb*[y]*ádo*           *camb*[y]*ándo*

| INDICATIVE | | SUBJUNCTIVE | |
|---|---|---|---|
| *cámb*[y]*o* | *camb*[y]*ámos* | *cámb*[y]*e* | *camb*[y]*émos* |
| *cámb*[y]*as* | | *cámb*[y]*es* | |
| *cámb*[y]*a* | *cámb*[y]*an* | *cámb*[y]*e* | *cámb*[y]*en* |

---

del siglo XIII; Berceo pronunciaba *signífica*, *sacrífica*. El italiano conserva siempre la acentuación clásica: *sacrífico*, *vivífica*, *cólloca*, *stérmino*, *consídero*, etc." (p. 274). The second step was the retraction of stress in the imperfect indicative and subjunctive, which was mentioned in Chapter 3, note 10. *Amabámos* and *amarámos*, for example, became *amábamos* and *amáramos*, thus destroying the last vestige of the relationship between verb stress and etymological vowel quantity. These are the facts, not an explanation of the facts, which still remains to be found and which would be an accomplishment of the highest order of interest in historical linguistics.

[9] A few other examples are *limpiar*, *aliviar*, *anunciar*, *remediar*, *rabiar*, *principiar*, *premiar*, *odiar*, *obsequiar*, *negociar*, *ensuciar*, *entibiar*, *envidiar*, *estudiar*, *fastidiar*, *incendiar*, *injuriar*, *lidiar*, *asediar*, *calumniar*, *codiciar*, *columpiar*, *contagiar*, *desperdiciar*, *diferenciar*, *divorciar*, *elogiar*, *beneficiar*.

If *cámb*[y]*o*, *cámb*[y]*as*, etc., were /cambio/, /cambias/ before stress was assigned, they would be incorrectly stressed as *\*cambío*, *\*cambías*, etc. The simplest assumption is that there is no penultimate *i* at the time stress is assigned: phonetic *y* is also underlying *y*, the root being *camby*.

The *cambiar* class may be contrasted with another class, which contains verbs like *ampliar*, "to enlarge."[10] The forms of *ampliar* relevant to the present discussion are given in (26):

(26)
| INFINITIVE | PAST PARTICIPLE | PRESENT PARTICIPLE |
|---|---|---|
| *ampl*[y]*ár* | *ampl*[y]*ádo* | *ampl*[y]*ándo* |

|  | INDICATIVE | SUBJUNCTIVE | |
|---|---|---|---|
| *ampl*[í]*o* | *ampl*[y]*ámos* | *ampl*[í]*e* | *ampl*[y]*émos* |
| *ampl*[í]*as* | | *ampl*[í]*es* | |
| *ampl*[í]*a* | *ampl*[í]*an* | *ampl*[í]*e* | *ampl*[í]*en* |

It is immediately obvious from the forms in (26) that the final stem segment in verbs of the *ampliar* class must be a vowel rather than *y*. The derivations in (27) illustrate the crucial difference between the *cambiar* class and the *ampliar* class:

(27)

| camby+a+mos | ampli+a+mos | camby+a | ampli+a | |
|---|---|---|---|---|
| á | á | á | í | (24*b*) |
| | y | | | (3:78*o*) |
| *cambyámos* | *amplyámos* | *cámbya* | *amplía* | |

Further evidence for this treatment is provided by the following facts. Verbs of the *ampliar* class may have related nouns or adjectives with penultimate stress—*rocío* (verb) and *rocío* (noun), *vacío* (verb) and *vacío* (noun or adjective)—or with antepenultimate stress—*amplío* (verb) but *ámplyo* (adjective), *varío* (verb) but *váryo* (adjective). Assuming that the nonverb forms are assigned stress by the LSR, those that receive penultimate stress must have underlying tense *i* and those that receive antepenultimate stress must have underlying lax *I* (which, as it remains unstressed, is changed to *y* by (3:78*o*)). Most of the verbs in the *cambiar* class also have clearly related nouns or adjectives, e.g., *cambio* [kámbyo] (noun). In contrast to the *ampliar* class, however, none of these related forms has antepenultimate stress.

---

[10] There are about thirty or forty verbs in this class, including *vigiar, vaciar, rociar, resfriar, pipiar, liar, expiar, estriar, enriar, enlejiar, variar, hastiar, criar, ciar, ataviar, descarriar, adiar, cuantiar, enviar.*

The complete lack of counterexamples in the 150 or so forms I have collected constitutes rather strong support for the hypothesis that the *cambiar* class of verbs has stem-final *y*.

### 4.3.3 Fraguar *versus* continuar

In the two classes of verbs just discussed, the stems end in a high front nonconsonantal segment. We now turn to two classes whose stems apparently end in a high back nonconsonantal segment. The verb *continuar*, "to continue," is representative of the first of these two groups, which contains about twenty verbs.[11] The relevant forms are given in (28):

(28)

| | INDICATIVE | | SUBJUNCTIVE | |
|---|---|---|---|---|
| | contin[ú]o | contin[w]ámos | contin[ú]e | contin[w]émos |
| | contin[ú]as | | contin[ú]es | |
| | contin[ú]a | contin[ú]an | contin[ú]e | contin[ú]en |

The stress patterns in (28) show that verbs of the *continuar* class have a stem-final high back vowel. This vowel is lax *U* in the stems of obviously related nouns and adjectives that are stressed on the antepenultimate syllable—*continúo* (verb), but *contínuo* (adjective), *perpetúo* (verb) but *perpétuo* (adjective), *individúo* (verb) but *indivíduo* (noun)—but it is tense *u* in the stem of the only obviously related form I have been able to find that is stressed on the penultimate syllable—*(des)-virtúo* (verb), *virtúd(Es)* (noun).

Verbs like *continuar* may be contrasted with those of the *fraguar* class, of which I have been able to find only the following examples: *fraguar, averiguar, santiguar, amortiguar, apaciguar, atestiguar, atreguar.* Forms of *fraguar*, "to forge (metal)," slightly simplified, are illustrated in (29):

(29)

| | INDICATIVE | | SUBJUNCTIVE | |
|---|---|---|---|---|
| | frágwo | fragwámos | frágwe | fragwémos |
| | frágwas | | frágwes | |
| | frágwa | frágwan | frágwe | frágwen |

It is clear that the stems of this class do not end in a vowel, for if they did the stress contour would be \**fragúo*, \**fragúas*, etc. Furthermore, there are no related nouns or adjectives like \**fragúa*, while there are related nouns like *frágua* and *trégua*. Now observe that the final consonantal segment in every stem is *g*. Thus, the underlying form of *fraguar* could be either /fragw-/ or /frag$^w$-/. Rounded velar consonants

---

[11] This class includes *actuar, exceptuar, habituar, insinuar, situar, anticuar, desvirtuar, evacuar, fluctuar, graduar, individuar, menstruar, oblicuar, perpetuar, puntuar, usufructuar.*

will be discussed in Section 5.2.5.3, when more data have been accumulated. Here we merely call attention to the matter and note that the stems of the *fraguar* class cannot end in a vowel.

4.3.4 *Stems with unstressed diphthongs:* adiestrar

Consider the forms of the verb *adiestrar*, "to make skillful," shown in (30):

(30) INFINITIVE       PAST PARTICIPLE      PRESENT PARTICIPLE
     *ad*[yĕ]*strár*       *ad*[yĕ]*strádo*          *ad*[yĕ]*strándo*

           PRESENT INDICATIVE
           *ad*[yé]*stro*    *ad*[yĕ]*strámos*
           *ad*[yé]*stras*
           *ad*[yé]*stra*     *ad*[yé]*stran*

The problem presented by these forms is that the diphthong [ye] occurs both stressed and unstressed. In fact, the diphthong in the stem of *adiestrar* is invariable, appearing not only in the forms of (30) but throughout all the paradigms. Recall, however, that rule (3:78*l*), the only diphthongization rule we have proposed, turns lax vowels into diphthongs just when stressed. The same problem is encountered in other verbs as well, for example, *am*[wĕ]*blár*, "to furnish (a house, apartment, etc.)," *av*[yĕ]*jár*, "to get old." One might at first propose that the diphthongs in question appear as such in systematic phonemic representations, rather than being derived from lax vowels. This cannot be the case, however, since these diphthongs alternate with simple vowels in categories other than verbs, as illustrated in (31):

(31)     VERB              NOUN, ADJECTIVE
       *ad*[ye]*strár*        *d*[yé]*stro*      *d*[ĕ]*stréza*
         to make skillful      skillful       skill
       *am*[we]*blár*       *m*[wé]*ble*     *m*[ŏ]*bláje*
         to furnish         (piece of)    (set of)
                       furniture      furniture
       *av*[ye]*jár*         *v*[yé]*jo*       *v*[ĕ]*jéz*
         to get old         old         old age

The verbs in (31) clearly have the same stems as the corresponding nouns and adjectives. Thus, the unstressed diphthongs of the verbs must be derived from systematic phonemic lax vowels.

General linguistic theory and the grammar of Spanish as so far developed here do provide a way to account for the verb forms in question. By making use of the cyclical application of rules, in particular, cyclical stress assignment, we may derive the correct phonetic representations of the forms of *adiestrar* as in (32) (where irrelevant details have been omitted). Note that no rules other than those that assign stress need apply cyclically.

(32)    $[_V\#a\ [_A\#dEstr\#]_A\ a+mos\#]_V$    1ST CYCLE
          É                                      (24*a*)

        $[_V\#a+dÉstr+a+mos\#]_V$               2ND CYCLE
              á                                  (24*b*)
            yé                                   (3:78*l*)
            yĕ                                   (3:78*p*)
        *adyestrámos*

All other forms of *adiestrar* and of *amueblar* and *aviejar* can obviously be accounted for in the same way.

Stress cycles internal to a word are apparently also needed in Spanish for categories other than verbs, for example for superlatives of adjectives—*b*[wĕ]*nísimo*, superlative of *b*[wé]*no*, "good" (cf. *b*[ŏ]*ndád*, "goodness"); *f*[wĕ]*rtísimo*, superlative of *f*[wé]*rte*, "strong" (cf. *f*[ŏ]*rtaléza*, "strength")—and for diminutives of nouns and adjectives—*v*[yĕ]*jíto*, diminutive of *v*[yé]*jo*, "old," "old man" (cf. *v*[ĕ]*jéz*, "old age"); *p*[wĕ]*blíto*, diminutive of *p*[wé]*blo*, "town" (cf. *p*[ŏ]*blación*, "town," "populated area").

These cases of internal stress cycles suggest a natural way to account for some extremely marginal phenomena. In all forms of the verb *piar*, "to chirp," "to peep," the stem *i* is always syllabic, that is, it is never changed to [y], even when unstressed.[12] Thus there exist such contrasts as bisyllabic [pi]*ár* versus monosyllabic [gy]*ár* (infinitives), trisyllabic [pi]*ádo* versus bisyllabic [gy]*ádo* (past participles), and the completely minimal pair of trisyllabic *p*[i]*ára* (imperfect subjunctive of *piar*) versus bisyllabic *p*[y]*ára*, "herd of animals (especially pigs)." If verbs like *cambiar* have stem-final /y/, verbs like *vaciar* have stem-final tense /i/, and verbs like *ampliar* have stem-final lax /I/, then it is not immediately obvious what the stem-final vowel of *piar* can be. Note, however, that there exists a noun *pío*, "chirp," "peep." Thus, with an internal noun cycle for *piar*, the contrast between, say, the imperfect subjunctive form *p*[i]*ára* of *piar* and the unrelated noun *p*[y]*ára* can be accounted for as in (33) (where it is assumed that the final *o* of the noun *pío* is the gender vowel rather than part of the stem):

---

[12] There is much dialect variation here. For some speakers the stem *i* of *piar* does in fact become [y] when not stressed. Furthermore, there are speakers for whom *piar* with always-syllabic *i* is unique, while for others some of the verbs mentioned in note 10 also have unstressed syllabic stem *i*, for example *l*[i]*ár*.

(33)  $[_V\# \,[_N\#\text{pi}\#]_N\ \text{a}+\text{ra}\#]_V$  $\quad[_N\#\text{piar}+\text{a}\#]_N$  1ST CYCLE
$\qquad\quad$ í $\qquad\qquad\qquad\qquad\qquad\qquad\qquad\qquad$ (24$a$)

$\quad[_V\#\text{pí}+\text{a}+\text{ra}\#]_V$ $\qquad\qquad\qquad\qquad$ 2ND CYCLE
$\qquad$ á $\qquad\qquad\qquad\qquad$ á $\qquad\qquad$ (24$b$, $a$)
$\qquad$ − $\qquad\qquad\qquad\qquad$ y $\qquad\qquad$ (3:78$o$)
$\qquad$ ĭ $\qquad\qquad\qquad\qquad\qquad\qquad\qquad$ (3:78$p$)
$\quad$ *piára* $\qquad\qquad\qquad$ *pyára*

## 4.4 Morphological subclasses

Rules (3:78$g$), (3:78$h$), (3:78$l$) of Chapter 3 and rules (20$a$) and (22) of this chapter have been described as applying only "under certain conditions." Examples have been given to show, on the one hand, that each of these rules is highly motivated in a grammar of Spanish, but, on the other hand, that incorrect results will be produced if these rules are allowed to apply to all forms that meet the structural descriptions. Several more such rules and similar sets of examples will be given in the next chapter. In order to clarify past obscurities and to facilitate subsequent exposition, I will at this point present a hypothesis concerning the rules and examples in question.

The set of forms that do not undergo each of the rules just mentioned is far too large to plausibly consist of idiosyncratic exceptions; in fact, they far outnumber the cases where the rule does apply. It would then be reasonable to argue that each rule $R_i$ of the set under discussion is a "minor" rule, and it therefore applies only to a relatively small class of forms marked as exceptionally undergoing $R_i$. I will, however, make a much stronger claim, namely, that the rules in question belong to a specially designated subset of rules that are applicable to all and only the members of a specially designated subset of formatives. Conversely, all and only the members of a specially designated subset of formatives undergo all of the applicable rules of a specially designated subset of the total set of phonological rules. Let us be somewhat more precise.

(a)  All formatives are subcategorized with respect to the morphological feature [S], mnemonic for "special": all formatives are either [+S] or [−S].[13]

---

[13] See Chomsky and Halle (1968, Chapter Four, Section 2.2, and Chapter Eight, Section 7) for discussion of the formal properties of diacritic features such as [S] whose domain is an entire formative rather than a single segment. See also Kiparsky (1968) for extremely illuminating discussion of some of Chomsky and Halle's proposals, as well as comments on some of the discussion in Sections 4.2 and 4.3.1 of this chapter, which Kiparsky has read in manuscript.

(b) Formatives subcategorized as [+S] are subject to all phonological rules that [−S] formatives are subject to. Formatives subcategorized as [+S] are also subject to an additional designated subset of rules that [−S] formatives are not subject to.

(c) Rules that apply to [+S] formatives only are so designated by the inclusion of [+S] in the structural description. That is, such rules are of the form $[A, +S] \rightarrow B/X$——$Y$ or, equivalently, $A \rightarrow B/X[$——$, +S]Y$, where $A$, $B$, $X$, $Y$ are interpreted in the usual way.[14] These rules are not all contiguously ordered; they are interspersed among other rules.

(d) Items in the lexicon are either marked or unmarked for [S]. By convention, $[m\ S] \rightarrow [+S]$, $[u\ S] \rightarrow [−S]$. (A glance through a dictionary is sufficient to show that the vast bulk of the lexicon is [−S], that is, unmarked. Heuristically, a lexical formative is assumed to be unmarked until one is forced to the conclusion that it is marked.)

(e) Inflectional formatives (complexes of features for person, number, mood, aspect, etc.) are automatically assigned the feature [+S]. The features [+S], [−S] are features of formatives, not words: [+S] affixes may be attached to [−S] stems.[15]

Perhaps it would be helpful to illustrate the difference between a "special" rule, as just described, and a "minor" rule. Case (*a*) of rule (20) is "special"—the environment, when properly formulated, is [——, −tense, +S], with [+S] taking the place of "under certain conditions"—and applies to all lax vowels in all [+S] formatives. Case (*c*) of rule (20), on the other hand, is "minor," and it applies only to the set of formatives marked to undergo this particular case of this particular rule, which set is not coextensive with the set of [+S] formatives. For example, (20c) applies neither to the stem of *residir*, which is [−S], nor to that of *recibir*, which is [+S] (cf. *recipiente*). Similarly, (20c) applies to (*cor*)*regir* but not to (*di*)*rigir*, although both are [−S], as will be argued in Sections 5.2.3.4 and 5.2.3.6.

No doubt some readers will have noticed that the categorizations imposed by the feature [S] correspond in part to the distinction made

---

[14] It may prove necessary to allow also rules of the form $A \rightarrow B/[X, +S]$——$Y$ or $A \rightarrow B/X$——$[Y, +S]$. Compare, for example, the third person preterit forms *ri*[xyé]*ron* and *di*[xé]*ron* of *regir* and *decir*, respectively. The [y] of the ending -*tron* → -*Éron* → -*yéron*, which must be [+S] in both forms, is apparently deleted after the [+S] stem of *decir* but not after the [−S] stem of *regir*. At this point such evidence is premature, however, since the correct derivation of the highly irregular preterit forms of *decir* is not known.

[15] For a slightly different proposal for French see Schane (1968, pp. 26–27).

in traditional studies of Spanish philology between "vulgar" and "erudite" words (see Menéndez Pidal (1962, Chapter One), Lapesa (1959, pp. 75 ff.)): [+S] corresponds roughly to "vulgar," and [−S] to "erudite." As the terms "vulgar" and "erudite" are well entrenched in historical studies, I have rejected them in favor of the neutral terminology "special" in order to emphasize three facts. First, synchronically [+S] formatives constitute a rather small part of the total lexicon (although the bulk of historical discussion is devoted to "vulgar" words since their development is more interesting than that of "erudite" words). Second, the feature [S] is motivated in a synchronic grammar completely independently of a priori assumptions based on historical data. Finally, the correspondence between the historical and the synchronic distinctions is actually not a very close one. Many formatives known to have undergone "vulgar" historical processes are not marked [+S] in a synchronic grammar for the simple reason that they are not involved in any synchronic alternations that would require their being so marked.

The second of the points just made is particularly important and perhaps deserves further comment. Language learners do not have access to historical data as such. Consequently, such data can in no way figure in the motivation or justification of a synchronic grammar. It is entirely another matter when grammars based wholly on synchronic data happen to reflect, to whatever extent, historical processes. What has motivated the use of the feature [S] in the present study is simply the fact that certain clear *synchronic* generalizations will be lost if a relatively small set of forms is not distinguished that undergo a relatively small set of rules not applicable to other forms.[16]

Actually, the bipartitioning of the lexicon of Spanish into just the two classes imposed by the feature [±S] is not quite adequate. There exist, in fact, "semi-special" forms, that is, forms that undergo some applicable "special" rules but not all. Consider, for example, *lacrimoso,* "lachrymose," *lacrimógeno,* "tear producing," and *lágrima,* "tear." The stem must be /lakrIm/ in all three forms. In *lacrimoso* and *lacrimógeno* this stem appears phonetically as [lakrim], and these forms are clearly [−S]. In *lágrima,* however, systematic phonemic /k/ appears as $g$, which suggests that *lágrima* is [+S], $k$ being changed to $g$ by the [+S] rule (3:78$h$). But now we face a contradiction: *lágrima* is stressed on the

---

[16] In addition to Schane's treatment of French mentioned in the previous note, morphological subclasses have been proposed in recent studies for English (Chomsky and Halle (1968)), Russian (Lightner (1965)), Yawelmani (Kuroda (1967)), Mohawk (Postal (1968)), and other languages. The most extensive theoretical discussion is to be found in Postal (1968).

antepenultimate syllable. This indicates that the penultimate vowel is lax, yet this lax *I* is not lowered to *e* by the first case of rule (20), which applies to "special" morphemes. A good many other examples of this sort can be found, involving various "special" rules. The correct descriptive mechanism for handling "semi-special" forms may be a set of redundancy statements that impose a hierarchy of rule applicability. For example, applicability of the first case of (20), high lax vowel lowering, implies applicability of (3:78*h*), obstruent lenition, *but not conversely.* Study of "semi-special" forms has only recently begun, and I do not believe it would be productive to go into more detail at this time. We will therefore continue to operate with the [±S] system described above, which is sufficiently accurate to allow us to proceed without difficulty.

## 4.5 Summary of rules

There follows a list of all the rules discussed in this chapter, re-numbered as (34). Where appropriate, notational changes are made in accordance with the discussion of the feature [D] in Section 4.2 and the feature [S] in Section 4.4. A cumulative list of all the rules proposed in this study will be given at the end of Chapter 6.

(34)

$$
a. \quad \begin{bmatrix} V \\ -\text{low} \end{bmatrix} \rightarrow \begin{bmatrix} +\text{high} \\ +\text{tense} \end{bmatrix} \Bigm/ \left\{ \begin{array}{l} \underline{\hspace{1em}}[+\text{past}] \\ \left[\underline{\hspace{1em}\atop 3\text{conj}}\right] C_0 V]_V \end{array} \right\} \qquad \begin{array}{l} (3{:}78a), \\ (2), (8) \end{array}
$$

$$
b. \quad V \rightarrow \phi \Bigm/ + \left[\underline{\hspace{1em}\atop \langle +\text{irreg}\rangle}\right] + \left\{ \begin{array}{l} \begin{bmatrix} V \\ +\text{tense} \end{bmatrix} \\ \langle r\#[+\text{fut}]\rangle \end{array} \right\} \qquad (3{:}78c)
$$

$$
c. \quad V \rightarrow [\text{1stress}] \Bigm/ \underline{\hspace{1em}} \left\{ \begin{array}{l} (C_0(\check{V}C_0^1(L))V)C_0\#]_{N,A} \\ (([-\text{perf}])C_0V)C_0\#]_V \end{array} \right\} \qquad \begin{array}{l} (3{:}78f), \\ (24) \end{array}
$$

$$
d. \quad \begin{bmatrix} V \\ +\text{low} \\ +S \end{bmatrix} \rightarrow \begin{bmatrix} -\text{low} \\ \alpha\text{back} \end{bmatrix} \Bigm/ \underline{\hspace{1em}} \begin{bmatrix} -\text{cons} \\ +\text{high} \\ \alpha\text{back} \end{bmatrix} \qquad (3{:}78g)
$$

$$
e. \quad \begin{bmatrix} +\text{obstr} \\ +S \end{bmatrix} \rightarrow [-\text{tense}] \Bigm/ V\underline{\hspace{1em}}[-\text{obstr}] \qquad (3{:}78h)
$$

*(continued)*

*(34 continued)*

*f.* $\begin{bmatrix} e \\ -\text{tense} \end{bmatrix} \rightarrow \phi \ / \ V \begin{bmatrix} +\text{cor} \\ +\text{ant} \end{bmatrix}_0^1 \underline{\phantom{xx}} \#$  (3:78*i*)

*g.* $\begin{bmatrix} V \\ +\text{stress} \\ +S \end{bmatrix} \rightarrow \begin{bmatrix} -\text{high} \\ -\text{tense} \end{bmatrix} \ / \ \underline{\phantom{xx}} \left\{ \begin{matrix} rV \\ \begin{bmatrix} +\text{cons} \\ -\text{obstr} \end{bmatrix} \begin{bmatrix} -\text{voc} \\ +\text{ant} \end{bmatrix} \end{matrix} \right\}$  (3:78*k*),
(22)

*h.* $\left\{ \begin{matrix} e \\ {}_1 o \end{matrix} \right\}_1 \rightarrow \left\{ \begin{matrix} ye \\ {}_1 we \end{matrix} \right\}_1 \ / \ \begin{bmatrix} \underline{\phantom{xx}} \\ +\text{stress} \\ -\text{tense} \\ +S \end{bmatrix}$  (3:78*l*)

*i.* $V \rightarrow [-\text{high}] \ / \ \left\{ \begin{matrix} \begin{bmatrix} \underline{\phantom{xx}} \\ -\text{tense} \\ +S \end{bmatrix} \\ \begin{bmatrix} \underline{\phantom{xx}} \\ -\text{stress} \end{bmatrix} C_0 \left\{ \begin{matrix} \# \\ i \end{matrix} \right\} \end{matrix} \right\}$  MINOR  (3:78*n*), (4),
(11), (20)

*j.* $\begin{bmatrix} -\text{cons} \\ +\text{high} \\ -\text{stress} \end{bmatrix} \rightarrow [-\text{voc}] \ / \ \left\{ \begin{matrix} \underline{\phantom{xx}} V \\ V \underline{\phantom{xx}} \end{matrix} \right\}$  (3:78*o*)

*k.* Erase all stresses but the rightmost in a word.  (3:78*p*)

# 5. Consonantal Alternations in Derivational Morphology

## 5.1 Preliminary remarks

In this chapter we will examine consonantal alternations that occur when certain derivational suffixes are attached to certain stems. In general, vowel alternations will be ignored since most of those that appear here are handled by rules already given and the remainder are rather marginal. The suffixes with which we will be primarily concerned are the following:

(a) the nominalizing suffix *-ión*

(b) the agentive suffix that appears as *-tor*, *-dor*, *-sor*, or *-or*

(c) the suffix *-(t)ivo*, which corresponds closely to English "-ive" and which forms adjectives that will be called "performatives," for want of a better term

(d) miscellaneous adjective- and noun-forming suffixes

A small sample of the kind of data that will be presented in this chapter is given in (1).

In order to restrict the data to unquestionably related forms, I have used the *Vox Diccionario general ilustrado de la lengua española* as a reference to guarantee identity of stems in a given paradigm. For every stem S, every *-ión* nominalization cited here is defined by *Vox*, on at least one reading, simply as "acción y efecto de S," every agentive as "que S," and so on. Any deviation, however slight, is sufficient

132

(1)

| VERB | NOMINALI-<br>ZATION | AGENTIVE | PERFORMA-<br>TIVE | MISCELLA-<br>NEOUS |
|---|---|---|---|---|
| generar | generación | generador | generativo | |
| succionar | succión | | | |
| unir | unión | unidor | unitivo | |
| | punición | | punitivo | |
| | inmersión | | | |
| | erudición | | | erudito(A) |
| adaptar | adaptación | | | |
| adoptar | adopción | adoptador | adoptivo | |
| atender | atención | atendedor | | atento(A) |
| extender | extensión | extensor | extensivo | extenso(A) |
| abortar | | | abortivo | aborto(N) |

to exclude a form from consideration. For example, *comparador*, defined by *Vox* as "FÍS. Instrumento para señalar las más pequeñas diferencias entre las longitudes de dos reglas," is excluded from the set *comparar*, "to compare," *comparación, comparativo.* Thus, blanks in the sets of examples to be given could be filled, in many cases, by forms with the expected shape but not with the expected syntactic and semantic properties. Such scrupulousness is no doubt excessive in some cases, but I feel that the study of Spanish has not progressed to the point where one can take lightly the familiar admonition to build a theory on absolutely clear data.[1]

I will not deal with the matter of hypothetical but nonoccurring forms such as the nonoccurring verb *\*punir*, "to punish," corresponding to occurring *punición*, "punishment," and *punitivo*, "punitive." Interesting questions are involved here, but it would be a mistake to pursue them in an exploratory phonological study. Also I will have nothing further to say about sets like *succión*, "suction," *succionar*, "to suck," in which the verbal affixes, in this case *-ar*, are added to a base that already contains the nominalizing element *-ión.* (There is no

[1] Herein lies the most serious shortcoming of Foley's (1965) work, the only other large-scale study of Spanish phonology within the theory of generative grammar: elaborate, often ingenious theoretical machinery is set up on a factual basis whose weakness could hardly be exaggerated. Foley's arguments include nonexistent words (*\*credible, \*baptista, \*admiso*, etc.) and even phonologically inadmissible forms (*\*telegraf*). Furthermore, synchronic morphological relatedness is taken to be clear in such cases as the following: *luna*, "moon," and *lucir*, "to shine"; *tiple*, "soprano," "small guitar," and *triángulo*, "triangle."

verb *sucar or *suctar.) There is a sizable class of such sets: *confección–confeccionar, congestión–congestionar, contorsión–contorsionar, decepción–decepcionar, evolución–evolucionar, selección–seleccionar* are only a few of the possible examples. It is of some interest that these sets are unlike their English counterparts, but we exclude them from consideration since there are no consonantal alternations in the environments we are investigating, namely, at the boundary indicated by $+$ in *succion$+$ar*, for example.[2]

## 5.2 Some derivational paradigms

There is a large mass of data to be considered in this chapter. For clarity of exposition we will present the examples in relatively small sets, with a tentative analysis sometimes accompanying a set. It should be kept in mind throughout that final judgment of such analyses must be reserved until all the data have been given.

### 5.2.1 Athematic nominalizations

There is a small class of examples, shown in (2), in which the nominalization affix *-ión* is attached directly to a stem, with no intervening segments. In particular, the theme vowel of the verb form does not appear in the nominalization.

(2)    *un-ir*      *un-ión*      *un-idor*      *un-itivo*
       *rebel-ar*   *rebel-ión*                                *rebel-de*
       *opin-ar*    *opin-ión*

In the agentive *unidor* and the adjective *unitivo*, we observe that the theme vowel occurs after the stem, although it does not in the *-ión* nominalizations nor in the noun *rebelde*.

The apparently final stress of *-ión* (like that of the infinitives) is accounted for by the presence of an underlying final $E$, which is deleted by rule (4:34$f$) and which actually occurs in plurals (e.g.,) *uniones, rebeliones, opiniones*), where the environment of this rule is not met. Note, incidentally, that it could well be that *-ión* should have the underlying representation /yonE/ rather than /ionE/ (with /i/ being changed to [y] by rule (4:34$j$)) since $+$GVCV$+$ is presumably less

---

[2] This is not to say that I am unaware that *confección*, for example, has an interesting etymology. If it should turn out that on the basis of clear synchronic evidence /fak/ may figure in the phonological representation of both *confección* and *hacer*, then one must pursue the question further; however, to include this as an a priori assumption is to render without interest a putatively synchronic grammar of Spanish.

marked than $+$VVCV$+$.[3] We will not pursue this matter here, and for the sake of readability we will write simply *-ión* henceforth.

### 5.2.2 *Quasi-productive patterns*

The examples in (3) represent a small sample of the hundreds of sets formed on the basis of the most productive pattern:

(3)
| | | | |
|---|---|---|---|
| *generar* | *generación* | *generador* | *generativo* |
| *formar* | *formación* | *formador* | *formativo* |
| *afirmar* | *afirmación* | *afirmador* | *afirmativo* |
| *acumular* | *acumulación* | *acumulador* | *acumulativo* |
| *comparar* | *comparación* | | *comparativo* |
| *acelerar* | *aceleración* | *acelerador* | |
| *ventilar* | *ventilación* | *ventilador* | |
| *radiar* | *radiación* | *radiador* | |
| *explotar* | *explotación* | *explotador* | |
| *fundar* | *fundación* | *fundador* | |
| *obligar* | *obligación* | | |
| *eructar* | *eructación* | | *eructo* |

The pattern illustrated in (3) can be represented schematically as in (4):

(4)
$$\text{stem} + \text{theme vowel} + \begin{Bmatrix} ción \\ dor \\ tivo \end{Bmatrix}$$

This pattern is called "quasi-productive" to emphasize the fact that not all combinations of stem $+$ theme vowel $+$ suffix are actually in use (*\*acelerativo*, *\*explotativo*), although some of those not officially recognized may be heard occasionally as nonce creations and are readily understood as such.

All of the verbs of (3) belong to the first conjugation, the class to which the vast bulk of the verbs in the lexicon belong, and the one to which new words and nonce inventions are assigned. Examples from the third conjugation constructed on the pattern of (4) are less numerous. A sample is given in (5):

(5)
| | | | |
|---|---|---|---|
| *abolir* | *abolición* | | |
| *fruir* | *fruición* | | *fruitivo* |
| *cohibir* | *cohibición* | | |
| *definir* | *definición* | *definidor* | *definitivo* |

*(continued)*

---

[3] See Chomsky and Halle (1968, Chapter Nine).

*(5 continued)*

| | | | |
|---|---|---|---|
| exhibir | exhibición | | |
| expedir | expedición | expedidor | |
| prohibir | prohibición | | prohibitivo |

There are only a few clear examples from the second conjugation, as in (6):

(6)   perder      perdición      perdedor
      demoler     demolición

Note, incidentally, that the *e* ∼ *i* alternation of the theme vowel in these forms might be handled by an extension of rule (4:34*a*), which raises nonlow vowels to high in certain environments (see the end of Section 4.1.2.2). With so few clear cases, however, it is difficult to make a firm decision.

A few forms that follow this pattern show alternations between tense and lax obstruents in the stem, as shown in (7):

(7)   nadar       natación       nadador
      saludar     salutación
      pedir       petición       pedidor

We already have in the grammar a rule to account for this alternation, namely, rule (4:34*e*), which laxes obstruents in intervocalic position in [+S] formatives. Thus the stems /nat/, /salut/, and /pet/ are marked [+S] in verbs and in agentive nouns but [−S] in *-ión* nominalizations. We might speculate that these stems are lexically marked [+S], and some sort of redundancy rule changes this to [−S] (or simply erases the feature) in the *-ión* nominalizations.

### 5.2.3 *Nonproductive patterns with* -ción

We now turn to sets of examples in which *-ción*, not *-ión* (as in the forms of Section 5.2.1), occurs directly after the stem, without an intervening theme vowel. The examples are subdivided according to the final consonant or consonant cluster of the stem. There seems to be no reason to separate the three conjugations.

5.2.3.1. We shall first consider forms in which the final stem consonant is *n*. The only examples I have found are compounds of the highly irregular *tener* and *venir*, which are given in (8):

(8)   detener     detención      detenedor
      obtener     obtención      obtentor
      retener     retención      retenedor      retentivo

*(continued)*

*(8 continued)*

| | | | |
|---|---|---|---|
| *contener* | *contención* | *contenedor* | *contentivo* |
| *intervenir* | *intervención* | *interventor* | |
| *contravenir* | *contravención* | *contraventor* | |
| *convenir* | *convención* | | |

Note that although *-ción* is always added directly to the stem, without the theme vowel, the agentive suffix may or may not be separated from the stem by the theme vowel: *deten*ed*or* versus *obtentor*. Thus the appearance or nonappearance of the theme vowel is apparently an idiosyncratic property of each compound, not of the stem. The agentive suffix must be /torE/, with the property [+S]. The final *E* appears in plurals (e.g. *detenedores, obtentores*) but is deleted in the singular forms by rule (4:34*f*). Initial *t* of the suffix is changed to *d* by rule (4:34*e*) when preceded by a vowel.

5.2.3.2. The final stem consonant is *m* in forms such as shown in (9):

| (9) | *redimir* | *redención* | *redentor* | | |
|---|---|---|---|---|---|
| | *presumir* | *presunción* | | *presuntivo* | *presunto* |
| | *consumir* | *consunción*<br>*consumición* | *consumidor* | | *consunto* |

Note the variants *consunción* and *consumición*, which the *Vox* dictionary cites as synonyms. Thus it is clear that the presence or absence of the theme vowel in *-ción* nominalizations, as well as in the agentive nouns, is lexically rather than phonologically determined and is in some cases optional. The nasal assimilation rule (2:69*f*) handles the *m ∼ n* alternations.

5.2.3.3. The final stem consonant alternates between [s] and [k] in forms such as those in (10). (The letter *c* stands for [s] before a front nonconsonantal segment, [k] in all other environments.)

(10)

| | | | | |
|---|---|---|---|---|
| *sedu*[s]*ir* | *sedu*[ks]*ión* | *sedu*[k]*tor* | *sedu*[k]*tivo* | |
| *producir* | *producción* | *productor* | *productivo* | *producto* |
| *conducir* | *conducción* | *conductor* | *conductivo* | *conducto* |
| *deducir* | *deducción* | | *deductivo* | |
| *traducir* | *traducción* | *traductor* | | |
| *contradecir* | *contradicción* | *contradictor* | | |
| *predecir* | *predicción* | | | |
| *satisfacer* | *satisfacción* | | | |
| *cocer* | *cocción* | | | |

The $s \sim k$ alternation is handled by a rule we have already stated in vague form, namely, (3:78*b*), which changes *k* to *s* before a front nonconsonantal segment. (This rule will be discussed in detail in Section 6.3.) Thus the stems in (10) are /. . .duk/, /. . .dik/, /. . .fak/, and /kOk/ (with lax *O* because of present indicative [kwéso], etc.) *K* is not changed to *s* in other than verb forms since the environment of (3:78*b*) is not met.

5.2.3.4. The final stem consonant alternates between [x] and [k] in forms such as those in (11). (The letter *g* stands for [x] before a front nonconsonantal segment.)

(11)

| | | | | |
|---|---|---|---|---|
| *prote*[x]*er* | *prote*[ks]*ión* | *prote*[k]*tor* | *prote*[k]*tivo* | |
| *corregir* | *corrección* | *corrector* | *correctivo* | *correcto* |
| *eregir* | *erección* | *erector* | | *erecto* |
| *dirigir* | *dirección* | *director* | *directivo* | |
| *elegir* | *elección* | *elector* | *electivo* | *electo* |
| *colegir* | *colección* | *colector* | | *colecta* |
| *afligir* | *aflicción* | | *aflictivo* | *aflicto* |

Since we already have rule (3:78*b*), which changes *g* to *x* before a front nonconsonantal segment, we assume that all the stems in (11) have final /g/. This /g/ is changed to *k* in the nonverb forms by the familiar rule (12):

(12)    $[+\text{obstr}]$  →  $[+\text{tense}]$  $/ \underline{\hspace{1cm}} \begin{bmatrix} +\text{obstr} \\ +\text{tense} \end{bmatrix}$ *where have we seen this before?*

5.2.3.5. The final stem consonant alternates between *b* (actually [β] after spirantization) and *p* in forms such as those in (13):

(13)

| | | | | |
|---|---|---|---|---|
| *recibir* | *recepción* | { *receptor*<br>{ *recibidor* | *receptivo* | |
| *percibir* | *percepción* | *perceptor* | *perceptivo* | |
| *concebir* | *concepción* | | *conceptivo* | *concepto* |
| *describir* | *descripción* | *descriptor* | *descriptivo* | { *descripto*<br>{ *descrito* |
| *proscribir* | *proscripción* | *proscriptor* | | { *proscripto*<br>{ *proscrito* |
| *prescribir* | *prescripción* | | *prescriptivo* | { *prescripto*<br>{ *prescrito* |

At first glance we seem to be faced with an indeterminacy: the final stem consonant could be /b/, which is tensed to *p* in certain

environments by (12), or it could be /p/, which is laxed to *b* by rule
(4:34*e*) in certain environments. In the case of *recibir*, "to receive,"
the choice is made by *recipiente*, "recipient," formed with the common suffix -(*i*)*ente*. Since the [p] in this form is followed by a vowel, it
could not have come from /b/ by (12). Thus the underlying consonant
in question must be /p/, which is laxed by (4:34*e*), and *recibir* must be
[+S]. The other cases are not so clear. One might take the position
that *percibir* and *concebir* share the formative /cep/, "-ceive," with
*recibir*. This is not implausible, but it begs the question of the identity
of this formative since *recibir*, *percibir*, and *concebir* do not behave
alike in all respects. In particular, *concebir*, but not *recibir* or *percibir*,
undergoes the last case of (4:34*i*). Having recorded this caveat, and
in the absence of further negative evidence, we will, however, make
the tentative assumption that all three examples have underlying
/p/ and, concomitantly, that they are [+S].

In the case of *describir*, *proscribir*, and *prescribir*, however, I can find
absolutely no evidence for postulating underlying /p/. We therefore
make the simplest assumption, namely, that these verbs are [−S]
and that the underlying stem-final consonant is /b/, which is tensed
in the appropriate environment by (12).

This leaves the variants *descripto–descrito*, *proscripto–proscrito*, and
*prescripto–prescrito* to be accounted for. (Not all speakers have the first
member of each pair.) On the basis of examples like *séptimo*, "seventh,"
*siéte*, "seven," and *seténta*, "seventy," I take it that the forms without
the cluster are [+S] and that there is a rule with the effect of (14):

(14)
$$\begin{bmatrix} p \\ +S \end{bmatrix} \rightarrow t \ / \ \text{---} t$$

The resulting *tt* cluster is then simplified by a rule with the effect
of (15):[4]

---

[4] *Siéte* must be [ +S] because of the stressed diphthong that alternates with unstressed *e*. The presence of intervocalic tense [t] is no problem if (4:34*e*), which laxes
intervocalic obstruents in [ +S] formatives, is ordered before rule (15). Rule (15) must
apparently be restricted in some way that is not entirely clear at present. The need for
some restriction arises from the fact that there are occurrences in phonetic representations of long consonantal segments (despite Foley's (1965, p. 7) statement to the
contrary, which is simply an error) which presumably derive from geminate clusters.
For example, there is the apparently unique adjective *pere*[n:]*e*, "perennial," and,
more importantly, a large number of examples involving the prefixes *en-* and *in-*:
*e*[n:]*egrecer*, *e*[n:]*oblecer*, *i*[n:]*ato*, *i*[n:]*ecesario*, *i*[n:]*umerable*. A large mass of complex
data is involved here which has not been carefully studied, including the identification
of the boundary between the prefixes and stems in question. Consider, for example,
*i*[n:]*ecesario*, *i*[n:]*umerable* but *i*[n]*ocente*, *i*[l]*egal* (*\*i*[n:]*ocente*, *\*i*[l:]*egal*); *pro*[R]*ogar*,
*a*[R]*ogar* but *e*[r]*ogar*, *de*[r]*ogar*.

(15) $\qquad$ $C_i C_j \;\Rightarrow\; C_k \;$ *where* $C_i = C_j = C_k$

5.2.3.6. There is a small class of examples such as those in (16):

(16)

| destruir | destru[ks]ión | $\begin{cases} destru[k]tor \\ destruidor \end{cases}$ | destru[k]tivo | |
|----------|----------------|-------------------|---------------|----------|
| instruir | instrucción | instructor | instructivo | |
| obstruir | obstrucción | obstructor | | |
| leer | | lector | | lectura |
| contraer | contracción | | contractivo | contracto |
| detraer | detracción | detractor | | |
| abstraer | abstracción | | | abstracto |

These stems must end in some consonant C* such that (17a) and (17b) are true:

(17) $\qquad$ *a.* $\;\; \text{C*} \;\rightarrow\; \phi \;/\; \text{V}\!\!-\!\!-\!\!-\!\!\begin{bmatrix} \text{V} \\ -\text{back} \end{bmatrix}$

$\qquad\qquad$ *b.* $\;\; \text{C*} \;\rightarrow\; \text{k} \;/\; -\!\!-\!\!-\!\!\begin{bmatrix} +\text{obstr} \\ +\text{tense} \end{bmatrix}$

It is unlikely that $\text{C*} = k$ because of the examples in Section 5.2.3.3, where underlying /k/ appears as [s] in the verb form. The next simplest assumption would be that $\text{C*} = g$, since (17b) would then be included in rule (12), which we already have. This assumption is strongly supported by the following set of forms: *leer*, "to read," *lector*, "reader," *lectura*, "reading," and, N.B., *legible*, "legible," *leíble*, "readable." The stem is /leg/; the *g* is tensed by (12) in *lector* and *lectura*, changed to *x* by (3:78b) in *legible*, and deleted in *leer* and *leíble*. Thus we conclude that the stems in (16) are /...trug/, /leg/, and /... trag/. But if this is correct, then these examples must be differentiated from those of (11), in which stem-final /g/ is not deleted. Let us assume that the stems in (11) are [−S], that those in (16) are [+S], and that (17a) should be stated as (18):

(18) $\qquad$ $\begin{bmatrix} \text{g} \\ +\text{S} \end{bmatrix} \;\rightarrow\; \phi \;/\; \text{V}\!\!-\!\!-\!\!-\!\!\begin{bmatrix} \text{V} \\ -\text{back} \end{bmatrix}$

The difference, then, between *legible* and *leíble* is that the former is [−S] while the latter is [+S]. Similarly, the variants *destructor* and *destruidor* in (16) are accounted for if the first form is [−S] and the theme vowel does not appear, while the second form is [+S] and the theme vowel does appear.

5.2.3.7. The examples in (19) bear some similarity to those of (16):

(19)

| | | | |
|---|---|---|---|
| *instituir* | *institución* | *instituidor* | *instituto* |
| *restituir* | *restitución* | *restituidor* | |
| *constituir* | *constitución* | *constituidor* | *constitutivo* |
| *prostituir* | *prostitución* | | *prostituta* |
| *atribuir* | *atribución* | *atributivo* | *atributo* |
| *distribuir* | *distribución* | *distribuidor* | *distributivo* |
| *contribuir* | *contribución* | *contribuidor* | *contributivo* |
| *retribuir* | *retribución* | *retributivo* | |
| *disminuir* | *disminución* | | |

Apparently the difference between (19) and (16) is that the stems of the present examples end in the vowel *u*, rather than in *g*, and there is no reason to assign to them the feature [+S].

5.2.3.8. Consider, now, the stem-final consonants in (20):

(20)

| | | | |
|---|---|---|---|
| *absorber* | *absorción* | | *absorto* |
| *compungir* | *compunción* | *compungivo* | |
| *fungir* | *función* | | |
| *ungir* | *unción* | | |
| *esculpir* | | *escultor* | *escultura* |

Apparently the stems are /absorb/, /kompung/, /fung/, /ung/, and /skulp/.[5] In the forms having a suffix that begins with a consonant, e.g., /absorb/+*ción*, /kompung/+*ción*, /skulp/+*tor*, the final stem consonant is deleted by a cluster simplification rule:

$$(21) \qquad \begin{bmatrix} +\text{obstr} \\ -\text{cont} \end{bmatrix} \rightarrow \phi \ / \ [+\text{cons}]\text{———}[+\text{obstr}]$$

---

[5] The initial [e] of the last stem is epenthetic, being inserted by the relatively uninteresting rule

$$\phi \rightarrow e \ / \ \#\text{———}s[+\text{cons}]$$

(The specification [+cons] allows the inclusion of ———*sl*: cf. *checoslovaco*, *eslovaco*.) Thus no phonetic representation has an initial cluster consisting of *s* plus a consonantal segment. If this epenthesis rule is ordered after stress assignment, a few instances of apparently exceptional stress placement can be accounted for: for example, *escuéla*, *está* from *skOla*, *sta*, respectively. Also, a generalization can be made about the final *y* of *estoy*, as well as of *doy*, *soy*, *voy* (and presumably *he* and *sé*, from *ha*+*y* and *sa*+*y*): *y* is added to all *monosyllabic* first person singular present indicative forms.

That this rule applies only to noncontinuant obstruents can be seen from such forms as *monstruo, instrumento, yu*[ks]*taposición, e*[ks]*tra, e*[ksk]*luir.*[6]

5.2.3.9. We now summarize our observations about the relatively nonproblematic examples of stem+*ción.*

(a) We have found examples with the following underlying stem-final consonants:

*n*  (*detener, detención*)
*m*  (*redimir, redención*)
*k*  (*sedu*/k/*ir, seducción*)
*g*  (*proteger, protección; destru*/g/*ir, destrucción; fungir, fun*φ*ción*)
*p*  (*reci*/p/*ir, recepción; esculpir, escul*φ*tor*)
*b*  (*describir, descripción; absorber, absor*φ*ción*)

(b) We have found examples with stem-final *u: instituir, institución.* We saw in Section 5.2.1 that there are a few examples in which the form of the nominalization affix is -*ión* rather than -*ción*. This suggests that what we have written as -*ción* should be -*c*+*ión*, where *c* is some sort of augment that appears in some forms but not in others.

At least one example can be found in which the agentive noun affix seems to be -*or* rather than -*t*/*dor: contend-er, contend-or.* Again this suggests that the affix is -*t*+*or*, where *t* is some sort of augment.

One example has been given in which the "performative adjective" affix is -*ivo* rather than -*tivo: compung-ir, compung-ivo* (20). Other examples can be found: *abus-ar, abus-ivo; in*+*noc*+*uo, noc*+*ente, noc-ivo.* Thus, once more, the suffix seems to be -*t*+*ivo*, where the *t* is an augment.

If the affixes are of the form *c*+*ión, t*+*or,* and *t*+*ivo,* then it is quite plausible, though not necessarily true, that what we have represented with orthographic *c* in *c*+*ión* is the same augment /t/ that occurs in *t*+*or* and *t*+*ivo.* We would then need a rule to change *t* to *s* in the environment ——*ión.* But such a rule has independent motivation, as we can see from the examples in (22):

(22)     *torren*[t]*e–torren*[s]*ial*     torrent–torrential
         *Mar*[t]*e–mar*[s]*iano*         Mars–Martian
         *Egip*[t]*o–egip*[s]*io*         Egypt–Egyptian

The appropriate rule is, then, (23):

---

[6] In the dialect under study, orthographic *x*C is regularly pronounced [ksC]. This may be surprising to those familiar with any of the numerous dialects in which *x*C is regularly pronounced [sC].

(23)

$$t \;\rightarrow\; s \;\; / \;\; \underline{\quad\quad} + \begin{bmatrix} -\text{cons} \\ +\text{high} \\ -\text{back} \end{bmatrix} V$$

Thus it is both possible and plausible that the nominalizing suffix is *t+ión*. So far, however, we have no argument that this *must* be the case, that is, that the affix *cannot* be *s+ión*. Indeed, there are clearly other instances of morphemic *+s+*: for example, plural *s* (*la casa*, *las casas*) and the second person singular verbal inflection (*hablas*, *hables*, *hablabas*, etc.) We discuss this matter further as we proceed.

There are other sets of examples with stem+*ción* words that are of considerable interest. However, these data contain problems that are best studied after some insight is gained into the more straightforward cases. We therefore postpone discussing them until Section 5.2.5.

### 5.2.4 *Patterns with* -sión

We turn now to sets of examples in which the phonetic forms of the agentives, performatives, and miscellaneous nouns and adjectives contain *s* rather than *t/d* and in which the [s] of the nominalizing suffix is orthographically represented as *s* rather than as *c*. In Castilian, of course, there is a phonetic as well as an orthographic difference between -*ción* and -*sión*: the former is [θyón], the latter [syón]. Although this particular distinction does not occur in the dialect studied here, the appearance of [s] rather than *t/d* in the agentives, performatives, and so on shows that the examples to follow differ in some fundamental way from those of preceding sections.

5.2.4.1. The stem-final consonant is *d* in the examples of (24), as we shall see in Section 5.2.4.3:

(24)

| | | | | |
|---|---|---|---|---|
| *dividir* | *división* | *divisor* | *divisivo* | |
| *disuadir* | *disuasión* | | *disuasivo* | |
| *persuadir* | *persuasión* | { *persuadidor* / *persuasor* | *persuasivo* | |
| *conceder* | *concesión* | | *concesivo* | |
| *exceder* | | | *excesivo* | *exceso* |
| *acceder* | *accesión* | | | |
| *evadir* | *evasión* | *evasor* | *evasivo* | |
| *invadir* | *invasión* | *invasor* | | |
| *agredir* | *agresión* | *agresor* | *agresivo* | |
| *aludir* | *alusión* | | *alusivo* | |

*(continued)*

*(24 continued)*

| | | | | |
|---|---|---|---|---|
| *eludir* | *elusión* | | | |
| *coludir* | *colusión* | *colusor* | | |
| *elidir* | *elisión* | | | |
| *decidir* | *decisión* | | *decisivo* | *(in)deciso* |
| *circuncidar* | *circuncisión* | | | *circunciso* |

5.2.4.2. In the examples of (25), the stem ends in *nd*:

(25)

| | | | | |
|---|---|---|---|---|
| *expandir* | *expansión* | | *expansivo* | |
| *suspender* | *suspensión* | *suspendedor* | *suspensivo* | *suspenso* |
| *comprender* | *comprensión* | $\left\{ \begin{array}{l} comprendedor \\ comprensor \end{array} \right.$ | *comprensivo* | |
| *aprehender* | *aprehensión* | *aprehensor* | | |
| *ofender* | | $\left\{ \begin{array}{l} ofendedor \\ ofensor \end{array} \right.$ | *ofensivo* | *ofensa* |
| *defender* | | $\left\{ \begin{array}{l} defendedor \\ defensor \end{array} \right.$ | *defensivo* | $\left\{ \begin{array}{l} (in)defenso \\ defensa \end{array} \right.$ |
| *extender* | *extensión* | *extensor* | *extensivo* | *extenso* |
| *descender* | *descensión* | | | *descenso* |
| *ascender* | *ascensión* | | | *ascenso* |

5.2.4.3. Let us now compare the examples of (24) and (25) with those of (26):

(26)

| | | | | |
|---|---|---|---|---|
| *incluir* | *inclusión* | | *inclusivo* | *incluso* |
| *excluir* | *exclusión* | *excluidor* | *exclusivo* | |
| *concluir* | *conclusión* | | *conclusivo* | *(in)concluso* |
| *recluir* | *reclusión* | | | *recluso* |
| *corroer* | *corrosión* | | *corrosivo* | |
| *poseer* | *posesión* | *poseedor* | *posesivo* | |

Taking (24), (25), and (26) together, the simplest assumptions seem to be the following:

(a) The verb stems in (24) are [−S] since there seems to be no evidence to the contrary. Suffixal [s] is derived from /...d+t.../ by rules to be given directly, that is, /divid+tion/→*división*, /divid+tor/→*divisor*, etc.

(b) Some of the verb stems in (25) are [−S], some are [+S]. For example, *defend-* must be [+S], as is shown by the [ĕ] ∼ [yé] alternation in *def*[ĕ]*ndemos*, "we defend," *def*[yé]*nde*, "(he) defends." On the other hand, there is no reason to assign the feature [+S] to *ofend-*: *of*[ĕ]*ndemos,* "we offend," *of*[é]*nde,* "(he) offends." Suffixal [s] in (25) is derived from /d+t/, as in (24).

(c) All of the verb stems in (26) are [+S]. In systematic phonemic representations all of these stems end in /d/. A rule to be given directly will then delete this /d/ in intervocalic position when the following vowel is [−back]. (Note that stem-final /d/ in [+S] *defender* is not deleted because it is not intervocalic.) Again, suffixal [s] is derived from /d+t/.

We already have in the grammar a rule that can be simplified so that it deletes /d/ in the appropriate examples of (26). This is rule (18), which deletes /g/ in [+S] forms in just the environment in which /d/ is deleted in (26). Thus (18) is replaced by (27):

(27)
$$\begin{bmatrix} +\text{obstr} \\ -\text{tense} \\ \alpha\text{cor} \\ \alpha\text{ant} \\ +\text{S} \end{bmatrix} \rightarrow \phi \ / \ \text{V}\underline{\hspace{2em}}\begin{bmatrix} \text{V} \\ -\text{back} \end{bmatrix}$$

The rule that accounts, in part, for the appearance of underlying /d+t/ as [s] in (24), (25), and (26) can be stated, as a first approximation, as (28):

(28)
$$\begin{array}{ccc} d & + & t \\ 1 & 2 & 3 \end{array} \Rightarrow \begin{array}{ccc} s & + & s \\ 1 & 2 & 3 \end{array}$$

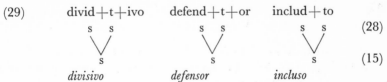

*why not*
*d+t ⟶ s*
*1 2 3* ?

Rule (28) will be altered slightly in Section 5.2.4.5 and discussed in more detail in Section 5.2.5.2. For the moment its role in accounting for appropriate forms of (24)–(26) can be clarified with the partial derivations in (29):

(29)

| divid+t+ivo | defend+t+or | includ+to | |
|---|---|---|---|
| s   s | s   s | s   s | (28) |
| \  / | \  / | \  / | |
| s | s | s | (15) |
| *divisivo* | *defensor* | *incluso* | |

5.2.4.4. The final stem consonant seems to be *t* in the examples in (30), as will be discussed in the following section:

(30)

| *emitir* | *emisión* | *emisor* | |
|---|---|---|---|
| *omitir* | *omisión* | | *omiso* |

(continued)

*(30 continued)*

| | | |
|---|---|---|
| *remitir* | *remisión* | *remisivo* |
| *admitir* | *admisión* | |
| *dimitir* | *dimisión* | |
| *cometer* | *comisión* | *cometedor* |
| *discutir* | *discusión* | |
| *explotar* | *explosión* | *explosivo* |

5.2.4.5. In the examples of (31) stem-final *t* is preceded by *r* or *n:*

(31)

| | | | | |
|---|---|---|---|---|
| *pervertir* | *perversión* | *pervertidor* | | *perverso* |
| *convertir* | *conversión* | *convertidor* | *conversivo* | *converso* |
| *invertir* | *inversión* | | | $\begin{cases} inverso \\ inversa \end{cases}$ |
| *divertir* | *diversión* | | | |
| *asentir* | | | | *asenso* |
| *disentir* | *disensión* | | | *disenso* |

The examples in (30) and (31) show that rule (28) might be revised as in (32):

(32)
$$\begin{Bmatrix} d \\ t \end{Bmatrix} + t \Rightarrow s + s$$
$$1 \quad 2 \quad 3 \qquad 1 \ 2 \ 3$$

However (32) duplicates part of the work of (12), which tenses obstruents before other tense obstruents. Thus we restate (32) as (33), which is ordered after (12):

(33)
$$t + t \Rightarrow s + s$$
$$1 \ 2 \ 3 \qquad 1 \ 2 \ 3$$

Further modification of (33) will be suggested in Section 5.2.5.2.

With the rules as they now stand, appropriate examples from (24), (26), and (30) are derived as in (34):

(34)

| agred+t+or | reclud+ir | reclud+to | remit+ir | remit+t+ivo | |
|---|---|---|---|---|---|
| t | | t | | | (12) |
| s  s | | s  s | | s  s | (33) |
| \\/ | φ | \\/ | | \\/ | (27) |
| s | | s | | s | (15) |
| *agresor* | *recluir* | *recluso* | *remitir* | *remisivo* | |

5.2.4.6. This concludes the survey of relatively straightforward forms with stem$+s\{$-*ión, -or, -ivo*$\}$. Let us summarize. We have found examples with the following underlying stem-final consonants and consonant clusters:

| | |
|---|---|
| *d* | (*dividir, división; inclu*/d/*ir, inclusión*) |
| *nd* | (*expandir, expansión*) |
| *t* | (*emitir, emisión*) |
| *rt* | (*pervertir, perversión*) |
| *nt* | (*disentir, disensión*) |

Thus all the examples with *s* in the affixes have stems that end with the dental obstruent *d* or *t*. Recall from Section 5.2.3.9 that none of the forms with *t*, *c*( $=$ [s]) in the affixes have stems that end in *d* or *t*. The crucial difference between these two sets of examples is that rule (33) applies to certain forms of the set with stem-final *d* or *t* but does not apply to forms of the other set.

We also note in passing that of all the stems in (24)–(26), (30), (31) only two are first conjugation: *circuncidar* and *explotar*.

5.2.5 *Real and apparent anomalies*

5.2.5.1. There is another class of examples with stem-final *nd* that contains, as far as I know, only the forms in (35):

(35)

| | | | |
|---|---|---|---|
| *atender* | *atención* | *atendedor* | *atento* |
| *contender* | *contención* | $\begin{cases} contendedor \\ contendor \end{cases}$ | *contienda* |

Orthographic *c* in *atención* and *contención* in (35) is a surprise, but there is no phonological problem in these two forms. *Contendor* is also slightly odd, since one would have expected either \**contentor* or, more probably, \**contensor* (cf. *extender, extensor; defender, defensor*). Presumably the exceptionality of *contendor* consists in the lack of the *t* augment before the agentive suffix (see Section 5.2.3.9). The noun *contienda* may be simply /kon$+$tEnd$+$a/, and, if so, it presents no problem. The adjective *atento* is not so easy to explain away. However, there can be little doubt that the examples in (35), with the single stem -*tend*-, are the exceptional cases, as opposed to all the examples in (24)–(26), (30), (31). To get the form *atento*, it would suffice to make -*tend*- an exception to rule (33), as shown in (36):

(36)          atend$+$to

              t $\diagup$   (12)

            $-\diagdown\!\!\diagup-$   (33)

              t    (15)

         *atento*

Alternatives are certainly conceivable, but (36) is as little *ad hoc* as any that readily come to mind. One formative is not worth further concern unless some greater generalization is involved, which does not seem likely in this case.

5.2.5.2. The set of examples represented by (37) is quite large and must be taken into account.

(37)

| editar | edición | editor | | (in)édito |
|---|---|---|---|---|
| dilatar | {dilatación / dilación | dilatador | dilatativo | |
| objetar | objeción | | | |
| sujetar | sujeción | sujetador | | sujeto |
| ejecutar | ejecución | ejecutor | | |
| excretar | excreción | | | excreto |
| secretar | secreción | secretor | | |
| redactar | redacción | redactor | | |
| proyectar | proyección | proyector | | proyecto |
| inyectar | inyección | inyector | | |
| infectar | infección | | infectivo | infecto |
| adoptar | adopción | adoptador | adoptivo | |
| eruptar | erupción | | eruptivo | |
| optar | opción | | optativo | |
| desertar | deserción | desertor | | |
| cantar | canción | | | canto |
| inventar | invención | inventor | inventivo | invento |
| untar | unción | untador | | {unto, untura / untadura |
| abortar | | | abortivo | aborto |
| relatar | relación | relator | | relato |
| detractar | | detractor | | |
| delatar | delación | delator | | |
| consultar | consultación | consultor | | consulta |
| adjuntar | | | | adjunto |
| pintar | | pintor | | pintura |
| raptar | | raptor | | rapto |

Now consider the contrasts in (38):

| (38) FORMS FROM (37) | FORMS FROM (30), (31) |
|---|---|
| editar, edición, editor | emitir, emisión, emisor |
| desertar, deserción, desertor | convertir, conversión, converso |
| inventar, invención, invento | disentir, disensión, disenso |

The problem posed by the examples in (38) is the following. The stems in (37) apparently end in -t, -rt, or -nt, as do those in (30) and (31). Yet only the stems in (30) and (31) undergo rule (33), with the ultimate result that phonetic [s] appears in forms with affixes beginning with /t/. Thus we must find some way of distinguishing the stems of (37), which do not undergo rule (33), from the stems of (30) and (31). It is not immediately obvious how this should be done. Two alternative ways of accounting for the contrasts illustrated in (38) will now be proposed, and evidence will be sought that might provide grounds for rejecting one of these proposals in favor of the other.

First, consider the vowel alternation in *cometer, comisión* of (30). Recall that we have in the grammar rule (4:34*i*), the first case of which is repeated for convenience here as (39):

(39)
$$ V \rightarrow [-\text{high}] \quad / \quad \left[ \begin{array}{c} \underline{\phantom{xxxx}} \\ -\text{tense} \\ +S \end{array} \right] $$

Let us assume that the stem in question is /comIt/ and, furthermore, that this stem is [+S] in the verb but [−S] in the nominalization. (Cf. the remarks in Section 5.2.2 concerning the forms in (7).) Thus the stem *I* is lowered to *e* by (39) in the verb but not in the nominalization. Now however, we must ask why the [+S] stem /comIt/ of *cometer* does not undergo rule (4:34*e*), which laxes intervocalic obstruents in [+S] formatives, with the result *\*comeder*. Let us suppose, then, that the stem is actually /comItt/, where neither of the *t*'s is laxed by (4:34*e*) since neither is intervocalic.

If this analysis is correct, then it would be plausible, though not necessary, to assume that all the stems in (30), but not those in (37), end in geminate *tt*. Following this line of argument, we would have to revise the list of stem-final consonants and consonant clusters given in Section 5.2.4.6 to the following: *d, nd, tt, rt, nt*. We would then propose a redundancy rule to supply some feature [F] to all and only the stems ending in these consonants and restrict rule (33) so that it applies only to stems with the feature [+F]. In other words, rule (33) would be replaced by (40):

(40)
$$ \left[ \begin{array}{c} t \\ +F \end{array} \right] + t \Rightarrow s + s $$
$$ 1 \quad 2 \; 3 \qquad 1 \; 2 \; 3 $$

Thus rule (40) will apply to the appropriate forms in (30) to yield, ultimately, [s]. On the other hand, the stems in (37), with stem-final /t/ rather than /tt/, will not be marked [+F] by the suggested redundancy rule and therefore will not be subject to (40). The result in this case, as desired, will then be [t] rather than [s]. (The [s] in the -*ión* forms here, of course, will come from rule (23) rather than rule (40).)

But this is still inadequate. Note that a number of the stems in (37), to which the proposed redundancy rule (and consequently rule (40)) must *not* apply, seem to end in *rt* and *nt*, two of the clusters that, given the forms of (31), determine [+F] stems. Perhaps there is a way out of this difficulty. Several of the verbs in (37) are classified by lexicographers and philologists as "back formations." For example, the verb *cantar*, "to sing," is said to be derived from the noun *canto*, which consists of the root *can* plus noun-forming *-to* (actually *-t+o* since the final vowel is *o* in masculine nouns, *a* in feminine nouns). Similarly, the verb *untar*, "to smear (with something greasy)," is said to be derived from the root *ung*, which also occurs in *ungir*, "to anoint," the *t* of *untar* being the residue of noun-forming *-to*. Thus the stems in question may be /can+t/, /ung+t/, rather than /cant/, /un(g)t/.[7] If we assume this structure for all the stems of (37), we can then restrict the redundancy rule that supplies the feature [+F] (which in turn triggers rule (40)) to apply to stems that have the appropriate consonants *within a single morpheme*. Thus the stems of (37) with /r+t/ and /n+t/ will not be marked [+F], as opposed to the corresponding stems of (31), with /rt/ and /nt/, and rule (40) will apply as desired. In short, according to the proposal just sketched, the contrast between *t/c*-affixes and *s*-affixes depends ultimately on phonological representations such as in (41):

(41)

a.  /edi+t+a+rE/       /edi+t+ionE/       /edi+t+orE/
    →*editar*          →*edición*          →*editor*
    /emitt+i+rE/       /emitt+t+ionE/      /emitt+t+orE/
    →*emitir*          →*emisión*          →*emisor*

b.  /can+t+a+rE/       /can+t+ionE/        /can+t+o/
    →*cantar*          →*canción*          →*canto*
    /disent+i+rE/      /disent+t+ionE/     /disent+t+o/
    →*disentir*        →*disensión*        →*disenso*

c.  /abor+t+a+rE/      /abor+t+ivo/        /abor+t+o/
    →*abortar*         →*abortivo*         →*aborto*
    /convert+i+rE/     /convert+t+ivo/     /convert+t+o/
    →*convertir*       →*conversivo*       →*converso*

[7] The *g* in both /ung+t/ and /ungt/ would be deleted by rule (21).

The occurrence of three *t*'s in the underlying representations of forms such as *emisión* and *emisor* will be dealt with at the end of this section.

Let us now turn to an alternative proposal. It is a fact that all of the stems in (37) belong to the first conjugation, that is, they have the lexical property [+1conjugation]. On the other hand, all of the stems in Section 5.2.4, which have *s*-affixes rather than *t/c*-affixes, are second or third conjugation—that is, they have the lexical property [−1conjugation]—with the exception of *circuncidar* in (24) and *explotar* in (30).[8] Thus, by considering these two *-ar* verbs to be exceptional, we may propose that the occurrence of affixal *s* is due not to the final consonant or consonant cluster of the stem but rather to conjugation class membership. According to the present proposal, then, (33) is replaced not by (40) but by (42):

(42)
$$
\begin{bmatrix} t \\ -1\text{conj} \end{bmatrix} + t \;\Rightarrow\; s + s
$$
$$
\quad 1 \qquad\quad 2 \; 3 \qquad 1 \; 2 \; 3
$$

With rule (42) in the grammar there is no need for any internal analysis of stems such as *edit-*, *cant-*, and *abort-*.

We shall now consider the relative merits of the two proposals just discussed and proceed to make the necessary refinements in the alternative selected as the better of the two.

We first note that the two versions of the crucial rule in each case, (40) and (42), are of equal complexity. The first proposal, however, requires in addition to rule (40) an *ad hoc* redundancy rule to supply certain formatives with the *ad hoc* feature [F]. The second proposal requires no *ad hoc* machinery at all: the feature [−1conjugation], which plays the same role in (42) that [F] does in (40), is already one of the features of the stems in question. All other things being equal, these considerations would suffice to reject the first proposal in favor of the second.

The following comments are only suggestive, but they also lend at least intuitive support to the second proposal. Stems that belong to the nonproductive second and third conjugation—{that is, those characterized by the feature [−1conjugation]—are vaguely felt to be somewhat unusual. It would seem natural, then, that they should

[8] The *explotar* of (30) means "to explode," and, according to Corominas (1961), it was coined in 1916 as a back formation from *explosión*. This new verb was assigned to the first conjugation, as are all new coinages. Note that in (3) there is another *explotar*, which means "to exploit" and is unrelated to the *explotar* of (30). The *explotar* of (3), of course, causes no problems. *Circuncidar* is from Latin *circumcīdĕre*. The date of its switch to the first conjugation is not documented.

be subject to phonological processes to which formatives belonging to the productive first conjugation are not subject. This vague feeling is represented more directly in the second proposal, which makes use of the feature [−1conjugation] rather than an arbitrary feature. Furthermore, the slightly more complex lexical representations of stems such as *edit-*, *cant-*, and *abort-* required by the first proposal are highly counterintuitive. Even more serious is the fact that there seems to be no independent synchronic motivation for representations like *edi+t, dila+t, excre+t, secre+t, adop+t, erup+t, can+t, abor+t* for the examples of (37). The philological considerations mentioned previously certainly do not constitute synchronic evidence. Similarly, it is not at all convincing to point to etymological doublets such as *ungir,* "to anoint," and *untar,* "to smear . . ." since the former (like *unción*) refers to a religious rite, while the latter might refer to bread and butter. In other words, *ungir* and *untar* have different meanings, and there is no more motivation for positing a morpheme common to both than there is for English pairs such as "father"–"paternal," "ear"–"hear," "footstool"–"pedestal," "serpent"–"herpetology," "wine"–"vintage."

Let us therefore accept, at least tentatively, the correctness of the second proposal and attempt to clarify certain details.

The conjunction of several sets of facts seems to indicate that rule (42) must be revised slightly. Observe first that the sequence [ts] does not occur at all in the language (aside from a few loan words such as *A*[ts]*capo*[ts]*alco, que*[ts]*al*). We have as yet no rule in the grammar to account for this fact, but (42) could do so if it were broken into two steps as in (43). (Note that the + must be present in (43*a*) but absent in (43*b*).)

(43)

$$a. \quad t \rightarrow s \ / \begin{bmatrix} t \\ -1\text{conj} \end{bmatrix} +\underline{\qquad}$$

$$b. \quad t \rightarrow s \ / \underline{\qquad} s$$

Recall that we have a rule in the grammar with the same effect as (43*b*), namely, rule (23), which converts *t* to *s* in the environment $\underline{\qquad}+$[i,y]V. There seems to be no reason why rules (43*b*) and (23) cannot be combined as in (44), thus cutting down the additional complexity involved in breaking (42) into two steps.

(44)

$$t \rightarrow s \ / \underline{\qquad} \left\{ \begin{array}{ll} + \begin{bmatrix} -\text{cons} \\ +\text{high} \\ -\text{back} \end{bmatrix} V & a \\ \\ s & b \end{array} \right.$$

Cases (*a*) and (*b*) of (44) must be ordered as shown, as will become clear directly.

It was argued at the beginning of this section that the [+S] stem of the verb *cometer* must be /comItt/, with geminate *tt*. This argument still stands, although the proposal in which it was embedded has been rejected. If this is correct, and if one is to avoid special statements about the distribution of the *t* augment that occurs before *-ión*, *-ivo*, etc., then some phonological representations will have a sequence of three *t*'s, as in /comItt+t+ionE/. This, however, is no problem. We already have in the grammar a cluster simplification rule, rule (21), which if properly ordered will delete the middle *t*. The ordering of (21) and the operation of the various rules that play a role in producing the forms discussed in this section are illustrated in the derivations in (45) (in which irrelevant details are omitted):

(45)

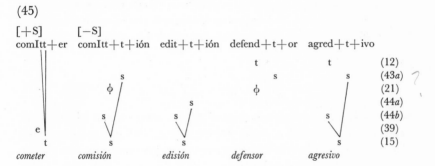

5.2.5.3. We will look at one further set of examples of *-ión* nominalizations, agentives, etc. This set is small and somewhat marginal. We investigate it not so much for the intrinsic interest of the examples themselves as for the light they shed on certain areas of Spanish phonology to be discussed here and in subsequent sections.

Consider the examples in (46). (Note that [g]—or [γ] in case the Spirantization rule has applied—is spelled *gu* before a front vowel and *g* elsewhere):

(46)

| | | | | |
|---|---|---|---|---|
| *perse[γ]ir* | *perse[k]ución* | *perse[γ]idor* | | |
| *conseguir* | *consecución* | | | |
| *extinguir* | *extinción* | *extinguidor* | | *extinto* |
| *distinguir* | *distinción* | | *distintivo* | *distinto* |

The alternation between *g* in *per-*, *con-seguir* and *k* in *per-*, *con-secución* is readily accounted for on the assumption that the former (and *perseguidor*) are [+S] while the latter are [−S], as has frequently been seen to be the case, and that the consonant in question is tense in its underlying form but is laxed in the [+S] verbs by rule (4:34*e*). There are other questions, however, that are not so easily answered. (For ease of reference I shall temporarily use $K$ as the symbol for the stem-final segments in (46).)

(a) Why is $K$ unaffected by rule (3:78*b*), which, as provisionally formulated, changes *k* to *s* and *g* to *x* before front vowels? That is, how is *perse*[γ]*ir*, for example, rather than \**perse*[x]*ir* or \**perse*[s]*ir*, to be accounted for?

(b) What is the origin of the *u* in *per-, con-secución*?

(c) Why are $K$ and *u* both absent in *extinción, distinción, distintivo*, etc.?

(d) What is the systematic phonemic representation of $K$?

The answers to these questions involve inferences from a fairly wide range of data. Let us begin by considering the forms in (47), all of which presumably share the formative *lok* or *loK*:

(47)           *lo*[kw]*áz*    loquacious
                *lo*[ku]*ción*    locution
                *ventrílo*[kw]*o*    ventriloquist

As was observed in Section 2.4.5.1, stress cannot be assigned correctly to *ventrílocuo* if orthographic *u* is also phonological *u* in this case. Thus the phonemic representation of [kw] must be either /kw/ or the single rounded velar segment /k$^w$/.

Consider now *ex-, dis-tinguir, ex-, dis-tinción*, and the related forms with the same stems. The phonetically lax stem-final consonant must also be phonemically lax since the only obstruent-laxing rule, (4:34*e*), cannot apply here. If this lax obstruent were the single segment /g$^w$/, then there would be an easy way to account for the absence of both $K$ and *u* in *ex-, dis-tinción, distintivo*, etc. When the stems in question are followed by a suffix beginning with /t/, stem-final /g$^w$/ is deleted by the cluster simplification rule (21) (after having been tensed, irrelevantly, by rule (12)), as shown in (48):

(48)     exting$^w$+ción    disting$^w$+tivo    exting$^w$+to
           k$^w$                k$^w$            k$^w$        (12)
           φ                 φ             φ        (21)
      *extinción*     *distintivo*     *extinto*

We have thus found two independent sets of facts that suggest that the set of systematic phonemes of Spanish may well include the rounded velar obstruents /k$^w$/ and /g$^w$/: (a) stress placement in *ventrílocuo*, and (b) deletion of the stem-final velar segment of *distintivo*, *extinto*, etc., by rule (21). Before considering (46) and (47) further, let us examine additional evidence for the existence of underlying rounded velars.

The distribution of *w* in phonetic representations seems, at first glance, to be inexplicably skewed. In native words there appear to be three sources of phonetic *w* in postconsonantal position. Two of these are:

(a) From the diphthongization of lax stressed /O/. Phonetic *w* from /O/ occurs after any consonant: *podemos–puedo, volamos–vuelo, forzamos–fuerzo, movemos–muevo, torcemos–tuerzo, dolía–duele, soltamos–suelto, llover–llueve, pañoleta–pañuelo, contamos–cuento,* etc.

(b) From unstressed *u* followed by a vowel. Phonetic *w* in this case occurs after labial and dental as well as velar consonants: *atrib*[ú]*yo–atrib*[w]*ír, fluct*[ú]*a–fluct*[w]*ár, individ*[ú]*o–indivíd*[w]*o insin*[ú]*o–insin*[w]*ámos, menstr*[ú]*a–menstr*[w]*ár, incl*[ú]*yo–incl*[w]*ír, evac*[ú]*a–evac*[w]*ár,* etc.

Otherwise—and this is the third source—postconsonantal [w] follows only velar consonants: *agua, tregua, antiguo, cuando, cuota, ventrílocuo,* etc. There are extremely few exceptions (and, interestingly enough, they seem to occur mainly after *s: suave, persuadir*). In short, while there are words like [kw]*ando,* [kw]*ota* in which [w] must come from some source other than *O* or *úV,* there are no words like *\*[pw]ado, \*[tw]orzo, \*[yw]ave.* Apparently this can be accounted for in part by the fact that Spanish has the rounded velars /k$^w$/ and /g$^w$/, but not rounded labials and dentals */p$^w$/, */t$^w$/, etc.

The phonetic manifestations of the velar-glide sequences in *cuánto, trégua,* for example, which are presumably derived from underlying /k$^w$/, /g$^w$/, are not distinct from those of words like *cuénto, agüéro,* which are derived from underlying /kO/, /gO/ (cf. *cŏntár, agŏrár*). In order to provide nondistinct phonetic representations for these sequences with distinct origins, a rule is needed with the effect of (49):

(49)
$$\begin{bmatrix} +\text{obstr} \\ +\text{round} \end{bmatrix} \phi \;\Rightarrow\; [-\text{round}] \; w$$
$$\quad\quad 1 \quad\quad 2 \quad\quad\quad 1 \quad\quad 2$$

Further motivation for (49) can be adduced as follows. We observed that the stems in (46) are not affected by rule (3:78*b*), the effect of which is *k→s, g→x* before front vowels. This can be accounted for quite naturally now, and without complicating rule (3:78*b*), by ordering the rules so that (3:78*b*) follows (49). As illustrated in the partial derivations of (50), once rule (49) has applied to a rounded velar the segment will be followed by $w$ rather than by a front vowel and therefore will not fall into the environment of rule $(3:78b)$.

(50)   persek$^w$+ir      exting$^w$+ir      persek$^w$+idor
      kw                      gw                      kw                    (49)
      –                        –                        –                     $(3:78b)$

We must now account for the appearance of $u$ in *persecución, consecución,* as opposed to *extinción, distinción.* Recall that in the latter forms stem-final $/g^w/$ is deleted by the cluster simplification rule (21). Thus we have assumed that these forms do not have $u$ because the source, namely, $/g^w/$, is deleted. In *persecución* and *consecución,* on the other hand, the stem-final rounded velar ($/k^w/$ in these cases) is preceded by a vowel and is thus not deleted by (21). Instead, $k^w$ is changed to $kw$ by rule (49), and all that must be done to obtain the correct result is to add rule (51), which is ordered after (49):

(51)   $\begin{bmatrix} -\text{cons} \\ +\text{round} \end{bmatrix} \rightarrow [+\text{voc}] \ / \ [+\text{cons}]\text{——}[+\text{cons}]$

Rule (51) changes $w$ to $u$ between consonants.[9] Illustrative partial derivations are given in (52):

(52)   persek$^w$+ción      exting$^w$+ción      disting$^w$+tivo
                    k$^w$                      k$^w$                  (12)
                    φ                        φ                    (21)
        kw                                                                (49)
        u                                                                 (51)
    *persekución*      *extinción*      *distintivo*

Finally, we must account for the fact that [γ] and [g], rather than [γ$^w$] and [g$^w$], appear in *perse[γ]ir, perse[γ]idor, conse[γ]ir, extin[g]ir, extin[g]idor,* and *distin[g]ir.* Consider the examples in (53), in which it is fairly clear that the words of each pair share a formative. Note that [kw] and [γw] before back vowels alternate with [k] before front vowels.

(53)      *li*[kw]*ar–li*[k]*idar*          liquefy–liquidate
         *li*[kw]*adora–lí*[k]*ido*      blender (liquifier)–liquid
                                *(continued)*

---

[9] Rule (51), or some refinement thereof, presumably figures also in the derivation of a few marginal examples such as *devol*[β]*er,* "to return (transitive)," *devol*[u]*ción,* "return," which have not been studied carefully.

*(53 continued)*

i[γw]*aldad–e*[k]*idad*        equality–equity
e[kw]*ación–e*[k]*ivalente*    equation–equivalent

*ye*[γw]*a–e*[k]*itación*        mare–horseback riding

[kw]*ál–*[k]*é*            which–what
[kw]*ándo–*[k]*ién*        when–who

These examples show clearly the need for a rule with the effect of (54):[10]

(54)

$$ w \rightarrow \phi \ / \ \begin{bmatrix} +\text{obstr} \\ +\text{back} \end{bmatrix} \text{---} \begin{bmatrix} V \\ -\text{back} \end{bmatrix} $$

Rule (54) must obviously be ordered after rule (3:78*b*), which would otherwise change these velars to [s] or [x], and before rule (4:34*h*), diphthongization, so that *w* is not deleted in (*kOnto→*) *kwento*, etc.

To conclude this section, I give sample derivations in (55) illustrating all the rules that have been proposed in connection with the examples in (46). Irrelevant details are omitted.

(55)

| [+S] | [−S] | [−S] | [−S] | |
|------|------|------|------|------|
| persek^wir | persek^wción | exting^wir | exting^wción | |
| | | | k^w | (12) |
| | | | ф | (21) |
| kw | kw | gw | | (49) |
| – | – | – | | (3:78*b*) |
| | u | | | (51) |
| ф | | ф | | (54) |
| g | | | | (4:34*e*) |
| γ | | | | (2:69*h*) |
| *perseγir* | *persekución* | *extingir* | *extinción* | |

[10] There are a few extremely marginal instances of [kwi], spelled *cui*: *cuidar*, "to take care (of)"; *escuincle*, "baby, kid (slang)"; *cuico*, "cop (slang)"; *Cuicuilco, Cuicatlán, Ixcuintla* (place names). The stem *cuid-* is the only form of Latin origin that I know of with [kwi]. The other examples are of Mexican origin. Thus all these words might well be disregarded. Alternatively, there is no difficulty with considering the systematic phonemic representation of [kwi] to be /kui/, in which the /u/ is changed to [w] by the very late rule (4:34*j*).

There are also a few forms of Mexican origin with sequences realized phonetically as [γ^wi] in Andante and [wi] in Allegretto and spelled *hui* or *güi*: *huipil, huisache, Huicho/Güicho, Coahuila, güiro*. These may be considered to have systematic phonemic /wi/. (Rules with the effect of *w→γ^w* (*→w*) were discussed at length in Section 2.4.)

## 5.3 Summary of rules

The rules that play a crucial role in the derivation of the forms discussed in this chapter are here collected, ordered, and renumbered as (56). In Chapter 6 some of these rules will be refined and their order with respect to rules of previous chapters determined.

(56)

a.  $[+\text{obstr}] \rightarrow [+\text{tense}] \quad / \underline{\quad} \begin{bmatrix} +\text{obstr} \\ +\text{tense} \end{bmatrix}$    (12)

b.  $t \rightarrow s \quad / \begin{bmatrix} t \\ -1\text{conj} \end{bmatrix} + \underline{\quad}$    (28), (32), (33), (42), (43a)

c.  $\begin{bmatrix} +\text{obstr} \\ -\text{cont} \end{bmatrix} \rightarrow \phi \quad / \ [+\text{cons}]\underline{\quad}[+\text{obstr}]$    (21)

d.  $t \rightarrow s \quad / \underline{\quad} \left\{ \begin{matrix} + \begin{bmatrix} -\text{cons} \\ +\text{high} \\ -\text{back} \end{bmatrix} V \\ \\ s \end{matrix} \right\}$    (23), (28), (32), (33), (42), (43b), (44)

e.  $\begin{bmatrix} p \\ +S \end{bmatrix} \rightarrow t \quad / \underline{\quad}t$    (14)

f.  $\begin{bmatrix} +\text{obstr} \\ +\text{round} \end{bmatrix} \phi \ \Rightarrow \ [-\text{round}] \ w$    (49)
  $\quad\quad 1 \quad\quad 2 \quad\quad\quad 1 \quad\quad 2$

g.  $\begin{bmatrix} +\text{obstr} \\ -\text{tense} \\ \alpha\text{cor} \\ \alpha\text{ant} \\ +S \end{bmatrix} \rightarrow \phi \quad / \ V\underline{\quad}\begin{bmatrix} V \\ -\text{back} \end{bmatrix}$    (18), (27)

h.  $\left\{ \begin{matrix} k \\ {}_1g \end{matrix} \right\}_1 \rightarrow \left\{ \begin{matrix} s \\ {}_1x \end{matrix} \right\}_1 \ / \ \underline{\quad}\begin{bmatrix} -\text{cons} \\ -\text{back} \end{bmatrix}$    (3:78b)

i.  $\begin{bmatrix} -\text{cons} \\ +\text{round} \end{bmatrix} \rightarrow [+\text{voc}] \quad / \ [+\text{cons}] \ \underline{\quad} \ [+\text{cons}]$    (51)

*(continued)*

(56 *continued*)

*j.*  w  →  φ  /  $\begin{bmatrix} +\text{obstr} \\ +\text{back} \end{bmatrix}$——$\begin{bmatrix} V \\ -\text{back} \end{bmatrix}$    (54)

*k.*  φ  →  e  /  #——s [+cons]    (note 5)

*l.*  $\begin{bmatrix} +\text{obstr} \\ +S \end{bmatrix}$  →  [−tense]  /  V——[−obstr]    (4:34*e*)

*m.*  $\begin{bmatrix} e \\ -\text{tense} \end{bmatrix}$  →  φ  /  V$\begin{bmatrix} +\text{cor} \\ +\text{ant} \end{bmatrix}_0^1$——#    (4:34*f*)

*n.*  V  →  [−high]  /  $\left\{ \begin{matrix} \begin{bmatrix} \quad\quad \\ -\text{tense} \\ +S \end{bmatrix} \\ \begin{bmatrix} \quad\quad \\ -\text{stress} \end{bmatrix} C_0 \begin{Bmatrix} \# \\ i \end{Bmatrix} \end{matrix} \right\}$    (4:34*i*), (39)

MINOR

*o.*  $C_i C_j$  ⇒  $C_k$  *where* $C_i = C_j = C_k$    (15)

# 6. The Set of Rules: Refinements and Summary

## 6.1 Preliminary remarks

A number of the rules proposed in the course of this study have been formulated only loosely for purposes of illustration. Such formulation, although it facilitates exposition, in some cases may mask a good deal of complexity and provide no real insight into the phonological processes of Spanish or general phonological theory. Take, for example, rule (5:56*h*), repeated here for convenience as (1):

$$(1) \qquad \begin{Bmatrix} k \\ _1g \end{Bmatrix}_1 \rightarrow \begin{Bmatrix} s \\ _1x \end{Bmatrix}_1 \quad / \underline{\hspace{1cm}} \begin{bmatrix} -\text{cons} \\ -\text{back} \end{bmatrix}$$

Rule (1) restates certain easily observable facts, but it gives no hint about the relation of these facts to other facts, either particular to Spanish or of more general concern. In this chapter we shall look more closely at (1) and at a few other rules where it seems that further study would be profitable.

Many rules will not be refined although they could be. For example, rule (5:56*e*), which assimilates *p* to a following *t* in [+S] formatives, could be stated more generally as in (2):

$$(2) \qquad \begin{bmatrix} +\text{obstr} \\ +\text{ant} \\ -\text{cont} \\ +\text{S} \end{bmatrix} \rightarrow [+\text{cor}] \quad / \underline{\hspace{1cm}} \begin{bmatrix} +\text{obstr} \\ +\text{tense} \\ +\text{cor} \\ -\text{strid} \end{bmatrix}$$

160

I will not bother with such reformulations, however, since nothing of any great interest seems to be involved.[1]

Other loose formulations and unclarities will be allowed to remain when it seems to me that my understanding of the data is limited to the point where I would have to make *ad hoc* decisions in order to achieve an illusion of greater precision.

## 6.2 Diphthongization

Early in this study a rule of diphthongization was proposed that was last stated in Chapter 4 (rule $(34h)$) as in (3):

(3)

$$
\begin{Bmatrix} e \\ {}_1 o \end{Bmatrix}_1 \rightarrow \begin{Bmatrix} ye \\ {}_1 we \end{Bmatrix}_1 \Big/ \begin{bmatrix} \underline{\qquad} \\ +\text{stress} \\ -\text{tense} \\ +\text{S} \end{bmatrix}
$$

One's first thought would be that the proper formulation of this rule should include two steps, the first of which inserts a glide that agrees in backness with the vowel, and the second of which converts the resulting *wo* to *we*. These steps are given in (4):

(4)

$$
a. \quad \phi \rightarrow \begin{bmatrix} G \\ \alpha\text{back} \end{bmatrix} \Big/ \underline{\qquad} \begin{bmatrix} +\text{stress} \\ -\text{tense} \\ -\text{high} \\ -\text{low} \\ \alpha\text{back} \\ +\text{S} \end{bmatrix}
$$

$$
b. \quad \text{o} \rightarrow \text{e} \ / \ \text{w}\underline{\qquad}
$$

The choice of features in (4*a*) is somewhat arbitrary, but not entirely so. The inserted glide is specified as [αback] rather than [αround]

---

[1] Suppose, on the other hand, that in addition to [p, $+$S]$\rightarrow t/$——$t$ there were also the rule [p, $+$S]$\rightarrow s/$——$s$. Then a generalization about assimilation would be captured by combining these two rules as:

$$
\begin{bmatrix} +\text{obstr} \\ +\text{ant} \\ -\text{cont} \\ +\text{S} \end{bmatrix} \rightarrow \begin{bmatrix} +\text{cor} \\ \alpha\text{cont} \end{bmatrix} \Big/ \underline{\qquad} \begin{bmatrix} +\text{obstr} \\ +\text{tense} \\ +\text{cor} \\ \alpha\text{cont} \end{bmatrix}
$$

I have not chosen this example at random. The assimilation of *p* to *s* in "vulgar" words is a historical change, but I am not aware of any clear evidence that it is also a synchronic process.

since the marking conventions for glides proposed by Chomsky and
Halle (1968, Chapter Nine, Section 2.1) supply the specification
[αround] in the environment ——[αback], but not vice versa. For
the vowel before which the glide is inserted, the choice of [ —low]
rather than [αround] is arbitrary.[2]

It was observed in Section 5.2.5.3 that rule (5:56*j*), which deletes
*w* in certain environments, must apparently be ordered before
diphthongization so that the *w* in words like (/kOnta/→) [kw*enta*], "(he)
tells," is not deleted. Now note that this same rule must also be
ordered after (5:56*f*), which changes *k*$^w$ and *g*$^w$ to *kw* and *gw*, respectively. In other words, forms such as *quiere*, "(he) wants," *cuota*, "quota,"
and *cuenta* show the need for the transitive ordering relation indicated
in (5). (The underlying representation of *quiere* is assumed to be
/k$^w$Ere/, with initial /k$^w$/, because of the failure of this segment to
undergo velar softening.)

(5)        (5:56*f*)   *k$^w$Ere* → *kwEre, k$^w$ota* → *kwota*
           (5:56*j*)   *kwEre* → *kEre, kwota* unaffected
           (4*a*)      *kEre* → *kyere, kOnta* → *kwonta*
           (4*b*)      *kwonta* → *kwenta, kyere* unaffected
                       *kwota* → *\*kweta*

[2] There may be interesting material for historical and dialectological study here.
In some non-Castilian dialects of Spain, the diphthongization of lax *o* has ended up
variously as [wo], [wɔ], [wa], [wæ], and even [wö]. Although there is much disagreement among philologists, it seems likely that either before or after glide insertion,
*É* and *Ó* became low æ and ɔ, respectively, and then different dialects added different
versions of rule (4*b*). It also seems that there was at times an interaction between
the historical analogues of (4) and those of the rule that changes unstressed vowels to
glides before vowels: that is, *ia* sometimes had the same fate as *É*, namely, [ye] or
[yæ], as in *com*[yé]*mos* or *com*[yæ]*mos* for Castilian *com*[ía]*mos*.

There are a few interesting examples in which a restructuring of lexical representations seems to have taken place. For instance, the interrogative (and relative) *como*,
"how," is believed to have come from Latin *quō mōdō*. At an early stage in the history
of Spanish this became [kwomo], presumably /k$^w$omo/, sharing initial /k$^w$/ (corresponding to English *wh-*) with other interrogatives whose modern forms are:

|           |           |           |
|-----------|-----------|-----------|
| /k$^w$alE/ | [kwal]    | which     |
| /k$^w$ando/ | [kwando]  | when      |
| /k$^w$anto/ | [kwanto]  | how much  |
| /k$^w$EnE/ | [kyen]    | who       |
| /k$^w$e/   | [ke]      | what      |

Later, "how" appears as [kwemo], apparently because (a) the phonetic sequence
[wo] has been affected by the historical analogue of (4*b*), and (b) the lexical representation has been restructured as /kOmo/. Then [kwemo] is replaced by [komo]
in both stressed and unstressed positions, the lexical representation having again
been restructured, this time to /komo/.

Given the order in (5), sequences of *kwo* produced by rule (5:56*f*) will be subject to rule (4*b*), along with sequences of *wo* produced by rule (4*a*). But this is wrong, as is shown by the incorrect form \**kweta* rather than *kwota*. Apparently, then, (4*b*) must be restricted so as to apply only to those instances of *wo* that result from the diphthongization of stressed lax *O*. Since, as we have seen, we cannot achieve this by ordering rule (5:56*f*) after rule (4*b*), we must instead somehow restrict (4*b*) itself so that it applies only to the output of (4*a*). One might attempt to accomplish this by limiting the application of (4*b*) to [+S] formatives since only these undergo diphthongization in the first place. This will fail, however, because of [+S] forms such as *agwoso*, "watery," and *agwosidad*, "wateriness" (cf. [−S] *akwático*, where *k* from /k$^w$/ is not laxed by (5:56*l*)), which would become \**agweso*, \**agwesidad* even with the proposed restriction. It seems, then, that the correct solution is to state both steps of (4) as the single transformation (6):

(6)
$$\phi \begin{bmatrix} +\text{stress} \\ -\text{tense} \\ -\text{high} \\ -\text{low} \\ \alpha\text{back} \\ +\text{S} \end{bmatrix} \Rightarrow \begin{bmatrix} \text{G} \\ \alpha\text{back} \end{bmatrix} [-\text{back}]$$

      1      2            1     2

## 6.3 Velar softening, palatalization

"Velar softening" is the term that will be used for convenience to refer to the phonological processes summarized as rule (1). "Palatalization" will be clarified shortly. A rather wide range of data and a number of rules are involved in these processes. As the exposition proceeds, data relevant to each step will be given. The real force of the argument, however, rests not so much in the motivation for the individual steps, which is not always overwhelming, as in the total tightly interlocking system of rules, which, if correct, succeeds in uniting quite a number of apparently disparate facts into a coherent relationship. I will discuss first the phonological processes themselves, and then examine in some detail certain of the cases in which velar softening does not occur although the rules predict that it should.

### 6.3.1 *The phonological processes*

Rule (1) could, in principle, be "translated" into distinctive feature notation as it stands. As we shall see in this section, however, such a "translation" would not only be quite complex, but it would also provide no insight into the phonological processes involved. It will be shown here that (1) is actually a summary of the following steps:

(7)     $k \rightarrow t^s \rightarrow (d^z \rightarrow z \rightarrow) \ s$

     $g \rightarrow \check{\jmath} \rightarrow \check{z} \rightarrow \check{s} \rightarrow x$

The motivation for each of these steps will be given in detail, and it will be seen that, broken down as in (7), rule (1) involves in part familiar phonological processes such as "palatalization," "assimilation," and "lenition."

6.3.1.1. The first step in (7) is effected by rule (8):

(8)     $\begin{bmatrix} +\text{obstr} \\ -\text{ant} \\ -\text{cor} \\ \langle +\text{tense} \rangle \end{bmatrix} \rightarrow \begin{bmatrix} -\text{back} \\ \langle +\text{ant} \rangle \end{bmatrix} \ / \ \underline{\hspace{2em}} \begin{bmatrix} -\text{cons} \\ -\text{back} \end{bmatrix}$

Given the theory of rule application and marking conventions proposed in Chomsky and Halle (1968, Chapter Nine, Section 4), rule (8) converts tense $k$ into the tense, strident, noncontinuant, dental obstruent $t^s$; and it converts lax $g$ into the lax, strident, noncontinuant, alveolopalatal obstruent $\check{\jmath}$. Thus (8) is essentially an assimilation rule: velar obstruents assimilate in frontness to a following front nonconsonantal segment.

Note that (8) must be ordered before rule (5:56*l*), which laxes intervocalic obstruents in [+S] formatives. Otherwise (5:56*l*) would convert instances of intervocalic /k/ in [+S] formatives to $g$, which would then ultimately become [x] in the environment of (8), which is incorrect.

Since noncontinuant /k/ and /g/ ultimately become continuant [s] and [x] in the environment of (8), justification must be given for not specifying [+continuant] in the output of this rule. Furthermore, lax /g/ ultimately becomes tense [x]. Therefore the exclusion of [+tense] from the output of (8) must also be justified. We turn now to the first of these matters.

6.3.1.2. Consider the examples in (9), all of which contain [x], represented orthographically as $j$:

(9)     | *Japón* | Japan | *jacaranda* | jacaranda (tree) |
| --- | --- | --- | --- |
| *japonés* | Japanese | *jaguar* | jaguar, tiger |
| *jardín* | garden | *Jaime* | James |
| *jabalina* | javelin | *Jamaica* | Jamaica |
| *jabón* | soap | *jamón* | ham |

*(continued)*

*(9 continued)*

| | | | |
|---|---|---|---|
| *jacal* | shack | *jaque (mate)* | check(mate) |
| *jazmín* | jasmine | *jade* | jade |
| *jalea* | jelly | *Java* | Java |
| *jaula* | cage | *Jorge* | George |
| *José* | Joseph | *Juan* | John |

In these examples, and many others like them, the systematic phonemic representation of phonetic [x] is not at all obvious. It seems that /g/ must be ruled out since nowhere in (9) is [x] followed by a front nonconsonantal segment, nor is there the slightest reason to suppose that [x] in these words is followed by a front nonconsonantal segment at any stage of derivation (except of course for the second [x] in *Jorge* [xorxe]). There is, in fact, no segment that occurs in phonetic representations of Spanish that could be the systematic phonemic source of [x] here but *x* itself.[3] If /x/ were in fact a systematic phoneme of Spanish, then the dialect under study would apparently have the set of systematic phonemic obstruents shown in (10):[4]

[3] Some qualification is required here. Consider the following curious contrasts:

> *dis*[y]*unción–con*[x]*unción*    disjunction–conjunction
> *in*[y]*ección–inter*[x]*ección*    injection–interjection

Such contrasts suggest that in a specially marked subset of forms systematic phonemic /y/ or /i/ undergoes a minor rule with the effect of [i,y]→[j]. This is vastly more plausible than a rule with the effect of [i,y] → [x] or any other alternative that I can think of. The existence of dozens, perhaps hundreds, of words such as *ya, yacer, yo, yodo, yuca, yugo, yugoeslavo, yunque, yunta, yute, yuxtaposición, Ayala, epopeya, plebeyo, pompeyano, Maya, mayo, tocayo, chirimoya, aleluya, cuyo, suyo, tuyo,* in which the only imaginable source for *y* is /y/ or /i/, shows clearly enough that the forms in which /y/ or /i/ is realized as [x] are idiosyncratic.

It is possible that systematic phonemic /i/ or /y/ is the source of phonetic [x] in forms like those of (9), and that these forms should also be included in the set that undergoes the suggested minor rule [i,y]→[j]. It is not obvious, however, what would be gained by this move, and, in any event, the discussion of the rules involved in velar softening would remain entirely unaffected.

Incidentally, it will be shown in Section 6.3.1.4 that /ks/ is also a source of phonetic [x]. It is hardly likely, however, that anyone would seriously consider, say, /ksapon/, /ksamaika/, /ksava/ as the systematic phonemic representations of *Japón, Jamaica, Java,* and so on for the rest of the examples in (9), or /kon+ksuntionE/ for *conjunción,* etc.

[4] The status of *č* as a systematic phoneme of Spanish does not seem to me to be open to question. A glance through a dictionary is all that is needed to find a very large number of words in which *č* is involved in no alternations at all and for which the only reasonable source is /č/. It will be argued in Section 6.3.1.4 that some instances of [č] derive from /kt/, but surely this source is out of the question for words like *muchacho, chinche, chocho, cachondo, salchicha, chucho* or in fact for any of the thousand or so words listed in the *Vox* dictionary with initial [č].

(10)    p  t  č  k  kʷ
        b  d     g  gʷ
        f  s     x

But now consider that there are instances of [x] that clearly come from systematic phonemic /g/, and that one of the steps in the derivation of [x] from /g/ is ǰ. Thus it would be reasonable to argue that the systematic phonemic representation of [x] in the examples of (9) is /ǰ/ rather than /x/. Underlying /ǰ/ would be converted to [x] by the same rules that convert (/g/→)ǰ to [x]. Perhaps some additional plausibility is lent to this proposal by the fact that the underlying system of obstruents would be somewhat more symmetrical with /ǰ/ instead of /x/, as shown in (11):

(11)    p  t  č  k  kʷ
        b  d  ǰ  g  gʷ
        f  s

If these suggestions are correct, then the exclusion of [+continuant] from rule (8) is justified: since there is no x at the point when the early rule (8) applies, all velars will be noncontinuant and the feature [continuant] is therefore not mentioned in the rule. But now $t^s$ and ǰ resulting from (8) and systematic phonemic /ǰ/ must be converted into continuants by a later rule.

After (8) has applied, there will be representations containing the following obstruents: $p$, $b$, $f$, $t$, $d$, $t^s$, $s$, $č$, $ǰ$, $k$, $g$, $k^w$, $g^w$. Of these, all of the strident segments except č are manifested phonetically as continuants. We may therefore propose rule (12):

(12)
$$
\begin{bmatrix}
+\text{strid} \\
\begin{cases} -\text{tense} \\ +\text{ant} \end{cases}
\end{bmatrix} \rightarrow [+\text{cont}]
$$

This rule states that all segments that are strident and also either [−tense] (ǰ) or [+anterior] ($t^s$,$f$,$s$) are realized as continuants. It applies vacuously to $f$ and $s$ and changes $t^s$ and ǰ to $s$ and ž, respectively. Actually, rule (12) applies nonvacuously to another segment as well. It will be shown in Section 6.4 that this rule must follow rule (5:56$l$), which laxes intervocalic obstruents in [+S] forms. Thus certain instances of $t^s$ from /k/ will have been converted by (5:56$l$) to $d^z$ at the point when rule (12) is reached. Being strident and lax (as well as anterior), $d^z$ will be changed to $z$ by (12). This explains the two steps in the derivation of $s$ from $k$ that were parenthesized in (7). The final step of converting $z$ to $s$ will be taken care of in the following section.

6.3.1.3. We must now account for the fact that the instances of /g/ affected by rule (8) and all instances of /ǰ/ are realized phonetically as tense segments. We note that *all* strident segments are [+tense] in phonetic representations. (The tense, voiced, strident segments $s^z$ and $f^v$ appear phonetically—see Section 2.5.2—but lax, voiced, strident $v, z, ž$ do not.) Since both /ǰ/ and the instances of /g/ in question have been converted to strident $ž$ by rule (12), we may postulate the completely general rule (13):

(13)                    [+strid]   →   [+tense]

Rule (13) gives not only $š$ from $ž$ in the case of underlying /g/ and /ǰ/, but also $s$ from $z$ in the case of underlying /k, +S/.

There is no reason why (12) and (13) cannot be combined as (14), with the cases applying in the order given:

(14)

$$[+\text{strid}] \quad \rightarrow \quad \left\{ \begin{array}{l} [+\text{cont}] \quad / \quad \left[ \overline{\left[ \begin{array}{l} \{-\text{tense}\} \\ \{+\text{ant}\ \} \end{array} \right]} \right] \\ [+\text{tense}] \end{array} \right\} \quad \begin{array}{l} a \\ \\ b \end{array}$$

Before further discussion of (14), let us pause to summarize the steps in the process of velar softening so far accounted for. These are as follows:

| /k/ | /k, +S/ | /g/ | |
|---|---|---|---|
| $t^s$ | $t^s$ | ǰ | (8) |
| | $d^z$ | | (5:56*l*) |
| s | z | ž | (14*a*) |
| | s | š | (14*b*) |
| *s* | *s* | *x* | PHONETIC FORM |

(The phonetic reflex of underlying /ǰ/ is also derived by the same rules, except for rule (8), of course, which is not relevant.) Thus, only $š→x$ remains to be accounted for, which will be done in the next two sections.

It is important to note at this point that (13) = (14*b*) must be in the grammar completely independently of velar softening and systematic phonemic /ǰ/. Rule (5:56*l*), which laxes obstruents in intervocalic position in [+S] formatives, has been formulated as simply as possible. That is, this rule has not been restricted so that it applies only to the noncontinuant obstruents $p, t, k, k^w$ to the exclusion of $f$ and $s$.[5] But $f$ and $s$ are always realized as tense segments in phonetic representations, even in [+S] forms. Even so, it is clearly incorrect to complicate

---

[5] It will become clear in Section 6.3.1.4 why rule (5:56*l*) never applies to $č$.

rule (5:56*l*) so that it does not apply to *f* and *s*. The reasons are the following. Instances of lax /g/ that undergo velar softening must be made tense at some point since they ultimately become tense [x]. Thus a single rule, namely, rule (14*b*), may be used to tense (a) *v* and *z* produced by (5:56*l*) from /f/ and /s/ in [+S] forms, (b) *ž* resulting from /g/ and /ĵ/, and also (c) *z* resulting from /k/→*t*ˢ→*d*ᶻ in [+S] forms. Furthermore, it will be argued in Section 6.4 that there is motivation for (14*b*) completely aside from the question of the simplicity of the formulation of (5:56*l*).

Let us summarize what we have done so far with the sample derivations in (15), in which the examples used are orthographic *japonés*, "Japanese," *laringe*, "larynx," *opacidad*, "opacity," *cuece*, "(he) cooks," and *mies*, "ripe grain." (Irrelevant details are omitted.)

| (15) | [−S] | [−S] | [−S] | [+S] | [+S] | |
|---|---|---|---|---|---|---|
| | ĵaponés | laringe | opakidad | kOke[6] | mEsE[7] | |
| | | ĵ | tˢ | tˢ | | (8) |
| | | | | dᶻ | z | (5:56*l*) |
| | | | | | φ | (5:56*m*) |
| | ž | ž | s | z | | (14*a*) |
| | š | š | | s | s | (14*b*) |
| | | | | we | ye | (6) |
| | šaponés | larinše | opasidad | kwese | myes | |

Nothing further must be done to *opasidad*, *kwese*, and *myes*. However, *šaponés* and *larinše* must still be converted into [x]*aponés* and *larin*[x]*e*, and we turn in the next two sections to a discussion of this change.

6.3.1.4. Before actually formulating the rule that effects the change *š*→*x*—the only step in the process of velar softening that remains to be accounted for (see (7))—we shall consider a set of facts relevant to this rule. We shall see that these data provide strong independent support for the rule under discussion in that they show that: (a) the segment *š* will be produced in the derivation of certain forms quite apart from velar softening and systematic phonemic /ĵ/; and (b) this *š*

---

[6] The form /kOke/ = *cuece* is the third person singular present indicative of the verb *cocer*, "to cook (especially by boiling)," which was mentioned previously in Section 5.2.3.3. The stem must be [+S] because of the diphthong (cf. *cocémos*, first person plural present indicative); the final segment of the stem must be /k/ because of the nominalization *co*[k]*ción*.

[7] The form /mEsE/ = *mies* must be [+S] because of the diphthong (cf. *meseguéro*); it must end in /E/ because of the plural *mieses*; the stem must have a single (intervocalic) /s/ because final *E* is deleted (in the singular *mies*) after at most one dental consonant.

must be converted into [x], just like the *š* produced in derivations such as those in (15).

Consider first the examples in (16), which show an alternation between [ks] and [x]:

(16)     *a*[ks]*ial–e*[x]*e*         axial, axile–axle
          *ane*[ks]*ar–ane*[x]*o*    to annex–annex (noun)
          *refle*[ks]*ivo–refle*[x]*o*    reflexive–reflex

Note that *a* alternates with *e* in a*xial–eje*. We already have in the grammar rule (4:34*d*), which changes *a* to *e* in the environment ——[i,y] in [+S] formatives. This fact, together with the fact that we must have a rule in the grammar in any event to convert *š* to *x*, suggests that (a) the left-hand members of the pairs in (16) are [−S] while the right-hand members are [+S], (b) systematic phonemic /ks/ underlies both [ks] and [x] in (16), (c) there are rules with the effect of /ks/→*š*(→*x*) in [+S] formatives, and, finally, (d) one of the steps involved in /ks/→*š* is *k*→*y*, so that the observed alternation between *a* and *e* can be accounted for in part by (4:34*d*). These suggestions are illustrated roughly in (17), with the form *eje*:

(17)          [+S]
               akse
               ayse     k → y *in some environment*
               ayše     s → š /y——
               eyše     (4:34*d*)
               eše      y → φ /——š
               exe      š → x

Extremely strong support for the proposals outlined in (17) is provided by examples such as those in (18), which show an alternation between [kt] and [č]:

(18)     *lá*[kt]*ico–le*[č]*e*       lactic–milk
          *no*[kt]*urno–no*[č]*e*    nocturnal–night
          *o*[kt]*avo–o*[č]*o*        eighth–eight

Note that the alternation between *a* and *e* in *láctico–leche* parallels that of a*xial–eje*. Other parallels between (18) and (16) are fairly obvious, and they suggest derivations like that of (19) for the right-hand members of the pairs in (18):[8]

---

[8] Consider also the irregular past participles *di*[č]*o* and *he*[č]*o* of [+S] *decir* and *hacer*. The irregularity of these forms stems ultimately from their athematicity; that is, the systematic phonemic representations are /dik+to/ and /hak+to/, with no theme vowel before the participial ending *-to* (see Section 3.4.1). Underlying *kt* in both forms and *a* in *hakto* are converted to [č] and [e], respectively, as suggested in (19).

(19)          [+S]
              lakte
              layte    k → y *in some environment*
              layče    t → č /y——
              leyče    (4:34*d*)
              leče     y → φ /——č

The primary difference between the derivations in (17) and (19) is that the step *š→x* is lacking in (19); otherwise they are quite comparable. Let us therefore propose, as a first approximation, that the first step in each is handled by rule (20), which changes *k* to *y* before *t* or *s* in [+S] forms:[9]

(20)    $\begin{bmatrix} +\text{obstr} \\ +\text{high} \\ +\text{S} \end{bmatrix} \rightarrow \begin{bmatrix} -\text{cons} \\ -\text{back} \end{bmatrix} \quad / \quad \text{——} \begin{bmatrix} +\text{obstr} \\ +\text{cor} \end{bmatrix}$

The second of the steps in derivations (17) and (19) can be stated as (21), which converts *t* to *č* and *s* to *š* after *y*:

(21)    $\begin{bmatrix} +\text{obstr} \\ +\text{cor} \\ +\text{S} \end{bmatrix} \rightarrow [+\text{high}] \quad / \quad \begin{bmatrix} -\text{voc} \\ -\text{back} \\ +\text{high} \end{bmatrix} \text{——}$

Now, the conjunction of several facts indicates that (20) and (21) must be collapsed into the single transformation (22):

(22)    $\begin{bmatrix} +\text{obstr} \\ +\text{high} \\ +\text{S} \end{bmatrix} \quad \begin{bmatrix} +\text{obstr} \\ +\text{cor} \end{bmatrix} \Rightarrow \begin{bmatrix} -\text{cons} \\ -\text{back} \end{bmatrix} \quad [+\text{high}]$
        $\quad\quad\quad 1 \quad\quad\quad\quad\quad 2 \quad\quad\quad\quad\quad\quad 1 \quad\quad\quad\quad 2$

Formulation (22) seems to be required for the following reasons: (a) there is apparently no reason why rules (20) and (21) cannot be ordered contiguously; (b) rules (20) and (21) stated separately are unnecessarily complex—nearly every feature involved must be mentioned in both rules; (c) although the facts are not absolutely clear, there may be instances of *ys* and *yt* that do not derive from *ks*

——————

[9] In the distinctive feature framework assumed in this study, velars are characterized by the tongue-body features [+high, +back]. (Alveolopalatal *č* is [+high, −back].)

In rule (20), [+back] is not specified to the left of the arrow and [+anterior] is not specified to the right of the dash since *č* never occurs in either of these positions. Furthermore, tenseness need not be specified for either of these segments since there are no tense-lax clusters and lax clusters occur only exceptionally.

and *kt*, and these are not changed to *yš* and *yč*—*paisano, aceite*, for example. Note, furthermore, that the formulation (22) perhaps brings out more clearly than does a separate statement of (20) and (21) the phonological processes involved in the mutual attraction between *k* and *s* on the one hand and *k* and *t* on the other. That is, the process is one of palatalization, which is a special case of assimilation: the first segment in each case—*k*—assimilates to the nonback position of the second segment—*s* or *t*—and the second segment assimilates to the high position of the body of the tongue of the first.

Let us now consider the fourth step in the derivations under consideration, namely, the deletion of *y* before *š* in (17) and before *č* in (19). We already have in the grammar rule (3:78*j*), which deletes high unstressed vowels and glides in certain environments. It might seem at first glance that this rule effects the step in question, but closer inspection reveals that this is not the case. Rule (3:78*j*) applies only in the environment of a preceding nonlow vowel with which the segment to be deleted agrees in backness. This condition is of course met in *eyše* (→*eše*→*exe*), *aneyšo* (→*anešo*→*anexo*), *refleyšo* (→*refléšo*→ *reflexo*), and *leyče* (→*leče*), but it is not met in *noyče* (→*noče*) and other such words that have a back vowel before the nonback *y* in question. Thus we must propose rule (23), which deletes *y* before *š* and *č*:[10]

(23)
$$y \;\rightarrow\; \phi \;/ \;\underline{\hspace{2cm}}\; \begin{bmatrix} -\text{back} \\ +\text{high} \end{bmatrix}$$

As stated, rule (23) deletes *y* before *y* and *i*, as well as before *š* and *č*. It is apparently not necessary to add anything to (23) that would exclude these results. The sequence *yy* presumably does not occur, and the sequence *yi* occurs only in a few marginal forms such as some foreign words like *yidish*, diminutives like *rayita*, and a few other miscellaneous cases. We may of course disregard the foreign words entirely. The failure of (23) to apply to diminutives like *rayita* may be explained by the presence of the boundary # before the diminutive suffix, which blocks application of the rule. The presence of # before certain affixes is discussed in some detail in Section 6.3.2.3. The phonological process represented by (23) is sometimes called

[10] Now it can be seen why rule (5:56*l*) does not apply to *č* (see note 5). This rule is ordered after (22) but before (23). Thus, at the time (5:56*l*) applies, instances of *č* that ultimately appear in intervocalic position in [+S] formatives are preceded by [−vocalic] *y* rather than by a vowel. Instances of *č* in [−S] formatives and non-intervocalic *č* in [+S] formatives are of course unaffected by (5:56*l*).

"absorption." That is, the high nonback glide *y* is deleted or "absorbed" by another high nonback segment.[11]

6.3.1.5. Let us now formulate the rule that effects the change *š* to *x* required to complete our discussion of velar softening and palatalization. The desired conversion can be accomplished by the following rule:

$$(24) \qquad \begin{bmatrix} +\text{obstr} \\ -\text{ant} \\ +\text{cont} \end{bmatrix} \rightarrow [+\text{back}]$$

The features [−coronal] and [−strident] are supplied to the output of (24) by marking conventions (XXIII) and (XXVII), respectively, of Chomsky and Halle (1968, Chapter Nine, Section 2.1). There seems to be nothing further of interest to say about rule (24). In other words, it is apparently just a peculiar fact about phonetic representations in Spanish that segments that have reached the stage of derivation *š* go on to become the tense, nonstrident, continuant, velar obstruent [x].

Summarizing this section briefly, we have seen that quite a large number of apparently very peculiar consonantal and vocalic alternations can be accounted for by the interaction of five rules: (8), (14), (22), (23), and (24). Even if particular subsets of the total set of relevant data did not exist, each of these rules would still be necessary to account for the remaining data. Thus the proposed set of rules taken together receives quite strong support from the total body of data considered. Additional, and somewhat surprising, support for certain of these proposals will be given in Section 6.4.

---

[11] The question now arises as to whether *y* is "absorbed" also when it *follows* another high nonback segment. That is, perhaps (23) is a "mirror image" rule in the sense of Bach (1967). The facts are not entirely clear, so I will merely sketch some of the data that must be taken into account in future research. Consider the regular third person plural preterit forms *un*[ye]*ron*, "they united," versus *bruñ*[e]*ron*, "they burnished," and *pul*[ye]*ron*, "they polished," versus *bull*[e]*ron*, "they seethed." Apparently [y] is deleted after the palatal (high nonback) segments represented orthographically as *ñ* and *ll*. The same phenomenon is often invoked to explain the absence of [y] in irregular preterit forms like *condu*[xe]*ron*, "they led," which is presumably *condušyeron* at an earlier stage of derivation. But compare now many regular preterit forms like *cru*[xye]*ron*, "they creaked," and *ri*[xye]*ron*, "they ruled." These are presumably *crušyeron* and *rišyeron*, respectively, at the stage of derivation at which *condu*[xe]*ron* is represented as *condušyeron*. Thus it is not immediately obvious why [y] is deleted in *condu*[xe]*ron* but not in *cru*[xye]*ron* and *ri*[xye]*ron*. Perhaps all that is involved is that the stems of *crujieron* and *rigieron* are [−S], while that of *condujeron* is [+S]. (See in this regard note 14 of Chapter 4.)

[š] never appears in surface phonetic form in Spanish?

6.3.2 *Exceptions to velar softening*

A grammar of Spanish must clearly include rules that account for the alternations termed velar softening here. There are, however, many instances of [k] and [g] before front nonconsonantal segments in phonetic representations, apparently in contradiction to the rules that have just been proposed. We will examine these seemingly exceptional cases now, presenting them in order of increasing difficulty of explanation.

6.3.2.1. Whether the root-final consonant of verb forms undergoes velar softening or not is independent of the segment that follows it in *phonetic* representations, as can be seen from the examples in (25) (which are orthographically *sacar, saco, saque,* forms of "take out"; *pagar, pago, pague,* forms of "pay"; *cocer, cuezo, cueza,* forms of "cook," *cocción,* "cooking"; *proteger, protejo, proteja,* forms of "protect," *protección,* "protection"):

(25)      *sa*[ka]*r, sa*[ko]*, sa*[ke]
         *pa*[ga]*r, pa*[go]*, pa*[ge]
         *co*[se]*r, cue*[so]*, cue*[sa]  (cf. *co*[k]*ción*)
         *prote*[xe]*r, prote*[xo]*, prote*[xa]  (cf. *prote*[k]*ción*)

It was shown in some detail in Section 3.3 that the distribution of *k, g, s,* and *x* in these forms, which appears to be completely erratic in the phonetic representations, is predictable in a completely regular way from the systematic phonemic representations. This demonstration will not be repeated here.

6.3.2.2. There are many contrasts of the sort shown in (26):

(26)      *á*[x]*il–á*[g]*ila*       agile–eagle
         [x]*eranio–*[g]*erra*       geranium–war
         [x]*is–*[g]*isa*       chalk–manner, fashion
         [x]*itano–*[g]*itarra*       gypsy–guitar
         [s]*itar–*[k]*itar*       to cite–to remove
         [s]*eja–*[k]*eja*       eyebrow–complaint
         *leu*[s]*emia–*[k]*iste*       leukemia–cyst

The failure of velar softening in the right-hand members of the pairs in (26) cannot be accounted for in the same way as in the examples of (25). A possible explanation for the contrasts here has been given in Section 5.2.5.3, namely, that the forms with [x] and [s] have systematic phonemic /g/ and /k/, respectively, while those with [g] and [k] have /gʷ/ and /kʷ/. It was shown in detail in Chapter 5 that /gʷ/ and /kʷ/ do not undergo velar softening. Thus, when none of the considerations of the previous section or of the sections to follow are pertinent, systematic /gʷ/ and /kʷ/ can be assumed to be the source of [g] (and [γ] in case spirantization has occurred) and [k]—spelled *gu* and *qu*, respectively—before front nonconsonantal segments in phonetic representations. For example, /agʷIla/, /gʷerra/, /kʷitarE/ may be assumed for *águila, guerra, quitar*, respectively.

6.3.2.3. An extremely large number of examples can be found that show contrasts such as those in (27):

(27)

| [k] BEFORE BACK VOWEL | [k] BEFORE FRONT VOWEL | [k] BEFORE BACK VOWEL | [s] BEFORE FRONT VOWEL |
|---|---|---|---|
| *Puerto Ri*[k]*o* | *puertorri*[k]*eño* | *Costa Ri*[k]*a* | *costarri*[s]*ense* |
| *arran*[k]*ar* | *arran*[k]*e* | *api*[k]*al* | *ápi*[s]*e* |
| *acha*[k]*ar* | *acha*[k]*e* | *apendi*[k]*ular* | *apéndi*[s]*e* |
| *ata*[k]*ar* | *ata*[k]*e* | *heli*[k]*al* | *héli*[s]*e* |
| *to*[k]*ar* | *to*[k]*e* | *fau*[k]*al* | *fau*[s]*es* |

| [g] BEFORE BACK VOWEL | [g] BEFORE FRONT VOWEL | [g] BEFORE BACK VOWEL | [x] BEFORE FRONT VOWEL |
|---|---|---|---|
| *hidal*[g]*o* | *hidal*[g]*ía* | *larin*[g]*ólogo* | *larin*[x]*e* |
| *cie*[g]*o* | *ce*[g]*era* | *conyu*[g]*al* | *cónyu*[x]*e* |

The considerations of Section 6.3.2.1 are irrelevant for the forms in (27) since none of the instances of [k] or [g] followed by a front vowel are verb forms. (*Arranque, achaque, ataque, toque* are all nouns, even though they happen to be homophonous with the corresponding present subjunctive forms.) The discussion in Section 6.3.2.2 is not applicable here either, since if the segments that do not undergo velar softening were /kʷ/ and /gʷ/, then the phonetic realizations before back vowels would be [kw] and [gw]: \**Puerto Ri*[kw]*o*, \**arran*[kw]*ar*, \**hidal*[gw]*o*, \**cie*[gw]*o*, etc. (See rule (5:56*j*), which deletes this *w* only before a front vowel.) Thus we must look elsewhere for a solution to the problem of accounting for the contrasts illustrated in (27).

Since all of these contrasts obviously have to do with derivational affixes of one kind or another, one might be tempted merely to subcategorize derivational affixes with respect to some feature that would determine whether or not the stem to which a particular affix is attached is subject to velar softening. It is of course logically possible that this is the correct solution. However, to fall back on such an *ad hoc* approach without first investigating other possibilities would be to abandon hope from the outset of gaining any insight into the problem. A detailed study of the syntactic and phonological properties of a large number of derivational affixes would be required in order to give a fully motivated account of the contrasts in question, but, for the present, the following seems to be a promising direction for future research.

Consider the fact that there are several superlative and diminutive forms that have unstressed diphthongs: $b$[wĕ]$nísimo$, $f$[wĕ]$rtísimo$, $v$[yĕ]$jísimo$; $p$[wĕ]$blíto$, $v$[yĕ]$jíto$. Note further that velar softening does not occur before these superlative and diminutive affixes—$ri$[k]$o$: $ri$[k]$ísimo$, $ri$[k]$íto$; $fla$[k]$o$: $fla$[k]$ísimo$, $fla$[k]$íto$; $lo$[k]$o$: $lo$[k]$ísimo$, $lo$[k]$íto$; $po$[k]$o$: $po$[k]$ísimo$, $po$[k]$íto$; $lar$[g]$o$: $lar$[g]$ísimo$, $lar$[g]$íto$; $cie$[g]$o$: $cie$[g]$ísimo$, $cie$[g]$íto$. Observe particularly both the unstressed diphthong and the failure of velar softening in $cie$[g]$ísimo$, $cie$[g]$íto$. Recall now the proposals made in Section 4.3.4 to account for unstressed diphthongs in the phonetic representations of forms of a number of categories. These proposals, which have to do with the internal structure of such forms and the cyclical application of rules, provide a well-motivated way of accounting for the failures of velar softening under discussion now. For example, the underlying representations of $cieguísimo$, $cieguíto$ are roughly those shown in (28):

(28)     $[_A\# \ [_A\#cEg\#]_A \ isImo\#]_A$

         $[_A\# \ [_A\#cEg\#]_A \ ito\#]_A$

At the point when velar softening (8) is reached in the sequence of rules (which will be in the second cycle before the stress rules have applied to the whole form to place stress on the affix), the representations of (28) will have been converted into those of (29):

(29)     $[_A\#\#cÉg\#isImo\#]_A$

         $[_A\#\#cÉg\#ito\#]_A$

The internal $\#$ before -$isImo$, -$ito$, which must be present in (29) to account for diphthongization and stress placement in the phonetic forms, automatically explains the failure of velar softening: given the conventions regarding rule application and boundaries,[12] rule (8) as stated can apply to the strings $gi$ and $g+i$ but not to the string $g\#i$ of (29).

It would be quite plausible, then, to propose that contrasts such as those illustrated in (27) can be accounted for on the basis of whether

[12] See Chomsky and Halle (1968, p. 67).

*freely added suffixes?*

derivational affixes are preceded by # or by +. Freely added suffixes are preceded by #; affixes of more restricted, largely lexically determined distribution are preceded by +.[13] The forms in (30) provide some examples:

(30)    *a.*    *rik#isImo* → *ri*[k]*ísimo*          extremely rich
               *rik#eza* → *ri*[k]*eza*            wealth

               *flak#ito* → *fla*[k]*ito*           skinny
               *flak#eza* → *fla*[k]*eza*          thinness

               *sek#isImo* → *se*[k]*ísimo*         extremely dry
               *sek#ia* → *se*[k]*ía*             drought

               *larg#isImo* → *lar*[g]*ísimo*        extremely long
               *larg#ito* → *lar*[g]*ito*           longish

               *santiag#eño* → *santia*[g]*eño*       from Santiago
               *santiag#ista* → *santia*[g]*ista*      Santiaguist[14]
               *santiag#ismo* → *santia*[g]*ismo*      Santiaguism

        *b.*   *costarrik+ense* → *costarri*[s]*ense*   Costa Rican
               *apik+e* → *ápi*[s]*e*             apex
               *laring+e* → *larin*[x]*e*          larynx
               *conyug+e* → *cónyu*[x]*e*          spouse

*doesn't this seem suspicious?*

While these sketchily outlined suggestions obviously have some merit, they perhaps raise as many questions as they answer. For example, representations such as *arrank#e* (→*arran*[k]*e*) and *indIk+e* (→*índi*[s]*e*) imply a quite different derivational relationship between the verb *arrancar* and the noun *arranque* on the one hand and the verb *indicar* and the noun *índice* on the other. It may be worth noting that in verb-noun pairs like *arrancar–arranque, achacar–achaque, atacar–ataque* it is generally the case that there is no semantic difference between the verb and the corresponding noun other than that associated with category membership. This is less generally the case in pairs like *indicar*, "to indicate," *índice*, "index."

It seems to me pointless to pursue these matters further at this time since discussion must be almost completely speculative until much more is known about syntactic, and especially derivational, processes

[13] For discussion of # before freely added suffixes in English, see Chomsky and Halle (1968, Chapter Three, Section 1.3.1).

[14] *Santiaguista* and *santiaguismo* are nonce forms concocted to illustrate the predictable failure of velar softening in such inventions.

in Spanish.[15] I think it quite reasonable to assume, however, that the environment of rule (8) is correct as it stands and that restrictions on the applicability of the rule are determined by factors extrinsic to its formulation, such as occurrences of # in strings to which (8) would otherwise apply.[16]

## 6.4 Final *e* deletion

At several points in this study evidence has been cited for a rule that deletes final *e* in certain environments. This rule has been stated (see (5:56*m*)), as a first approximation, as in (31):

$$(31) \qquad \begin{bmatrix} e \\ -\text{tense} \end{bmatrix} \rightarrow \phi \ / \ V \begin{bmatrix} +\text{cor} \\ +\text{ant} \end{bmatrix}_0^1 \underline{\quad} \#$$

The motivation for a rule like (31) is quite strong. Without a rule to this effect, the following phenomena, among others, would be more difficult or impossible to account for:

(a) Plurals of nouns and adjectives. The single shape /s/, rather than the alternants /s/ ∼ /es/ ∼ φ, can be posited for the plural formative. For example

| SINGULAR | PLURAL |
|----------|--------|
| poste | poste+s |
| dios¢ | diose+s |
| dosis | dosis+¢ |

---

[15] Plausible alternatives to the proposals made here come to mind immediately. For example, the contrast between words like *arran*[k]*e* and words like *índi*[s]*e* might be accounted for roughly as follows:

| arrank+a+e | indik+e | |
|------------|---------|---|
| | s | *velar softening* |
| φ | | (3:78*c*) |

[16] There are still other types of cases in which velar softening fails for one reason or another. For example, the present indicative of the verb *caber* is [ke]*po, cabes, cabe, cabemos, caben*. The historical explanation for irregular [ke]*po* is as follows, where historical rules are identified by roughly equivalent synchronic rules:

| kapyo | |
|-------|---|
| yp | METATHESIS |
| – | VELAR SOFTENING |
| – | (5:56*l*) |
| e | (4:34*d*) |
| φ | (3:78*j*) |
| *kepo* | |

Since apparently idiosyncratic forms like *quepo* have not been studied carefully, it is not known how close or how far this historical account is from the correct synchronic account.

(For a more detailed and impressive discussion see Foley (1967).)

(b) Stress prediction. Apparently anomalous stress on the final syllable of the phonetic representation of a large number of words can be assigned in a fairly simple way by assuming an underlying final *e* that is later deleted in the appropriate forms. Thus, in all infinitives, nouns like *compás* (plural *compáses*), *albañíl* (plural *albañíles*), and adjectives like *feróz* (plural *feróces*), *azúl* (plural *azúles*), stress will be assigned to the penultimate syllable of representations like *andare*($+s$), *compase*($+s$), *albañile*($+s$), *feroce*($+s$), *azule*($+s$), and so on.

(c) Velar softening. Consider words like *vo*[s], "voice" (plural *vo*[s]*es*), *vo*[k]*al*, "vocal." The occurrence of [s] rather than [k] in the phonetic representation of *vo*[s] can be accounted for with the underlying representation *voke*($+s$).

Thus there can be little doubt that a grammar of Spanish must contain a rule similar to (31). Let us proceed, then, to examine the formulation of the rule more closely. As stated, rule (31) seems to be correct in at least the following details:

(a) The vowel deleted is lax /E/ rather than tense /e/. Some supporting evidence was given in Section 3.4.3.

(b) The only consonants after which word-final *e* is deleted are dental, that is, [+coronal, +anterior]. Evidence is provided by the fact that the dental consonants *d*, *s*, *n*, *r*, and *l* are the only consonantal segments that regularly occur in word-final position in phonetic representations.

(c) Word-final *e* is not deleted after more than one dental consonant. This point was argued briefly in Section 2.6.2.3.

Still, the formulation of (31) must be refined, as becomes obvious when the following sets of facts are considered:

(a) Final *e* is never deleted after voiceless *t*: *combate*, *confite*, *tomate*, *disparate*, *trámite*, *intérprete*, and many other examples. (Note that in *trámite*, *intérprete*, the reason for the failure of *e* deletion cannot be that the vowel in question is preceded by more than one consonant: if the [t] in question came from *tt*, then the Latin stress rule would assign stress to the penultimate vowel.)

(b) Final *e* is nearly always deleted after voiced *d*, *n*, *l*, and *r*: *ataúd* (plural *ataúdes*), *origen* (plural *orígenes*), *ágil* (plural *ágiles*), *cráter* (plural *cráteres*), and an enormous number of other examples. The exceptions appear to be restricted to words of Mexican origin such as *atole* and *mole* and a handful of learned Latin and Greek words such as *pene*, *prole*, *epipáctide*, *Melpómene*.

(c)  For no obvious reason, final *e* is sometimes deleted, sometimes not, after [s]. This is true both of [s] from /s/ and of [s] from /k/:

DELETION

*cortés* (plural *corteses*)
*bus* (plural *buses*)
*compás* (plural *compases*)
*ciprés* (plural *cipreses*)
*res* (plural *reses*)
*lápiz* (plural *lápices*)
*lombriz* (plural *lombrices*)
*voz* (plural *voces*)
*cruz* (plural *cruces*)

NO DELETION

*pose* (plural *poses*)
*base* (plural *bases*)
*envase* (plural *envases*)
*fase* (plural *fases*)
*frase* (plural *frases*)
*roce* (plural *roces*)
*ápice* (plural *ápices*)
*índice* (plural *índices*)
*cruce* (plural *cruces*)

(d)  In the extremely few examples that exist, final *e* is deleted after *y*: *ley* (plural *leyes*), *rey* (plural *reyes*), *buey* (plural *bueyes*), *ay* (plural *ayes*), *convoy* (plural *convoyes*), *mamey* (plural *mameyes*). In *ley*, "law," and *rey*, "king," *y* may possibly derive from systematic phonemic /g/—cf. *legal*, "legal," *regicidio*, "regicide" —although this is far from obvious. This question seems to have no bearing on the deletion of *e*, however, since there is not the slightest reason to suppose that the [y] of *buey*, *ay*, etc., derives from underlying /g/, or from anything but /y/.

Taking care of the most obvious things first, let us propose that (31) provisionally be replaced by (32):

(32)

$$
\begin{bmatrix} e \\ -\text{tense} \end{bmatrix} \rightarrow \phi \;/\; V \left\{ \begin{array}{l} \begin{bmatrix} +\text{cor} \\ +\text{ant} \end{bmatrix}_0^1 \\[6pt] y \end{array} \right\} \underline{\hspace{1em}} \# \quad \begin{array}{l} a \\[12pt] b \end{array}
$$

Now reconsider the fact that *e* is *never* deleted after voiceless *t*; *always* deleted after voiced *d*, *n*, *l*, *r*; *sometimes* deleted after voiceless *s*. There is thus at least a partial correlation between deletion of final *e* and voicing of the preceding consonant in phonetic representations. If we look at an earlier stage of derivation, however, we see that the correlation is actually complete. First, let us revise case (*a*) of (32) as in (33):

(33)

$$
\ldots \;/\; V \begin{bmatrix} +\text{cor} \\ +\text{ant} \\ +\text{voice} \end{bmatrix}_0^1 \underline{\hspace{1em}} \#
$$

Now let us assume that (33) is ordered after rule (5:56*l*), which laxes (voices) intervocalic obstruents in [+S] formatives, but before rule (14), which tenses (devoices) all strident consonants. Rule (33) will then delete *e* not only after all instances of *d, l, n, r*, but also after those dental obstruents in [+S] formatives that have been laxed by (5:56*l*). In particular, in [+S] forms that have phonetic [s] from underlying /k/ or /s/, the dental will be laxed by (5:56*l*) and *e* will be deleted in the environment (33) (after which (14) will apply to give [s]). On the other hand, in [−S] forms with phonetic [s] from underlying /k/ or /s/, the dental will not be laxed by (5:56*l*), the environment of (33) will not be met, and final *e* will not be deleted. Thus, while final *e* deletion is not itself a [+S] rule, its application depends crucially in many cases on the output of (5:56*l*), which *is* a [+S] rule.

A few sample derivations, in which all irrelevant steps (such as diphthongization, epenthesis of initial *e*) are omitted, are given in (34):

(34)

| [−S]     | [+S]  | [−S]     | [+S]     | [−S]   | [+S]       |          |
|----------|-------|----------|----------|--------|------------|----------|
| trámite  | líte  | ápike    | diéke    | ágile  | estiércole |          |
|          |       | $t^s$    | $t^s$    |        |            | (8)      |
|          | d     |          | $d^z$    |        |            | (5:56*l*)|
|          | φ     |          | φ        | φ      | φ          | (33)     |
|          |       | s        | s        |        |            | (14)     |
| *trámite*| *líd* | *ápise*  | *diés*   | *ágil* | *estiércol*|          |

The following are the considerations that determine the sub-categorization of the examples in (34) with respect to the feature [S]:

(a)  *trámite*, "transaction," because of the stress on the antepenultimate syllable, must have lax penultimate *i* followed by a single *t*. In [+S] formatives lax *i* is lowered to *e* (rule (5:56*n*)) and intervocalic *t* is laxed to *d* (rule (5:56*l*)). Therefore *trámite* must be [−S].

(b)  *lite → lid*, "contest," "fight," "dispute," must be [+S] because of the laxing of *t* (cf. [−S] *litigar*, "to litigate").

(c)  *ápike → ápi*[s]*e*, "apex," must be [−S] because penultimate *i*, which stress placement shows to be lax, is not lowered to *e*. The last consonant must be underlying /k/ rather than /s/ because of *apical*, "apical."

(d)  *dieke → die*[s], "ten," must be [+S] because of the diphthong (cf. *decéna*, "group of ten," analogous to *docena*, "dozen"). The last consonant must be underlying /k/ rather than /s/ because of *década*, "decade."

(e)  *ágile → ágil* must be [−S] because of phonetic [i], which stress placement shows to be lax. Also, /g/, which is deleted in [+S] formatives in the environment *a——i* (rule (5:56*g*)), is not deleted in this form (and becomes [x] after velar softening).

(f)  *estiércole→estiércol,* "manure," must be [+S] because of the diphthong (cf. *estercolar,* "to fertilize (with manure)").

Let us now incorporate environment (33) into the rule of final *e* deletion and restate (32) as (35):[17]

(35)

$$\begin{bmatrix} e \\ -\text{tense} \end{bmatrix} \rightarrow \phi \ / \ V \begin{Bmatrix} \begin{bmatrix} +\text{cor} \\ +\text{ant} \\ +\text{voice} \end{bmatrix}_0^1 \\ y \end{Bmatrix} \begin{matrix} \text{—\#} & a \\[2ex] & b \end{matrix}$$

It seems quite clear that (35) is closer to the correct rule than is (31) or (32). There remain, however, several unresolved questions, to which we now turn.

First let us consider a number of exceptions to (35) in which *e* is deleted although the rule predicts that it should not be. An example of this sort is *relo*[x], "clock," "watch," where the plural form *relo*[x]*es* indicates that the singular should be, roughly, *reloxe*. This is the only word with final [x] in the dialect under study. (There are a few other such forms in other dialects—*troj, borraj, boj,* for example, which are venerable conversation pieces among philologists.) Therefore we might view *reloj* as an isolated oddity and simply disregard it. Alternatively, we might postulate in addition to the "major" rule (35) a corresponding "minor" rule (35′) that deletes final *e* in certain environments in specially marked formatives. There is also a third possibility. It might be claimed that the base form is /reloj̆/, with no final vowel, the *e* of plural *relojes* being inserted by some rule. Such a rule is not implausible since it might help to account for the well-known stress shifts in *carácter–caractéres* (cf. *cadáver–cadáveres*), *régimen–regímenes, ínterin–intérines.* The same rule might furthermore play a part in some of the cases in (27) where velar softening fails: for example, the *e* of *arran*[k]e(+*s*), as well as that of such words as *tan*[k]e(+*s*), "tank," and the relatively recent borrowing *che*[k]e(+*s*), "check," might be inserted after the first rule of velar softening has been passed in the sequence of rules.

There are also examples in which *e* is not deleted although the rule

---

[17] I retain [+voice] rather than [−tense] in case (*a*) of (35) because I do not know whether *n* and *l* are [−tense] or [+tense] when the rule of final *e* deletion applies. As mentioned in Section 2.5.2, it is assumed that [+voice] is assigned to the output of the obstruent-laxing rule (5:56*l*) by marking convention. Thus the specification of [+voice] rather than [−tense] in rule (35) still allows it to apply as desired to the lax segments resulting from rule (5:56*l*).

of final *e* deletion predicts that it should be. Exceptions to rule (35) of this sort are more numerous than the type just discussed. The forms *pene, prole, epipáctide, Melpómene* have already been cited. For concreteness, let us look more carefully at *prole*, of Latin origin. In this case there are at least four possible ways to account for the nondeletion of final *e*:

(a)  Distinguish a set of "classical" words exempt from (35).

(b)  Make the *ad hoc* but historically correct claim that the final *e* is [+tense].

(c)  Make the *ad hoc* claim that the final vowel is /i/ rather than /E/ or /e/. After rule (35) has failed to apply, this *i* would be lowered by the second case of rule (5:56*n*) to give the correct phonetic form.

(d)  Make the *ad hoc* claim that the systematic phonemic representation is /prollE/, to which (35) cannot apply. Geminate *ll* would then be reduced to *l* by rule (5:56*o*) to give the correct phonetic form.

In short, the significant fact about these exceptions to (35) is not that a solution is difficult to find, but rather that there is a plethora of answers of roughly equal plausibility but no principled way of choosing the correct answer from among them.

Rule (35) as stated also predicts the deletion of final *e* after zero dental consonants, that is, after vowels. It is not clear that this is correct for the dialect under study. Foley (1967) has noted that the final stress of words such as *hindú,* "Hindu," *bajá,* "pasha," *café,* "coffee," might be accounted for by assigning stress to the tense penultimate syllable of representations like *hindue, bajae, cafee,* the final *e* then being deleted. In support of this account, Foley has pointed to the plurals *hindúes, bajáes, cafés* (from *cafées* by a rule that coalesces two contiguous identical vowels). For my informants, however, the plurals of such words vary between *hindús–hindúes, bajás–bajáes,* etc., the forms with *-es* being felt as somewhat odd, artificial, or archaic (in fact even the singulars of most such words except *café* are felt to be slightly odd) and the forms with V́s as more natural. Thus these examples seem to argue more strongly against than for the deletion of *e* after a vowel. Moreover, there are a number of completely acceptable words in which *e* is not deleted after a vowel: *héroe, oboe, nadie, carie, barbarie, serie, intemperie, calvicie, molicie, hematíe, planicie, superficie, efigie,* and so on. Thus, at least after superficial examination, the evidence seems to be overwhelmingly against deletion of final *e* after a vowel in Mexican Spanish, whatever the case may be in other dialects.

The issues involved in all these types of exceptions to (35) as it is now formulated are complex, and the range of relevant data extremely wide. Rather than give facile but unmotivated answers, I prefer to leave a number of questions open until research permits them to be answered in a principled way.[18] It seems fair to say, however, that significant new insight into the problem is afforded by the considerations that have led to the formulation of rule (35) as it now stands. Of particular interest, perhaps, is the suggestion made concerning the ordered sequence consisting of the obstruent laxing rule (5:56*l*), the rule of *e* deletion (35), and the strident tensing rule (14*b*), whose interaction accounts for the apparently erratic deletion of final *e* after phonetic [s].

## 6.5 Cumulative list of rules

(1)
$$\begin{bmatrix} V \\ -\text{low} \end{bmatrix} \rightarrow \begin{bmatrix} +\text{high} \\ +\text{tense} \end{bmatrix} \Bigg/ \left\{ \begin{array}{c} \underline{\quad\quad}[+\text{past}] \\ \begin{bmatrix} \underline{\quad\quad} \\ 3\text{conj} \end{bmatrix} C_0 V]_v \end{array} \right\}$$

3: (19), (27), (78*a*)
4: (2), (8), (34*a*)

(2)
$$[+\text{obstr}] \rightarrow [+\text{tense}] \Big/ \underline{\quad\quad} \begin{bmatrix} +\text{obstr} \\ +\text{tense} \end{bmatrix}$$

5: (12), (56*a*)

(3)
$$t \rightarrow s \Big/ \begin{bmatrix} t \\ -1\text{conj} \end{bmatrix} + \underline{\quad\quad}$$

5: (28), (32), (33),
(42), (43*a*), (56*b*)

---

[18] The only other detailed proposal known to me concerning final *e* deletion is that of Foley (1965, pp. 76–78; 1967). Foley's rule is restricted to "vulgar" ([+S]) forms but deletes lax *e* after vowels and any single consonant rather than after voiced dental consonants only. Unfortunately this formulation leads to a mass of contradictions. For example, *nieve*, "snow," and *nueve*, "nine," must be "vulgar" because of the diphthongs (cf. *nevar*, "to snow," *noveno*, "ninth," *noventa*, "ninety"), yet *e* is not deleted after the presumably single consonantal segment. Conversely, *ágil(E)* and all other words ending in unstressed -*il* must be "erudite," as pointed out in the discussion following (34), yet *e* is in fact deleted. (Even if *ágil*, etc., are bimorphemic *ag+ilE*, etc., +*ilE*+ must be "erudite" regardless of the subcategorization of +*ag*+, etc. To claim that *ágil* is trimorphemic *ag+il+E* of which only +*E*+ is "vulgar" would obviously be a meaningless artifice.) Foley claims that an early rhotacism rule converts intervocalic *s* to *r* in all "vulgar" words. How, then, do we account for the deletion of final *e* in words such as *compás*, "(geometric) compass," "(musical) measure, bar" (plural *compases*), *dios*, "god" (plural *dioses*), *res*, "beef," "head of cattle" (plural *reses*)? For Foley, such words must be "vulgar" for *e* deletion, and *e* deletion occurs after at most one consonant, but this one consonant must be intervocalic *s* which rhotacises in "vulgar" words. These observations are not exhaustive, but I believe they suffice to show the inadequacy of Foley's proposals.

(4) $\begin{bmatrix} +\text{obstr} \\ -\text{cont} \end{bmatrix} \rightarrow \phi \ / \ [+\text{cons}]\text{——}[+\text{obstr}]$     5: (21), (56$c$)

(5)
$$t \rightarrow s \ / \ \text{——} \left\{ \begin{matrix} + \begin{bmatrix} -\text{cons} \\ +\text{high} \\ -\text{back} \end{bmatrix} V \\ s \end{matrix} \right\}$$
5: (23), (28), (32), (33), (42), (43$b$), (44), (56$d$)

(6) $\begin{bmatrix} p \\ +S \end{bmatrix} \rightarrow t \ / \ \text{——}t$     5: (14), (56$e$)  
6: (2)

(7) $\begin{bmatrix} +\text{obstr} \\ +\text{round} \end{bmatrix} \quad \phi \ \Rightarrow \ [-\text{round}] \ w$     5: (49), (56$f$)  
    $\quad\quad 1 \quad\quad\quad 2 \quad\quad\quad\quad 1 \quad\quad 2$

(8) $\begin{bmatrix} +\text{obstr} \\ -\text{tense} \\ \alpha\text{cor} \\ \alpha\text{ant} \\ +S \end{bmatrix} \rightarrow \phi \ / \ V\text{——}\begin{bmatrix} V \\ -\text{back} \end{bmatrix}$     5: (18), (27), (56$g$)

(9) $\begin{bmatrix} +\text{obstr} \\ -\text{ant} \\ -\text{cor} \\ \langle +\text{tense}\rangle \end{bmatrix} \rightarrow \begin{bmatrix} -\text{back} \\ \langle +\text{ant}\rangle \end{bmatrix} \ / \ \text{——}\begin{bmatrix} -\text{cons} \\ -\text{back} \end{bmatrix}$     3: (14), (78$b$)  
5: (56$h$)  
6: (1), (8)

(10) $\begin{bmatrix} -\text{cons} \\ +\text{round} \end{bmatrix} \rightarrow [+\text{voc}] \ / \ [+\text{cons}]\text{——}[+\text{cons}]$     5: (51), (56$i$)

(11) $w \rightarrow \phi \ / \ \begin{bmatrix} +\text{obstr} \\ +\text{back} \end{bmatrix}\text{——}\begin{bmatrix} V \\ -\text{back} \end{bmatrix}$     5: (54), (56$j$)

(12) $\begin{bmatrix} +\text{obstr} \\ +\text{high} \\ +S \end{bmatrix} \begin{bmatrix} +\text{obstr} \\ +\text{cor} \end{bmatrix} \Rightarrow \begin{bmatrix} -\text{cons} \\ -\text{back} \end{bmatrix} [+\text{high}]$     6: (20), (21), (22)  
    $\quad\quad 1 \quad\quad\quad 2 \quad\quad\quad\quad\quad 1 \quad\quad\quad 2$

(13)
$$V \rightarrow \phi \ / \ + \begin{bmatrix} \underline{\quad\quad\quad} \\ \langle +\text{irreg}\rangle \end{bmatrix} + \left\{ \begin{matrix} \begin{bmatrix} V \\ +\text{tense} \end{bmatrix} \\ \langle r\#[+\text{fut}]\rangle \end{matrix} \right\}$$
3: (3), (17), (36), (70), (78$c$)  
4: (34$b$)

(14)
$$\phi \;\rightarrow\; d \;\; / \; \begin{bmatrix} +\mathrm{cons} \\ -\mathrm{obstr} \\ -\mathrm{cont} \end{bmatrix} + \text{——} r$$

3: (71), (78$d$)

(15) $b \;\rightarrow\; \phi \;\; / \; i + \text{——}$

3: (28), (78$e$)

(16)
$$V \;\rightarrow\; [1\mathrm{stress}] \;\; / \; \text{——} \left\{ \begin{array}{l} (C_0(\check{V}C_0^1(L))V)C_0\#]_{N,A} \\[6pt] (([-\mathrm{perf}])C_0V)C_0\#]_V \end{array} \right\}$$

3: (5), (25), (78$f$)
4: (24), (34$c$)

(17) $\phi \;\rightarrow\; e \;\; / \; \#\text{——}s[+\mathrm{cons}]$

5: (note 5), (56$k$)

(18)
$$\begin{bmatrix} V \\ +\mathrm{low} \\ +S \end{bmatrix} \;\rightarrow\; \begin{bmatrix} -\mathrm{low} \\ \alpha\mathrm{back} \end{bmatrix} \;\; / \; \text{——} \begin{bmatrix} -\mathrm{cons} \\ +\mathrm{high} \\ \alpha\mathrm{back} \end{bmatrix}$$

3: (38), (39),
   (48), (78$g$)
4: (34$d$)

(19)
$$\begin{bmatrix} +\mathrm{obstr} \\ +S \end{bmatrix} \;\rightarrow\; [-\mathrm{tense}] \;\; / \; V\text{——}[-\mathrm{obstr}]$$

3: (20), (78$h$)
4: (34$e$)
5: (56$l$)

(20)
$$\begin{bmatrix} e \\ -\mathrm{tense} \end{bmatrix} \;\rightarrow\; \phi \;\; / \; V \left\{ \begin{array}{c} \begin{bmatrix} +\mathrm{cor} \\ +\mathrm{ant} \\ +\mathrm{voice} \end{bmatrix}_0^1 \\ y \end{array} \right\} \text{——} \#$$

3: (23), (78$i$)
4: (34$f$)
5: (56$m$)
6: (31), (32),
   (33), (35)

(21)
$$[+\mathrm{strid}] \;\rightarrow\; \left\{ \begin{array}{l} [+\mathrm{cont}] \;\; / \; \left[ \overline{\left\{ \begin{array}{l} -\mathrm{tense} \\ +\mathrm{ant} \end{array} \right\}} \right] \\[12pt] [+\mathrm{tense}] \end{array} \right\}$$

6: (1), (12),
   (13), (14)

(22)
$$\begin{bmatrix} -\mathrm{cons} \\ -\mathrm{stress} \\ +\mathrm{high} \\ \alpha\mathrm{back} \end{bmatrix} \;\rightarrow\; \phi \;\; / \; \begin{bmatrix} V \\ -\mathrm{low} \\ \alpha\mathrm{back} \end{bmatrix} \text{——}$$

3: (38), (40), (78$j$)

(23) $y \;\rightarrow\; \phi \;\; / \; \text{——} \begin{bmatrix} -\mathrm{back} \\ +\mathrm{high} \end{bmatrix}$

6: (23)

(24)
$$\begin{bmatrix} +\mathrm{obstr} \\ -\mathrm{ant} \\ +\mathrm{cont} \end{bmatrix} \;\rightarrow\; [+\mathrm{back}]$$

6: (1), (24)

(25)
$$\begin{bmatrix} V \\ +\text{stress} \\ +S \end{bmatrix} \rightarrow \begin{bmatrix} -\text{high} \\ -\text{tense} \end{bmatrix} \Big/ \underline{\qquad} \left\{ \begin{matrix} rV \\ \begin{bmatrix} +\text{cons} \\ -\text{obstr} \end{bmatrix} \begin{bmatrix} -\text{voc} \\ +\text{ant} \end{bmatrix} \end{matrix} \right\}$$

3: (21), (31),
   (34), (78$k$),
4: (22), (34$g$)

(26)
$$\phi \begin{bmatrix} +\text{stress} \\ -\text{tense} \\ -\text{high} \\ -\text{low} \\ \alpha\text{back} \\ +S \end{bmatrix} \Rightarrow \begin{bmatrix} G \\ \alpha\text{back} \end{bmatrix} \begin{bmatrix} -\text{back} \end{bmatrix}$$
$$\quad 1 \quad\quad 2 \qquad\qquad 1 \qquad 2$$

2: (28$a$), (47$a$),
   (69$a$)
3: (78$l$)
4: (34$h$)
6: (3), (4), (6)

(27)
$$\begin{bmatrix} V \\ +\text{high} \\ +\text{stress} \end{bmatrix} \begin{bmatrix} V \\ +\text{high} \end{bmatrix} \Rightarrow \begin{bmatrix} -\text{stress} \end{bmatrix} \begin{bmatrix} +\text{stress} \end{bmatrix}$$
$$\quad 1 \qquad\qquad 2 \qquad\qquad 1 \qquad\qquad 2$$

3: (42), (78$m$)

(28)
$$V \rightarrow \begin{bmatrix} -\text{high} \end{bmatrix} \Big/ \left\{ \begin{matrix} \begin{bmatrix} \underline{\quad} \\ -\text{tense} \\ +S \end{bmatrix} \\ \begin{bmatrix} \underline{\quad} \\ -\text{stress} \end{bmatrix} C_0 \begin{Bmatrix} \# \\ i \end{Bmatrix} \end{matrix} \right\} \quad \text{MINOR}$$

3: (9), (44), (45),
   (78$n$)
4: (4), (11), (20),
   (34$i$)
5: (39), (56$n$)

(29) $g \rightarrow \phi \;/\; \underline{\qquad} w$

2: (29), (47$b$), (69$b$)

(30) $rr \Rightarrow R$

2: (67), (69$c$)

(31) $C_i C_j \Rightarrow C_k \quad \text{where } C_i = C_j = C_k$

5: (15), (56$o$)

(32)
$$\begin{bmatrix} \alpha\text{voc} \\ \alpha\text{cons} \\ -\text{lat} \end{bmatrix} \rightarrow \begin{bmatrix} -\alpha\text{obstr} \\ \alpha\text{tense} \end{bmatrix} \;/\; \#\underline{\qquad}$$

2: (28$b$), (44$a$), (47$c$),
   (58), (59), (60),
   (69$d$)

(33) $r \rightarrow \begin{bmatrix} +\text{tense} \end{bmatrix} \;/\; \begin{bmatrix} +\text{cor} \\ +\text{distr} \end{bmatrix} \underline{\qquad}$

2: (58), (66), (69$e$)

(34)

$$[+\text{nasal}] \rightarrow \begin{bmatrix} \alpha\text{cor} \\ \beta\text{ant} \\ \gamma\text{back} \\ \delta\text{distr} \end{bmatrix} \bigg/ \left\{ \begin{array}{l} \text{———} \begin{bmatrix} +\text{obstr} \\ \alpha\text{cor} \\ \beta\text{ant} \\ \gamma\text{back} \\ \delta\text{distr} \end{bmatrix} \text{ANDANTE} \\ \text{———}(\#) \begin{bmatrix} +\text{obstr} \\ \alpha\text{cor} \\ \beta\text{ant} \\ \gamma\text{back} \\ \delta\text{distr} \end{bmatrix} \text{ALLEGRETTO} \end{array} \right\}$$

2: (12),
(14),
(47$d$),
(69$f$)

(35)

$$1 \rightarrow \begin{bmatrix} \alpha\text{ant} \\ \beta\text{distr} \end{bmatrix} \bigg/ \left\{ \begin{array}{l} \text{———} \begin{bmatrix} +\text{obstr} \\ +\text{cor} \\ \alpha\text{ant} \\ \beta\text{distr} \end{bmatrix} \text{ANDANTE} \\ \text{———}(\#) \begin{bmatrix} +\text{obstr} \\ +\text{cor} \\ \alpha\text{ant} \\ \beta\text{distr} \end{bmatrix} \text{ALLEGRETTO} \end{array} \right\}$$

2: (19), (20),
(47$e$),  (69$g$)

(36)

$$\begin{bmatrix} +\text{obstr} \\ -\text{tense} \end{bmatrix} \rightarrow \begin{bmatrix} +\text{cont} \\ -\text{strid} \end{bmatrix} \bigg/ \left\{ \begin{array}{l} \left\{ \begin{bmatrix} +\text{obstr} \\ +\text{cont} \\ \langle[-\alpha\text{cor}]\rangle \end{bmatrix} \right\} \begin{bmatrix} \text{———} \\ \langle\alpha\text{cor}\rangle \end{bmatrix} \text{ANDANTE} \\ \left\{ \begin{bmatrix} +\text{obstr} \\ +\text{cont} \\ \langle[-\alpha\text{cor}]\rangle \end{bmatrix} \right\}(\#) \begin{bmatrix} \text{———} \\ \langle\alpha\text{cor}\rangle \end{bmatrix} \text{ALLEGRETTO} \end{array} \right\}$$

2: (49),
(50),
(69$h$)

(37)

$$\begin{bmatrix} -\text{cons} \\ +\text{high} \\ -\text{stress} \end{bmatrix} \rightarrow [-\text{voc}] \bigg/ \left\{ \begin{array}{l} \underline{\quad}\text{V} \\ \text{V}\underline{\quad} \end{array} \right\}$$

2: (28$c$), (47$f$), (69$i$)
3: (78$o$)
4: (34$j$)

(38)

$$\begin{bmatrix} \alpha\text{voc} \\ \alpha\text{cons} \\ -\text{lat} \end{bmatrix} \rightarrow \begin{bmatrix} -\alpha\text{obstr} \\ \alpha\text{tense} \end{bmatrix} \bigg/ \text{V———} \left\{ \begin{array}{l} (\#)[\alpha\text{cons}] \\ \| \end{array} \right\}$$

ANDANTE  2: (28$b$), (44$b$),
ANDANTE:    (45), (47$g$),
*obligatory*   (61), (62),
ALLEGRETTO:    (64),
*optional*   (69$j$)

(39) $\text{R} \rightarrow \begin{bmatrix} +\text{obstr} \\ -\text{ant} \end{bmatrix}$ ALLEGRETTO (*optional*)

2: (68), (69$k$)

(40)

$$\begin{bmatrix} -\text{cont} \\ +\text{tense} \end{bmatrix} \rightarrow \begin{bmatrix} +\text{voice} \\ +\text{h.s.press} \\ +\text{glott con} \end{bmatrix} \bigg/ \text{———}(\#) \begin{bmatrix} -\text{obstr} \\ -\text{nasal} \end{bmatrix}$$

2: (53), (69$l$)

(41)
$$\begin{bmatrix} +\text{obstr} \\ -\text{h.s.press} \end{bmatrix} \rightarrow \begin{cases} [\alpha\text{voice}] & / \underline{\quad}(\#) \begin{bmatrix} +\text{cons} \\ \alpha\text{voice} \end{bmatrix} \\ [-\text{voice}] & / \underline{\quad}\| \end{cases}$$

2: (28d), (35),
(47h), (47i),
(52), (54),
(69m)

(42)
$$\begin{Bmatrix} \gamma_1 \\ {}_1\gamma^w \end{Bmatrix}_1 \rightarrow \begin{Bmatrix} y \\ {}_1w \end{Bmatrix}_1 \quad \text{ALLEGRETTO}$$

2: (31), (47j),
(69n)

(43) Erase all stresses but the rightmost in a word.

3: (67), (78p)
4: (34k)

# 7. Historical Excursus: Reflexes of the Medieval Stridents

## 7.1 Preliminary remarks

Spanish underwent a rather complicated series of phonetic changes within the 150 or 200 years centering around the sixteenth century. In this chapter we will examine the evolution during this period of two dialects, the Mexican dialect studied in the earlier chapters and the prestige dialect of Central Spain usually referred to as Castilian.[1] As an introductory overview, the beginning and end points of the relevant series of changes are given in (1). (The phonetic symbols are explained in detail in the next section.)

[1] Castilian pronunciation is characterized by Navarro Tomás (1965) as "la que se usa corrientemente en Castilla en la conversación de las personas ilustradas . . . estudiada especialmente en el ambiente universitario madrileño" (p. 8). Madrid, however, has provided the norm for "received pronunciation" in Spain only in relatively modern times. During the turbulent eight centuries (711–1492) of the Arab occupation of Spain, the center of linguistic prestige shifted a number of times (for a convenient historical summary, see García de Diego (1961, pp. 14–21)), carrying along phonological peculiarities of diverse origins. Thus the modern prestige dialect is historically an amalgam rather than the direct lineal descendant of the dialect native to a particular region of Castilla la Vieja or Castilla la Nueva.

(1)    *a.*    MEDIEVAL    f    tˢ    dᶻ    S    Z    č    š    ž

MEXICAN    f         s              č    x

*b.*    MEDIEVAL    f    tˢ    dᶻ    S    Z    č    š    ž

CASTILIAN    f    θ         S         č    X

Examples of the changes sketched in (1) are given in (2):

(2)    | MEDIEVAL | MEXICAN | CASTILIAN |
|---|---|---|
| ele[f]ante | ele[f]ante | ele[f]ante |
| bra[tˢ]o | bra[s]o | bra[θ]o |
| de[dᶻ]ir | de[s]ir | de[θ]ir |
| pa[S]a | pa[s]a | pa[S]a |
| ca[Z]a | ca[s]a | ca[S]a |
| [č]í[č]aro | [č]í[č]aro | [č]í[č]aro |
| di[š]e | di[x]e | di[X]e |
| mu[ž]er | mu[x]er | mu[X]er |

There is something less than total agreement among scholars concerning the details of the data to be studied here.[2] However, the
arguments I shall give depend most heavily on clear facts and not at
all on those details that are disputed or admittedly unknown.

As we consider in detail each step of the evolution summarized in (1),
we shall see that the theoretical framework assumed throughout this
study allows us to gain certain insights into rather puzzling aspects of
the changes in question. Furthermore, facts will be revealed as we
proceed that have ramifications for certain theoretical issues:

(a)    The recently proposed (Chomsky and Halle (1968)) feature
[distributed] is seen to play a crucial role in sound change.

(b)    A set of marking conventions for the feature [distributed] is
proposed. (Chomsky and Halle provide none.)

(c)    A modification of Chomsky and Halle's marking conventions
for stridency is suggested that takes distributedness into account

[2] The following sources have been consulted: Ford (1900), Gavel (1920), Alonso
(1941; 1947; 1951a; 1951b; 1951c; 1955), Spaulding and Patt (1948), Martinet
(1949; 1951), Canfield (1950; 1952; 1962), García de Diego (1950; 1961), Alarcos
Llorach (1951; 1961), Contini (1951) Joos (1952), Catalán (1956; 1957), Lapesa
(1956; 1959), Galmés de Fuentes (1962), Menéndez Pidal (1962). These works vary
in informativeness and reliability, some being tertiary interpretations. I have relied
most heavily on Alonso (1955) because of his extraordinarily rich documentation
consisting of nearly four hundred pages of citations from medieval and early modern
phoneticians.

and makes a larger set of predictions than the original conventions.

(d) It is widely believed that in Latin American (in particular, Mexican) Spanish, [θ] and [s] have merged as [s]. This is seen to be incorrect. It is rather the appearance of [θ] in Castilian—perhaps a century after the fictitious merger is believed to have taken place—that is the relevant innovation.

The conception of sound change that underlies this entire chapter was first proposed by Halle (1962) and was subsequently developed in such works as Kiparsky (1965), Halle and Keyser (1966), Chomsky and Halle (1968, pp. 249–252), Kiparsky (1968), and Postal (1968). On this view, sound change is not thought of as change to be accounted for directly in terms of actual utterances produced by speakers, but rather as change in the internalized grammars that underlie these utterances. Looking ahead, the particular kind of change in grammars that will be observed in the present data is a very common one, namely, the addition of rules at or near the end of the sequence of rules that constitutes the grammar prior to the change.

## 7.2 Phonetic details

The symbols [f,tˢ,dᶻ,č,ž,θ] are used in (1) with their familiar values. It is essential to the ensuing discussion, however, to state in detail the intended values of [S,Z,s,z,X,x]. The descriptions to follow will be facilitated by reference to the drawings of (3):[3]

(3)

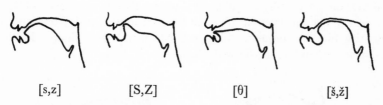

[s,z]          [S,Z]          [θ]          [š,ž]

The symbol [s] represents one of the "normal" types of *s*'s heard in most languages. The tongue is slightly convex, and the constriction is formed by the laminal or predorsal part against a fairly long section of the mouth at the upper alveolae. The symbol [z] stands for the lax counterpart of [s].

---

[3] These drawings are based on those of Navarro Tomás (1965), modified slightly in accordance with X rays by Wierzchowska (1965).

The [S] of Modern Castilian is strikingly different from [s] in auditory impression. ([S] is often perceived as [š] by phonetically unsophisticated observers, and it is sometimes described as "más palatal que [s]" by native writers.) According to Navarro Tomás (1965, pp. 105–108), the tongue is concave, with the apex—*not* the laminal or predorsal portion—raised to the posterior part of the upper alveolae. The symbol [Z] represents the lax counterpart of [S].

All of the segments illustrated in (3) are of course [+coronal], and all but [θ] are clearly [+strident].[4] The strident segments [s,z], [S,Z], and [š,ž] can be distinguished in a natural way with the features [distributed] and [anterior]. Comparing [s,z] and [S,Z], the zone of constriction where turbulence is produced is relatively long for [s,z], relatively short for [S,Z]; hence [s,z] (and [š,ž]) are [+distributed], while [S,Z] (and [θ]) are [−distributed]. In addition, it seems that [S,Z] should be further differentiated from [θ] and [s,z] in anteriority: [θ] and [s,z], with a forward tongue position, are [+anterior]; [S,Z], with a retracted, quasi-retroflex articulation, are [−anterior], which reflects the palatal-like auditory impression of [S] that was noted above. The segments [š,ž] are of course [−anterior]. Summarizing, the segments of (3) are characterized, in part, as in (4):

(4)

|  | [s,z] | [θ] | [š,ž] | [S,Z] |
|---|:---:|:---:|:---:|:---:|
| coronal | + | + | + | + |
| anterior | + | + | − | − |
| distributed | + | − | + | − |
| strident | + | − | + | + |

Mexican [x] and Castilian [X] are markedly different in auditory impression. (A Castilian speaker need utter only one word like *mu*[X]*er* or *naran*[X]*a* for even a phonetically unsophisticated Mexican to identify him as unquestionably non-Mexican.) The figures in (5) illustrate the differences in articulation:

(5)

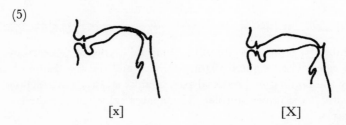

[x]                              [X]

---

[4] See Chomsky and Halle (1968, Chapter Seven) for definitions of all the features used here.

Mexican [x] is the "normal" nonstrident velar fricative found in a number of languages. Its point of articulation is essentially the same as that of velar [k,g,γ]. Navarro Tomás (1965, pp. 142–143) describes Castilian [X] as being articulated farther back than velar [k,g,γ], near the uvula. It can be seen in (5) that this results in a shorter constriction for [X] than for [x]. Thus it seems that [X] should be characterized as [−distributed], while [x] is [+distributed]. Navarro notes also that [X] is the most "áspera" of all the Spanish fricatives, even becoming "vibrante" rather than "fricativa" in energetic pronunciation. This suggests quite strongly that [X] is [+strident] while [x] is [−strident], technically as well as impressionistically.

To summarize the discussion in this section, and as a convenient reference for the following sections, the relevant feature specifications of all the segments mentioned are given in (6). Presumably the feature assignments other than those just discussed for [S], [X], etc., are not controversial.

(6)

| | f | θ | tˢ | dᶻ | s | z | S | Z | č | ǰ | š | ž | x | X |
|---|---|---|---|---|---|---|---|---|---|---|---|---|---|---|
| coronal | − | + | + | + | + | + | + | + | + | + | + | + | − | − |
| anterior | + | + | + | + | + | + | − | − | − | − | − | − | − | − |
| high | − | − | − | − | − | − | − | − | + | + | + | + | + | + |
| back | − | − | − | − | − | − | − | − | − | − | − | − | + | + |
| continuant | + | + | − | − | + | + | + | + | − | − | + | + | + | + |
| tense | + | + | + | − | + | − | + | − | + | − | + | − | + | + |
| distributed | − | − | + | + | + | + | − | − | + | + | + | + | + | − |
| strident | + | − | + | + | + | + | + | + | + | + | + | + | − | + |

## 7.3 Steps in the history of modern Mexican

The discussion here will proceed as follows. First there will be a statement of each step in the evolution of Mexican Spanish summarized as (1). Next the rule will be given that is added to the grammar with each change. In this section rules will be formulated as generally as possible but without regard for markedness. That is, each feature that actually changes will be mentioned in the rules, although it will be argued later that some of these features are supplied by convention. After the changes have been outlined, a few observations will be made concerning the chronology of the steps listed and certain other points in need of clarification.

### 7.3.1 *The changes*

(a)  f   tˢ   dᶻ   S   Z   č   š   ž
                  │   │
     f   tˢ   dᶻ   s   z   č   š   ž

$S \to s$, $Z \to z$; more generally, all nonhigh coronal stridents are [+anterior, +distributed]:

$$\begin{bmatrix} +\text{cor} \\ +\text{strid} \\ -\text{high} \end{bmatrix} \rightarrow \begin{bmatrix} +\text{ant} \\ +\text{distr} \end{bmatrix}$$

(b)  f   tˢ   s   dᶻ   z   č   š   ž
                    \  /
     f   tˢ   s     z     č   š   ž

$d^z \to z$; more generally, all lax stridents are continuants:

$$\begin{bmatrix} +\text{strid} \\ -\text{tense} \end{bmatrix} \rightarrow [+\text{cont}]$$

(c)  f   tˢ   s   z   č   š   ž
         \  /
     f    s    z   č   š   ž

$t^s \to s$; more generally, all anterior stridents are continuants:

$$\begin{bmatrix} +\text{ant} \\ +\text{strid} \end{bmatrix} \rightarrow [+\text{cont}]$$

(d)  f   s   z   č   š   ž
         \ /     \ /
     f    s       č   š

$z \to s$, $ž \to š$; more generally, all stridents are tense:

$$[+\text{strid}] \rightarrow [+\text{tense}]$$

(e)  f   s   č   š
                 │
     f   s   č   x

$š \to x$; it is not immediately obvious what the most general statement is in this case, but for the moment let us say:

$$\begin{bmatrix} +\text{obstr} \\ +\text{cont} \\ +\text{high} \end{bmatrix} \rightarrow \begin{bmatrix} -\text{cor} \\ +\text{back} \\ -\text{strid} \end{bmatrix}$$

All the Mexican changes just listed are brought together in (7):

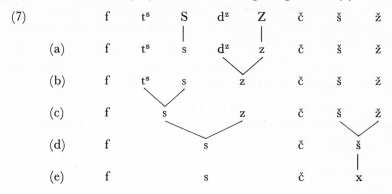

(7)        f      tˢ     S     dᶻ     Z     č     š     ž

(a)        f      tˢ     s     dᶻ     z     č     š     ž

(b)        f      tˢ     s           z     č     š     ž

(c)        f      s            z     č     š     ž

(d)        f            s           č     š

(e)        f            s           č     x

### 7.3.2 *Observations*

The first Mexican change ([S] → [s], [Z] → [z]) may have occurred long before the sixteenth century. Involved here is the extremely perplexing problem of the relative contribution of Northern and Southern Iberian dialects to New World Spanish. (For fuller discussion see Canfield (1962) and the references cited therein.) In any event, scholars do agree that the dialect in question had the [+anterior] continuants [s,z] at the beginning of the transitional period in question.

Spanish once had a noncontinuant [ǰ], which changed at some point to [ž]. It is not clear whether this change had already taken place before the sixteenth century. In any event, rule (b) would account for the change *ǰ→ž* along with *dᶻ→z*, which may be considered to define the starting point of the so-called sixteenth century evolution.

The changes *tˢ→s* and *dᶻ→z* are so similar that one would naturally assume that they are the result of the addition of a single rule. However, it seems clear that the change *tˢ→s* took place considerably later than *dᶻ→z*.[5] Thus the formulation of the rule for earlier *dᶻ→z* could not have been affected, at the time this change occurred, by the historically later change *tˢ→s*.

We may assume that all the rules of Section 7.3.1 except for the first (that is, the rule to effect the changes [S,Z] → [s,z]) remained in the grammar essentially unchanged. That is, there was no restructuring of the set of systematic phonemes except possibly for /S,Z/. This is evident from the fact that these rules are still synchronic rules in the modern dialect, as has been seen in previous chapters, especially Chapter 6.

[5] Alonso (1955, pp. 375–382).

Certainly by the time of change (b), probably centuries earlier, Spanish had the nonstrident continuant obstruents [β,δ,γ] in addition to the stops [p,t,k,b,d,g]. These will enter into the discussion at a later point, although only marginally.

## 7.4 Steps in the history of modern Castilian

The same format will be followed here as in Section 7.3: statements of each of the Castilian changes and the associated rules will be followed by a number of observations.

### 7.4.1 *The changes*

(a)  f   t$^s$   d$^z$   S   Z   č   š   ž

f   t$^s$   z   S   Z   č   š   ž

$d^z \rightarrow z$; more generally, all lax stridents are continuants:

$$\begin{bmatrix} +\text{strid} \\ -\text{tense} \end{bmatrix} \rightarrow [+\text{cont}]$$

(b)  f   t$^s$   z   S   Z   č   š   ž

f   t$^s$   s   S   č   š

$z \rightarrow s$, $\check{Z} \rightarrow S$, $\check{z} \rightarrow \check{s}$; more generally, all stridents are tense:

$$[+\text{strid}] \rightarrow [+\text{tense}]$$

(c)  f   t$^s$   s   S   č   š

f   s   S   č   š

$t^s \rightarrow s$; more generally, all anterior stridents are continuants:

$$\begin{bmatrix} +\text{ant} \\ +\text{strid} \end{bmatrix} \rightarrow [+\text{cont}]$$

(d)  f   s   S   č   š

f   θ   S   č   X

$s \rightarrow \theta$, $\check{s} \rightarrow X$; the most general statement seems to be:

$$\begin{bmatrix} \alpha\text{ant} \\ +\text{strid} \\ +\text{cont} \\ +\text{distr} \end{bmatrix} \rightarrow \begin{bmatrix} \alpha\text{cor} \\ -\alpha\text{back} \\ -\text{distr} \\ -\alpha\text{strid} \end{bmatrix}$$

All the Castilian changes just listed are shown in the single diagram (8):

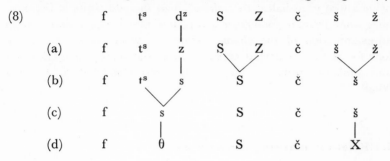

7.4.2 *Observations*

All but the first of the observations made concerning the Mexican developments are applicable also in the case of Castilian. Mexican rules (b), (c), and (d) are the same as Castilian rules (a), (c), and (b), respectively. Thus the innovations consisting of the addition of each of these rules are shared by the two dialects, although in a different order. The principal differences, then, between the history of Castilian and that of Mexican until relatively modern times are that Castilian has retained apical [S], the loss of lax stridents occurred earlier in Castilian than in Mexican, and Castilian developed nonstrident [θ] and strident [X] while Mexican did not.

This last divergence is of particular interest. Scholars have been unable to determine the chronology of [s] → [θ] with respect to [š] → [X], although there is some preference for considering [s] → [θ] as the later of the two changes.[6] Because of this uncertainty, I have given the single rule (d) to account for the two changes. It will be argued, however, that (d) must be split into two rules.

After change (c), Castilian had the five stridents [f,s,S,č,š], of which four were continuants ([f,s,S,š]) and four were coronal ([s,S,č,š]). It could very plausibly be argued that this delicate situation could not long resist change. Change did occur, but at a rather high price in terms of markedness. Not only was the unusual and presumably highly marked retracted apical [S] retained, but also both the relatively common segments [s] and [š] changed to the more unusual and presumably more highly marked nonstrident [θ] and strident [X]. By the same token, it is extremely difficult to tease out of rule (d) any obvious gain in the simplicity or symmetry of the resulting phonetic

[6] Alonso (1955, pp. 405 ff.), Lapesa (1959, pp. 245–248), Alarcos Llorach (1961, pp. 263–265), Canfield (1962, pp. 71–72), Menéndez Pidal (1962, p. 113).

system. Surely the appearance of [θ] and [X] either simultaneously or nearly so in a dialect that already had the odd segment [S] must obey some general phonological principle that is not apparent from an examination of the changes alone. It would seem natural to look for at least a partial explanation in the theory of markedness and "linking" proposed by Chomsky and Halle (1968, Chapter Nine).

## 7.5 Relevant marking conventions

The partial set of marking conventions postulated by Chomsky and Halle did not include reference to their newly proposed feature [distributed]. This feature, however, has figured prominently in our discussion thus far: it plays an important role in marking the distinctions among the segments of (3) and (5), and it has appeared in several of the rules given for the two dialects in question. Thus, if the sound changes just sketched are to be investigated in terms of the theory of markedness, provision must be made in this theory for the feature [distributed].

I will now tentatively propose a set of marking rules for [distributed]. The specifications relevant to predicting distributedness for a number of obstruents are given in (9). (The intended values of nonconventional symbols such as [P,T] are defined by the feature specifications shown.) Only those obstruents whose status as marked or unmarked for distributedness seems most clear are considered here. That is, the indications $u$ for "unmarked" and $m$ for "marked" that are given below the plus-minus values for [distributed] in (9) appear to me to be relatively noncontroversial.

(9)

| | $p^f$ | $p^\phi$ | | | $t^s$ | $t^\theta$ | | | | | | | | | | | |
|---|---|---|---|---|---|---|---|---|---|---|---|---|---|---|---|---|---|
| | f | φ | p | P | s | θ | t | T | S | š | č | $x_1$ | x | X | $k_1$ | k | K |
| coronal | − | − | − | − | + | + | + | + | + | + | + | − | − | − | − | − | − |
| anterior | + | + | + | + | + | + | + | + | − | − | − | − | − | − | − | − | − |
| high | − | − | − | − | − | − | − | − | − | + | + | + | + | + | + | + | + |
| back | − | − | − | − | − | − | − | − | − | − | − | − | + | + | − | + | + |
| delayed release | + | + | − | − | + | + | − | − | + | + | + | + | + | + | − | − | − |
| distributed | − | + | + | − | + | − | − | + | − | + | + | + | + | − | + | + | − |
| | $u$ | $m$ | $u$ | $m$ | $u$ | $m$ | $u$ | $m$ | $m$ | $u$ | $u$ | $u$ | $u$ | $m$ | $u$ | $u$ | $m$ |
| strident | + | − | − | − | + | − | − | − | + | + | + | − | − | + | − | − | − |

The conventions for interpreting "marked" and "unmarked" for distributedness can be stated as in (10):[7]

(10)

$$[u \text{ distr}] \rightarrow \left\{ \begin{array}{llll} [-\alpha\text{distr}] & / & \begin{bmatrix} -\text{cor} \\ +\text{ant} \\ \alpha\text{del rel} \end{bmatrix} & a \\\\ [\alpha\text{distr}] & / & \begin{bmatrix} +\text{cor} \\ +\text{ant} \\ \alpha\text{del rel} \end{bmatrix} & b \\\\ [+\text{distr}] & / & \begin{bmatrix} \phantom{-} \\ -\text{ant} \end{bmatrix} & c \end{array} \right\}$$

*this is just for Spanish? or for all logs?*

Convention (10) is of course a first approximation which will have to be extended to take into account sonorant consonants, and which perhaps must be modified in other ways. It does, however, make the correct predictions in the case of the obstruents of (9), which includes all the segments we are concerned with in the present discussion of Spanish, and other obstruents as well.

Let us turn now to stridency, for which Chomsky and Halle give the interpretive convention (11):

(11)

$$[u \text{ strid}] \rightarrow \left\{ \begin{array}{llll} [-\text{strid}] & / & \left\{ \begin{bmatrix} \phantom{-} \\ -\text{obstr} \end{bmatrix} \right. & a \\ & & \left. \begin{bmatrix} \phantom{-} \\ -\text{ant} \\ -\text{cor} \end{bmatrix} \right\} & b \\\\ [\alpha\text{strid}] & / & \begin{bmatrix} \alpha\text{del rel} \\ \left\{ \begin{array}{l} +\text{ant} \\ +\text{cor} \end{array} \right\} \end{bmatrix} & c \end{array} \right\}$$

Convention (11), which does not take distributedness into account, requires for its proper application that some of the segments in (9) be

---

[7] Recall from Chomsky and Halle (1968, p. 403) that marking conventions are interpreted differently from phonological rules in that the schema $[uF] \rightarrow [\alpha F]$ (where $\alpha = +$ or $-$ and F is some feature) represents the pair of rules $[uF] \rightarrow [\alpha F]$ and $[mF] \rightarrow [-\alpha F]$ (where $--=+$ and $-+=-$).

marked for stridency. I should like to claim, rather, that all of the segments shown in (9) are unmarked for stridency, the plus-minus value of which is predictable from the other feature specifications in (9), including those for distributedness. The line of reasoning that has led to this claim can be reconstructed roughly as follows. In early theories of distinctive features it was assumed that stridency was the unique feature that distinguishes, for example, strident labiodental [f] from nonstrident bilabial [ɸ], strident dorsoalveolar [s] from non-strident apicodental [θ], and strident alveolopalatal [š] from non-strident palatovelar [$x_1$]. It has often been observed, however, that stridency obviously does not account for the entirely analogous differences in point of articulation among nasals. Recent revisions of distinctive feature theory, in particular the introduction of the features [coronal], [anterior], and [distributed], have changed the picture: stridency is no longer the sole feature that distinguishes the pairs [f,ɸ], [s,θ], [š,$x_1$], and the three features just mentioned also characterize the distinctions among the corresponding pairs of nasals. This now suggests, at least, that stridency is not the "dominant" distinction between pairs of obstruents like [f,ɸ]; rather, given a particular articulatory configuration, the stridency or nonstridency of a segment follows, in the un-marked case, as a consequence of the geometry of the vocal organs, which includes of course the distributedness or nondistributedness of the zone of constriction.

I propose, then, that Chomsky and Halle's marking convention for stridency be replaced by (12):

(12)

$$[u \text{ strid}] \rightarrow \left\{ \begin{array}{l} [-\text{strid}] \quad / \left[ \overline{-\text{del rel}} \right] \qquad\qquad\qquad\qquad a \\[2em] \left\{ \begin{array}{l} [-\alpha\text{strid}] \quad / \left[ \begin{array}{l} \overline{\quad} \\ \alpha\text{distr} \\ -\text{cor} \end{array} \right] \qquad b \\[3em] [\alpha\text{strid}] \quad / \left[ \begin{array}{l} \overline{\quad} \\ \alpha\text{distr} \\ +\text{cor} \\ +\text{ant} \end{array} \right] \\[4em] [+\text{strid}] \quad / \left[ \begin{array}{l} \overline{\quad} \\ +\text{cor} \\ -\text{ant} \end{array} \right] \end{array} \right\} \quad / \left[ \overline{+\text{del rel}} \right] \quad c \\ \qquad\qquad\qquad\qquad\qquad\qquad\qquad\qquad\qquad\qquad\qquad d \end{array} \right.$$

Some of the empirical consequences of incorporating (10) and (12) into the set of marking conventions for consonants will be investigated in the next section.[8]

*skimmed*

## 7.6 The historical rules and "linking"

The theory of markedness assumed here defines a relationship not only between marking conventions and phonological matrices but also between the conventions and phonological rules (see Chomsky and Halle (1968, Chapter Nine, Section 4)). Let us now return to the rules given in Sections 7.3 and 7.4 and consider the effects of the interpretive conventions (10) and (12) proposed here in terms of Chomsky and Halle's theory of linking.

Mexican rule (a) is repeated here for convenience as (13):

$$(13) \qquad \begin{bmatrix} +\text{cor} \\ +\text{strid} \\ -\text{high} \end{bmatrix} \rightarrow \begin{bmatrix} +\text{ant} \\ +\text{distr} \end{bmatrix}$$

The effect of (13) is to change [S] to [s] and [Z] to [z]. Now suppose that the historical changes had instead been [S]→[θ], [Z]→[ð]. In this case the most general rule, ignoring linking, would be (14):

$$(14) \qquad \begin{bmatrix} -\text{ant} \\ +\text{strid} \\ -\text{high} \end{bmatrix} \rightarrow \begin{bmatrix} +\text{ant} \\ -\text{strid} \end{bmatrix}$$

Presumably, the changes [S]→[s], [Z]→[z] are more natural than [S]→[θ], [Z]→[ð], and the system resulting from the first set of changes is more natural than that resulting from the second set. This is not reflected in the rules, however, since rule (13) is not simpler than (14). Now let us make use of conventions (10) and (12) and the linking relation, which allow us to replace (13) by (15):

$$(15) \qquad \begin{bmatrix} +\text{strid} \\ -\text{high} \end{bmatrix} \rightarrow [+\text{ant}]$$

Rule (15) applies to the [−high] segments [S,Z], making them [+anterior]; case (b) of convention (10) supplies [+distributed]; and

---

[8] It must be asked at this point whether the feature [strident] really exists at all, that is, whether there are actually any two segments that differ *only* in stridency and whether there are any rules in which [strident] cannot be eliminated without loss of generality. These questions must obviously remain open at present, but some preliminary investigation suggests that [strident] may indeed be entirely redundant,

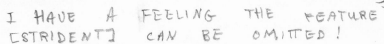

*I HAVE A FEELING THE FEATURE [STRIDENT] CAN BE OMITTED !*

case (*c*) of (12) vacuously reassigns [+strident]. Rule (15) also applies vacuously to [f,tˢ,dᶻ], and in each case conventions (10) and (12) vacuously reassign the correct values for distributedness and stridency. Note now that no comparable simplification of (14) is possible. Thus in this case conventions (10) and (12) together with the theory of linking have had the correct empirical consequences.

Mexican rule (e) is repeated here as (16):

(16)
$$
\begin{bmatrix} +\text{obstr} \\ +\text{cont} \\ +\text{high} \end{bmatrix} \rightarrow \begin{bmatrix} -\text{cor} \\ +\text{back} \\ -\text{strid} \end{bmatrix}
$$

The effect of (16) is to change [š] to [x]. Suppose now that the change had instead been [š]→[S], which seems wildly improbable. The most general rule would then be (17):

(17)
$$
\begin{bmatrix} +\text{obstr} \\ +\text{cont} \\ +\text{high} \end{bmatrix} \rightarrow \begin{bmatrix} -\text{high} \\ -\text{distr} \end{bmatrix}
$$

Rule (17) is simpler than (16), which is totally counterintuitive. Given the interpretive conventions, however, (16) may be replaced by (18):

(18)
$$
\begin{bmatrix} +\text{obstr} \\ +\text{cont} \\ +\text{high} \end{bmatrix} \rightarrow [+\text{back}]
$$

Rule (18) applies to [š], making it [+back], case (*b*) of Chomsky and Halle's convention (XXIII) supplies [−coronal], and case (*b*) of convention (12) supplies [−strident]. As was the case with rule (15), rule (18) is simpler than either (16) or (17), and no comparable simplification of (17) is possible. Thus again the correct empirical consequences follow from our assumptions.

We should note here that the grammar included a spirantization rule at the time when the innovation represented by (18) occurred. That is, the nonstrident continuants [β,δ,γ] were already in the language (in Castilian as well as Mexican). Thus rule (18) actually applied to [γ] as well as to [š], but it applied vacuously in the former case.

The next rule we shall consider is Castilian rule (d), which accounts for the changes [s]→[θ] and [š]→[X]. This rule is repeated here as rule (19):

(19)
$$
\begin{bmatrix} \alpha\text{ant} \\ +\text{strid} \\ +\text{cont} \\ +\text{distr} \end{bmatrix} \rightarrow \begin{bmatrix} \alpha\text{cor} \\ -\alpha\text{back} \\ -\text{distr} \\ -\alpha\text{strid} \end{bmatrix}
$$

It was noted at the end of Section 7.4.2 that the innovations effected by this rule and the resulting phonetic system are, on surface examination, extremely strange. This is reflected quite clearly in the extraordinary form of rule (19). Let us now discard this rule and, for the sake of argument, try a different approach to the changes in question. First let us assume that after change (c) Castilian shared with Mexican the innovation that consisted of the addition of (18) to the existing grammar. The effect of this change on the phonetic output of Castilian is shown in (20):

(20)
$$
\begin{array}{cccccc}
f & s & S & \check{c} & \check{s} & (\gamma) \\
 & & & & | & \\
f & s & S & \check{c} & x & (\gamma)
\end{array}
$$

Continuing the argument, let us now assume that the next change in Castilian was $s \rightarrow \theta$. The maximally general rule that effects this change is (21):

(21)
$$
\begin{bmatrix} +\text{tense} \\ +\text{cont} \end{bmatrix} \rightarrow [-\text{distr}]
$$

When rule (21) applies to [s], it assigns the feature [−distributed], which links (21) to case (c) of convention (12), which in turn assigns the feature [−strident], giving the desired segment [θ]. But this general rule also applies to [f] and [S], in this case vacuously, and to [x], giving, after application of case (b) of convention (12), strident [X]. Noncontinuant [č] and lax [γ], on the other hand, are not subject to rule (21). In short, when (18) and (21) apply, in the order given, to the Castilian segments existing after change (c), the result achieved is precisely that of change (d), that is, the relevant segments of modern Castilian, as shown in (22):

(22)
$$
\begin{array}{cccccc}
f & s & S & \check{c} & \check{s} & (\gamma) \\
 & & & & | & \\
f & s & S & \check{c} & x & (\gamma) \\
 & | & & & | & \\
f & \theta & S & \check{c} & X & (\gamma)
\end{array}
$$

Now, apparently, the puzzling situation described in Section 7.4.2 can be clarified to a great extent. Certain empirical proposals have been made about the form of phonological rules, about the status of certain segments as marked or unmarked for distributedness and stridency, and about the operation of linking—all of this, it should be noted, in complete independence of the history of Castilian Spanish. If these proposals are correct in relevant respects, then Castilian change (d) becomes less perplexing. The utterly incredible rule (d) may be replaced by the quite simple and general ordered rules (18) and (21). Furthermore, the Mexican change $š \rightarrow x$ and the corresponding Castilian change can now be seen as a shared innovation, accounted for by the addition of the same rule, rather than as innovations requiring quite different rules. We observed before that Mexican and Castilian shared three of the "sixteenth century changes," although in different orders; now the addition of rule (18) increases to four the number of shared rules. In short, the quite different results in the two dialects are due to (a) the absence of the change $[S,Z] \rightarrow [s,z]$ in Castilian, and (b) the absence of the change $[s] \rightarrow [\theta]$ in Mexican.

As mentioned in Section 7.4.2, scholars have not been able to determine the order of the changes $[s] \rightarrow [\theta]$ and $[š] \rightarrow ([x] \rightarrow) [X]$. Suppose, for a moment, that the order was the opposite of that just assumed. A little work with pencil and paper will show that the rules that must then be formulated are more complex than (18) and (21) and, furthermore, do not allow the velarization of $[š]$ to be considered as a single innovation shared by Mexican and Castilian. These facts, while by no means constituting a formal proof, suggest strongly that the relative chronology of these innovations was in fact that shown in (22). It seems, then, that this is a paradigm instance of a case in which theoretical considerations may be allowed to tentatively settle factual questions whose answers are underdetermined by clear data.

A little more work with pencil and paper will show that without the assumption that stridency is determined by distributedness, (in connection with other features,) there is no clear generalization to be made about the changes in question, under any assumption about their order. In other words, we would again be facing the puzzling situation described at the end of Section 7.4.2.

To conclude the present section, we may observe that if the proposals made here are correct, in particular rules (18) and (21), then there are a number of implications for linguistic theory. First, the still largely unfamiliar feature [distributed] must be granted recognition: generalizations concerning attested sound changes can be captured with reference to distributedness but not with reference to stridency, although on superficial examination the latter appears to be the feature most directly involved.[9] Secondly, and more generally, the proposals made here have assumed a phonological theory that includes a theory of markedness and the associated theory of linking. Given this general theory, which also includes an evaluation metric, we are forced to select rules (18) and (21) from the set of all possible rules compatible with the data since these are the most highly valued rules that are empirically correct. These rules in turn provide the basis for some amount of insight into a set of extraordinary sound changes. Considerable support is thereby provided for the phonological theory that makes this insight possible.

## 7.7 On θ in Mexican Spanish

The remaining discussion of this chapter is of little theoretical import but of considerable popular interest. It is widely believed that the historical development of Latin American, and in particular Mexican, Spanish included the addition of a rule with the effect of (23):[10]

(23)                              θ → s

The assumption that (23) is a historical rule of Latin American Spanish seems to be based on two facts: (a) [θ] occurs in modern Castilian, and (b) Spain colonized Latin America, not vice versa. In other words, no actual linguistic evidence has ever been presented in support of such a sound change.

The assertion has also been made that (23) is a rule in synchronic grammars of Latin American dialects.[11] However, while it has been convincingly argued that some instances of phonetic [s] in Latin American dialects are derived from some systematic phoneme other than /s/, it has never been shown that this phoneme is /θ/ or that θ appears at any step in the derivation of the instances of phonetic [s] in question. Certainly none of the matters examined in the preceding chapters of the present study indicate the existence of θ at any stage of derivation of any instance of phonetic [s].

Let us look more closely at the historical situation. As has been indicated in previous sections of this chapter, no factual basis for a historical rule such as (23) is to be found in the specialized literature on the

[9] There is, of course, considerable additional evidence for the feature [distributed]. See Chomsky and Halle (1968, Chapter Seven, Section 4.4), as well as Chapter 2 of the present study.

[10] See Sapir (1925), Sableski (1965), Saporta (1965).

[11] See Foley (1965), Sableski (1965), Saporta (1965).

subject. Alonso (1955, p. 410) has suggested that [θ] was not general in Castilian until perhaps as late as the middle of the eighteenth century. But this is an extreme estimate; let us be more conservative and push the date of the change [s]→[θ] back to the seventeenth century. Let us assume, for the sake of argument, that Mexican shared this change with Castilian and that Mexican had the additional innovation [θ]→[s], obviously not shared by Castilian. But it is known that Mexican had [s] rather than [θ] in the seventeenth century. Therefore, both (24a) and (24b) would have had to have been added to the grammar of Mexican in the seventeenth century:

(24)                       *a.*   s   →   θ
                              *b.*   θ   →   s

The absurdity of this claim is compounded by the fact that not one single historical datum has ever been offered in support of either (24a) or (24b).

Recall that Cortés reached Tenochtitlán, now Mexico City, on November 8, 1519. Shortly thereafter, colonists from various regions of Spain began arriving in large numbers. Certainly many of these were Castilians, although the majority probably were not.[12] At any rate, by the time of the most conservative estimate of the generalization of [θ] in Castilian, there had been several generations of native speakers of Mexican Spanish, which had had [s] for at least a century, possibly much longer. Thus it is hardly surprising that this dialect did not share with Castilian the innovation that replaced [s] by more marked [θ].

---

[12] See Canfield (1962, pp. 65–66).

# Bibliography

Alarcos Llorach, E. (1949). "El sistema fonológico español," *Revista de filología española 33*, 265–296.

———— (1951). "Esbozo de una fonología diacrónica del español," *Estudios dedicados a Menéndez Pidal 2*, 9–39.

———— (1958). "Quelques précisions sur la diphtongaison espagnole," *Omagiu lui Iorgu Iordan*, Bucharest, Editura Academiei Republicii Populare Romîne.

———— (1961). *Fonología española*, Madrid, Editorial Gredos.

Allen, W. S. (1964). "Transitivity and possession," *Language 40*, 337–343.

Alonso, A. (1941). "La pronunciación americana de la "z" y de la "ç" en el siglo XVI," *Revista de filología hispánica 3*, 78–99.

———— (1947). "Trueques de sibilantes en antiguo español," *Nueva revista de filología hispánica 1*, 16–27.

———— (1951a). "Cronología de la igualización c-z en español," *Hispanic Review 19*, 43–61.

———— (1951b). "Formación del timbre ciceante en la c-z española," *Nueva revista de filología hispánica 5*, 14–22.

———— (1951c). "Cómo no se pronunciaban las "ç" y "z" antiguas," *Hispania 34*, 51–53.

———— (1955). *De la pronunciación medieval a la moderna en español*, Madrid, Editorial Gredos.

Bach, E. (1967). "Two proposals concerning the simplicity metric in phonology," to appear in *Glossa*.

Bierwisch, M. (1966). "Regeln für die Intonation deutscher Sätze," *Studia Grammatica 7*, 99–201.

Bowen, J. D., and R. P. Stockwell (1955). "The phonemic interpretation of semivowels in Spanish," *Language 31*. (Reprinted in Joos (1963, pp. 400–402).)

—— (1956). "A further note on Spanish semivowels," *Language 32*. (Reprinted in Joos (1963, p. 405).)

—— (1960). *Patterns of Spanish Pronunciation*, Chicago, University of Chicago Press.

Bull, W. E. (1949). "Spanish verb forms, learning by contrast and analogy," *Language Learning 2*, 113–120.

—— (1960). *Time, Tense, and the Verb*, Berkeley, University of California Publications in Linguistics *19*, University of California Press.

Campbell, J. (undated). *A Sketch of Spanish Phonology*, unpublished mimeograph.

Canfield, D. L. (1950). "Spanish "ç" and "s" in the sixteenth century: a hiss and a soft whistle," *Hispania 33*, 233–236.

—— (1952). "Spanish American data for the chronology of sibilant changes," *Hispania 35*, 25–30.

—— (1962). *La pronunciación del español en America*, Bogotá, Publicaciones del Instituto Caro y Cuervo *17*.

Catalán, D. (1956). "El çeçeo-zezeo al comenzar la expansión atlántica de Castilla," *Boletim de filologia 16*, 305–334.

—— (1957). "The end of the phoneme /z/ in Spanish," *Word 13*, 282–322.

Chavarría-Aguilar, O. L. (1951). "The phonemes of Costa Rican Spanish," *Language 27*, 248–253.

Chomsky, N. (1957). *Syntactic Structures*, The Hague, Mouton.

—— (1964). *Current Issues in Linguistic Theory*, The Hague, Mouton.

—— (1965). *Aspects of the Theory of Syntax*, Cambridge, Mass., M.I.T. Press.

—— (1967). "Some general properties of phonological rules," *Language 43*, 102–128.

Chomsky, N., and M. Halle (1965). "Some controversial questions in phonological theory," *Journal of Linguistics 1*, 97–138.

—— (1968). *The Sound Pattern of English*, New York, Harper & Row.

Chomsky, N., M. Halle, and F. Lukoff (1956). "On accent and juncture in English," *For Roman Jakobson*, The Hague, Mouton.

Contini, G. (1951). "Sobre la desaparición de la correlación de sonoridad en castellano," *Nueva revista de filología hispánica 5*, 173–182.

Corominas, J. (1961). *Breve diccionario etimológico de la lengua castellana*, Madrid, Editorial Gredos.

Foley, J. A. (undated). *Spanish Verb Endings*, unpublished mimeograph.

—— (1965). *Spanish Morphology*, unpublished M.I.T. Ph.D. dissertation.

—— (1967). "Spanish plural formation," *Language 43*, 486–493.

Ford, J. D. M. (1900). "The old Spanish sibilants," *Harvard Studies and Notes in Philology and Literature 7*, 1–182.

Fudge, E. C. (1967). "The nature of phonological primes," *Journal of Linguistics 3*, 1–36.

Galmés de Fuentes, A. (1962). *Las sibilantes en la Romania*, Madrid, Editorial Gredos.

García de Diego, V. (1950). "El castellano como complejo dialectal y sus dialectos internos," *Revista de filología española 34*, 107–124.

—— (1961). *Gramática histórica española*, Madrid, Editorial Gredos.

Gavel, H. (1920). *Essai sur l'évolution de la prononciation du castillan depuis le XIV^me siècle*, Paris, E. Champion.

Gili y Gaya, S. (1964). *Curso superior de sintaxis española*, Barcelona, Biblograf.

Hall, R. A. (1945). "Spanish inflection," *Studies in Linguistics 3*, 24–36.

Halle, M. (1959). *The Sound Pattern of Russian*, The Hague, Mouton.

—— (1962). "Phonology in a generative grammar," *Word 18*, 54–72. (Reprinted in Fodor, J. A., and J. J. Katz (1964). *The Structure of Language: Readings in the Philosophy of Language*, Englewood Cliffs, N. J., Prentice-Hall.)

Halle, M., and S. J. Keyser (1966). "Chaucer and the study of prosody," *College English 28*, 187–219.

Hockett, C. F. (1947). "Problems of morphemic analysis," *Language 23*. (Reprinted in Joos (1963, pp. 229–242).)

Jakobson, R., and M. Halle (1956). *Fundamentals of Language*, The Hague, Mouton.

Jakobson, R., G. Fant, and M. Halle (1963). *Preliminaries to Speech Analysis*, Cambridge, Mass., M.I.T. Press.

Joos, M. (1952). "The medieval sibilants," *Language 28*. (Reprinted in Joos (1963, pp. 372–378).)

—— ed. (1963). *Readings in Linguistics*, New York, American Council of Learned Societies.

Katz, J., and P. Postal (1964). *An Integrated Theory of Linguistic Descriptions*, Cambridge, Mass., M.I.T. Press.

Kenyon, J. S., and T. A. Knott (1953). *A Pronouncing Dictionary of American English*, Springfield, Mass., Merriam.

Keyser, S. J. (1963). Review of Kurath, H., and R. I. McDavid (1961), *The Pronunciation of English in the Atlantic States*, in *Language 39*, 303–316.

Kim, C.-W. (1965). "On the autonomy of the tensity feature in stop classification," *Word 21*, 339–359.

King, H. V. (1952). "Outline of Mexican Spanish phonology," *Studies in Linguistics 10*, 51–62.

Kiparsky, R. P. V. (1965). *Phonological Change*, unpublished M.I.T. Ph.D. dissertation.

—— (1968). "How Abstract is Phonology?" unpublished mimeograph.

Kuroda, S.-Y. (1967). *Yawelmani Phonology*, Cambridge, Mass., M.I.T. Press.

Lakoff, G. (1965). *On the Nature of Syntactic Irregularity*, Cambridge, Harvard University Computation Laboratory Report No. NSF-16.

Lapesa, R. (1956). "Sobre el ceceo y el seseo en Hispanoamérica," *Revista Iberoamericana 21*, 409–416.

—— (1959). *Historia de la lengua española*, Madrid, Escelicer.

Lenz, R. (1944). *La oración y sus partes*, Santiago, Chile, Nascimento.

Lightner, T. M. (1965). *Segmental Phonology of Modern Standard Russian*, unpublished M.I.T. Ph.D. dissertation.

Lisker, L., and A. Abramson (1964). "A cross-language study of voicing in initial stops: acoustical measurements," *Word 20*, 384–422.

McCawley, J. D. (1967). "Sapir's phonologic representation," *International Journal of American Linguistics 33*, 106–111.

Malkiel, Y. (1966). "Diphthongization, monophthongization, metaphony: studies in their interaction in the paradigm of the Old Spanish -*ir* verbs," *Language 42*, 430–472.

Martinet, A. (1949). "Occlusives and affricates with reference to some problems of Romance phonology," *Word 5*, 116–122.

——— (1951). "The unvoicing of old Spanish sibilants," *Romance Philology 5*, 133–156.

Menéndez Pidal, R. (1962). *Manual de gramática histórica española*, Madrid, Espasa-Calpe.

Navarro Tomás, T. (1916). "Cantidad de las vocales acentuadas," *Revista de filología española 3*, 387–408.

——— (1917). "Cantidad de las vocales inacentuadas," *Revista de filología española 4*, 371–388.

——— (1918). "Diferencias de duración entre las consonantes españolas," *Revista de filología española 5*, 367–393.

——— (1965). *Manual de pronunciación española*, Madrid, Publicaciones de la Revista de Filología Española, Núm. III.

——— (1968). *Studies in Spanish Phonology*, Coral Gables, Fla., University of Miami Press.

Nida, E. A. (1948). "The identification of morphemes," *Language 24*. (Reprinted in Joos (1963, pp. 255–271).)

Perlmutter, D. (1968). *Deep and Surface Constraints in Syntax*, unpublished M.I.T. Ph.D. dissertation.

Postal, P. M. (1968). *Aspects of Phonological Theory*, New York, Harper & Row.

Rosenbaum, P. S. (1967a). *The Grammar of English Predicate Complement Constructions*, Cambridge, Mass., M.I.T. Press.

——— (1967b). "Phrase structure principles of English complex sentence formation," *Journal of Linguistics 3*, 103–118.

Sableski, J. A. (1965). *A Generative Phonology of a Spanish Dialect*, Seattle, University of Washington Press.

Sapir, E. (1925). "Sound Patterns in Language," *Language 1*, 37–51. (Reprinted in D. G. Mandelbaum (ed.), (1949). *Selected Writings of Edward Sapir in Language, Culture, and Personality*, Berkeley and Los Angeles, University of California Press.)

Saporta, S. (1956a). "A note on Spanish semivowels." *Language 32*. (Reprinted in Joos (1963, pp. 403–404).)

——— (1956b). "Problems in the comparison of the morphemic systems of English and Spanish," *Hispania 39*, 36–40.

——— (1959a). "Spanish person markers," *Language 35*, 612–615.

——— (1959b). "Morpheme alternants in Spanish," in Kahane, H. R., and A. Pietrangeli (eds.), *Structural Studies on Spanish Themes*, Salamanca, Acta Salmanticensia.

—— (1965). "Ordered rules, dialect differences, and historical processes," *Language 41*, 218–224.

Saporta, S., and H. Contreras (1962). *A Phonological Grammar of Spanish*, Seattle, University of Washington Press.

Saroïhandy, J. (1902). "Remarques sur la phonétique du "c" et du "z" en ancien espagnol," *Bulletin Hispanique 4*, 198–203.

Schane, S. A. (1968). *French Phonology and Morphology*, Cambridge, Mass., M.I.T. Press.

Silva-Fuenzalida, I. (1952). "Estudio fonológico del español de Chile," *Boletín de filología 7*, 153–176.

Sledd, J. H. (1966). "Breaking, umlaut, and the Southern drawl," *Language 42*, 18–41.

Spaulding, R., and B. Patt (1948). "Data for the chronology of 'theta' and 'jota'," *Hispanic Review 16*, 50–60.

Stockwell, R. P. (1960). "The place of intonation in a generative grammar of English," *Language 36*, 360–367.

Stockwell, R. P. and J. D. Bowen (1965). *The Sounds of English and Spanish*, Chicago, University of Chicago Press.

Stockwell, R. P., J. D. Bowen, and J. W. Martin (1965). *The Grammatical Structures of English and Spanish*, Chicago, University of Chicago Press.

Stockwell, R. P., J. D. Bowen, and I. Silva-Fuenzalida (1956). "Spanish juncture and intonation," *Language 32*. (Reprinted in Joos (1963, pp. 406–418).)

Trager, G. L. (1939). "The phonemes of Castilian Spanish," *Travaux du Cercle Linguistique de Prague 8*, 217–222.

*Vox Diccionario general ilustrado de la lengua española* (1964). Barcelona, Biblograf.

Wierzchowska, B. (1965). *Wymowa polska*, Warsaw, Panstwowe zaklady wydawnictw szkolnych.

# Index